Foreign Accent Synd

What does it feel like to wake up one day speaking with a foreign accent from a country one has never visited? Why does someone wake up doing this? This book seeks to portray the broad and diverse experiences of individuals with a rare neurological speech disorder called Foreign Accent Syndrome (FAS). Through a combination of personal testimony and scientific commentary, the book aims to shed unprecedented light on the understanding of FAS by elucidating the complex links between how the brain produces speech, how listeners perceive speech, and the role that accent plays in our perception of self and others.

The first part of the book provides a comprehensive introduction to FAS and covers a number of key subject areas, including:

- the definition and phenomenology of FAS
- a history of research on FAS
- the causes and psychosocial consequences of FAS
- a guide to further reading and a glossary of specialised terms.

The material in Part II provides a unique insight into the condition through personal testimony and accounts from family members. This collection of 28 testimonies from across the world underlines the importance of listening carefully to patients explaining their cases in their own words. The final section contains a questionnaire for use by clinicians to support case-history taking.

The authors are two leading global experts on FAS, and this is the first volume of its kind to provide such a broad and comprehensive examination of this rare and poorly understood condition. It will be of great interest to practising clinicians in neurology, psychiatry, psychology, and speech and language therapy/pathology, as well as students in health disciplines relevant to neuro-rehabilitation, linguists, and also to families and caregivers.

Jack Ryalls is Professor at the Department of Communication Sciences and Disorders at the University of Central Florida, USA. In addition to FAS, his research areas also include aphasia, normal aging, right hemisphere brain damage, Parkinsonism, Friedreich's ataxia and Alzheimer's disease.

Nick Miller is Professor of Motor Speech Disorders at the Institute of Health and Society, Newcastle University, UK. His teaching and clinical practice have covered all aspects of motor speech disorders as well as areas of neuro-psychology, aphasia and rehabilitation in neurological disorders. His main focus in research has been on speech, voice and swallowing changes in Parkinson's and after stroke, with involvement with FAS arising out of the latter.

Foreign Accent Syndromes

The stories people have to tell

Jack Ryalls and Nick Miller

Psychology Press
Taylor & Francis Group
LONDON AND NEW YORK

First published 2015
by Psychology Press
27 Church Road, Hove, East Sussex BN3 2FA

and by Psychology Press
711 Third Avenue, New York, NY 10017

Psychology Press is an imprint of the Taylor & Francis Group, an informa business

British Library Cataloguing in Publication Data
A catalogue record for this book is available from the British Library

Library of Congress Cataloging in Publication Data
Ryalls, John H., 1954–
    Foreign accent syndromes: the stories people have to tell/Jack Ryalls and Nick Miller. – 1 Edition.
    pages cm
    Includes bibliographical references and index.
    1. Speech disorders. 2. Communicative disorders. 3. Neurolinguistics.
    I. Miller, Nick. II. Title.
    RC423.R8962 2014
    616.85'5–dc23
    2013050466

ISBN: 978-1-84872-152-4 (hbk)
ISBN: 978-1-84872-153-1 (pbk)
ISBN: 978-1-315-87089-2 (ebk)

Typeset in Bembo and Gill Sans
by Florence Production Ltd, Stoodleigh, Devon, UK

Printed and bound in the United States of America by Publishers Graphics, LLC on sustainably sourced paper.

Contents

Acknowledgements and dedications   viii

PART I
Introduction   1

1   Introduction   3
    JACK RYALLS

2   All about Foreign Accent Syndrome   9
    NICK MILLER

    Definitions, phenomenology 9
    Historical perspective 16
    What causes Foreign Accent Syndrome? 24
    Psychosocial consequences of FAS 52
    Differential diagnosis 58
    Conclusions 65
    From the bookshelf 65
    Short glossary of some more specialised terms used in the text 69

PART II
Personal testimonies   71

3   Personal testimonies   73

    Australia 73
        Anonymous: *Starting over 73*

    Canada 85
        Ron Kochut: *Kelly's Vancouver Sun Run 2012 85*

    Costa Rica 88
        Jeffrey Barquero Salazar: *My mother and her foreign accent
            (Mi madre y su acento extranjero) 88*

Germany 90
  Martina Bodeck: *Lena Bodeck FAS 5.1.2011* 90

United Kingdom 94
  Annabel: *FAS, my friend* 94

  Claire Coleman: *'Relax, but how do I relax when I am so worried about my speech?'* 106

  Wendy Hasnip: *'1999 ... I used to become distraught, when the wiring on the hoover became quite loose ...'* 110

  Kath Lockett and family: *'Robbed of a precious gift, my identity'* 118

  June Maldonado: *'It does affect the family ... a little part of you goes with your voice change'* 124

  Julie Matthias and family: *'My glass is always half full, but I do shed the odd tear'* 128

  Debie Royston: *'Life isn't about waiting for the storm it's about learning to dance in the rain'* 132

  Kay Russell-Iliffe: *'Not everything is as it seem, not everything Is black/white'* 141

USA 147
  Teshera Bowser: *Dream turns into a nightmare* 147

  Kenley Byrd: *'I'm still me'* 150

  Gretchen Daniel and family: *My story of dealing with FAS* 155

  Julie Dieschbourg: *My FAS journey* 162

  Joy 'Curls' Garcia: *My new beginning* 164

  Nancy Haller: *In their perception* 168

  Kimberly Martens: *Thoughts on foreign accent syndrome* 175

  Karen Bailey Mullinix: *My story* 176

  Alice Murphy: *'The part of my brain that controlled a minor part was left in charge of everything and could not do the job thus everything shut down'* 179

  Cindy J. Neely-Langdon: *My stroke. My recovery* 182

  Cindylou Vedin Romberg: *Kindred spirits* 191

  Rose Shuff: *Foreign accent syndrome* 199

  Ellen Spencer: *This is not me!! (10 days)* 201

Bernadette West: *Living out dreams 208*

Paula Westberry and family: *FAS – my experience 212*

Venezuela 221
   Olga Boscán: *My history of foreign accent syndrome 221*

PART III
Additional resources   **225**

4   The psychosocial impact of FAS questionnaire – prototype   227
    JILL TAYLOR, CHLOE HOWE AND NICK MILLER

Index   241

Acknowledgements and dedications

I would like to acknowledge that part of the idea for this book was inspired by the popular and compelling course 'Brain Stories' given by my colleague Joe DiNapoli at my home institution, and the many stimulating conversations that Foreign Accent Syndrome has occasioned. It is especially appropriate for me to recognise my first exposure to Foreign Accent Syndrome through my mentor Sheila Blumstein more than thirty years ago (already!) — And, in turn, the debt to her mentors Harold Goodglass and Roman Jakobson. *Nanos gigantum humeris insidentes.* So, I would like to dedicate this book to her.

Jack Ryalls, Orlando, October 2013

With acknowledgement of the boundless insights into communication, its changes, and the human condition afforded by all those with Foreign Accent Syndrome whom I have had the privilege to encounter. With thanks for the inspiration of Jennifer Gurd, who has been a shining light in the field of FAS and neuropsychology for many decades.

Dedicated to the women in my life, Irene, Jane, Fiona, Catriona, Ōrla.

Nick Miller, Newcastle, October 2013

Part I

Introduction

Chapter 1

Introduction

Jack Ryalls

The purpose of this book is to relay the personal experience of Foreign Accent Syndrome (FAS). We seek to portray the broad and diverse experiences of those who have experienced this curious but compelling disorder; and who better to speak about this than those individuals who have lived with FAS themselves? For those who have, or have had FAS and for those who encounter these individuals, whether in clinic, home or the media, we also offer some insights from the history of FAS and comments from the science behind the condition.

We have purposely used 'syndromes' in the title, because it has become clear that there is more than one disorder, if disorder is the appropriate word. We wish to emphasise the breadth of experiences and aetiologies; to focus on how individual the experience is, despite the congruencies. While there are many different theories put forward to explain FAS, in this book we wanted to avoid a potentially turgid tome on the neurology, physiology, neuropsychology and phonetics of FAS, and gather together as many human experiences as possible. While it has been a century since a similar condition was described by the French neurologist Pierre Marie, there is not yet a single accepted theory for FAS.

In fact, a comprehensive account would probably have to be as diverse and individual as those who have written here about their experiences. We wanted to emphasise the individual and their personal experience. There have been some important historical developments in our understanding of this syndrome, as will be detailed below. But many attribute the first fully detailed case study where the psychosocial aspects of the condition were first brought to the fore, to the description by Monrad-Krohn of a Norwegian woman who lost her ability to produce the tonal accents of her native language. He established the term 'dysprosody' in 1947. His patient, Astrid, who ended up with a German-sounding accent, is probably the most famous and poignant case of FAS in the specialist literature. How much worse an experience can be imagined, than ending up with the accent of the occupying enemy army? Local shopkeepers refused her service, believing she was a collaborator.

There was also the notable coining of the term 'Foreign Accent Syndrome' by Whitaker in 1982 and his insistence on its neurological basis. For Whitaker, it was inappropriate to use the term 'Foreign Accent Syndrome' without clear evidence of a neurological basis. But oftentimes the aetiology is not clear, and not all neurological disturbances leave a clearly visible trail. As we have learned over the past few years, there are many cases of foreign accented speech related to all sorts of neurological disorders – migraine, dystonia and so forth, where brain consequences may be quite different to those in stroke or other head injury. While migraines are clearly recognised as neurologically based, there are no neuroimaging techniques to confirm the neurological basis of FAS associated with this disorder.

We are not seeking to solve the issues surrounding diagnosis or aetiology in the cases here. Rather our goal is to portray the broad existential content – what it feels like to experience this bewildering condition from the point of view of the speaker with FAS and the listener. Despite all the scientific scrutiny, we still know relatively little about this rare condition. But what we do know will be reviewed in the sections which follow.

While it has been claimed in various scientific publications that there are less than fifty cases of FAS in the world, from our experience we now know this condition to be hugely more prevalent than previously thought. Not only can a 'foreign accent' be associated with a much wider spectrum of conditions than previously suspected (drug interactions, a rather wide range of neurological conditions, even neurotoxins such as spider bites), but increased communication in the world has allowed us to hear from many more cases than ever previously possible.

One may well wonder why it is that human beings possess such an exquisite perception of different accents in the first place. It is tempting to speculate the existence of a 'module' in the human brain for detecting accent. Certainly the brain is highly skilled at detecting differences, whether they are changes in the visual, physical or auditory landscape. However, it is most likely several steps too far to assume there is some unique neurological substrate for 'accent'. Nevertheless, registering differences in accent is socially important in human intercourse. One could account for the biological motivation for such sensitivity to accent in the drive for diversification of the gene pool: alertness to threat identification of sameness and difference. Once one has allowed oneself to speculate on such a mechanism in the processing of speech, there are the roots of an account for the natural curiosity in different accents of the globe. It does not take too great a leap of the imagination to understand the natural 'attractiveness' of a foreign accent or interest listeners would have in it. Such an account may eventually explain why many of the contributors here have complained about the doggedness of listeners to find an acceptable 'explanation' or satisfactory account of their accent.

We cannot overemphasise the contribution of a private Facebook page to our cause. To the best of our knowledge, this was an outgrowth of the initial effort of Paula Westberry (a person living with FAS whom we will meet in her personal account) to establish an internet forum. The self-governed site has essentially nominated long-standing members to 'officiate'. Initially, the site served as an important information highway between the United States and Great Britain, but in recent years the network has broadened and is now truly global. Not only have people with FAS been able to reach out to each other around the world and exchange symptom relief information, but it has also served as a valuable and practical conduit of information, even in communicating various aspects of coordinating this book. It's no wonder that members now refer to themselves on this site as 'family'.

On the one hand, it is still true that there are precious few very well-documented and vetted cases which have undergone the full cycle of scientific scrutiny, including modern science's well-known 'peer review process'. On the other hand, both of us have heard from dozens of cases, which make it patently obvious just how under-reported this disorder really is. At the same time, though, there are too few true specialists dedicated to fully documenting all new cases. Oftentimes, the general public does not understand that it is not enough to simply report a new case. Rather, it is the more stringent requirement that each scientific article report something entirely new, in a systematic and rigorous fashion, which ultimately pushes science forward.

Our goal here has been to take inventory, to listen carefully to individuals explain their perception in their own words, and to share these experiences with the world – to be as broad and inclusive as possible. One may liken this role to medical cultural anthropologists investigating through personal stories. We endeavoured to keep editing of submissions to a bare minimum without judgement on what should or should not be told. Contributors were asked just to 'relate your story as you experienced it'.

While the original definition of FAS by Whitaker dictates a neurological aetiology, we embrace a somewhat wider view in this volume, one that does not clearly eliminate the important psychological consequences or origins of this often devastating condition. Eventually, it will become important to delineate subtypes to allow better scientific scrutiny and treatment. For the time being, we view at least three broad varieties: FAS which arises in association with a rather wide range of neurological conditions; FAS that accompanies structural changes to the vocal tract; and altered accent that appears for psychological or functional reasons. These are discussed in greater detail below.

It is important to point out that we do not feel that FAS from a functional or psychological origin is any less real in terms of its phenomenology compared to when it arises for neurological reasons. Furthermore, in some cases there is a definite blending of neurological and functional determinants of accent which is often difficult to disentangle. As the insightful neuropsychologist Kurt Goldstein so aptly pointed out more than a century ago, with neurological disorders such as aphasia (or here FAS) not only do we observe the direct neurological consequences of the disorder itself, but also the individual's adjustment to the devastating condition.

Many patients find their own coping mechanisms, and one can only admire the highly creative and adaptive manners in which they have got on with their lives. We are happy and proud to be able to showcase their tenacity of human spirit in this book. For this and many more reasons, it is misguided, even simply wrong to speak of 'patients' or 'sufferers'. Let us call them 'persons with FAS'.

As we shall see in the personal accounts and in the introduction to psycho-social effects, there are many routes to adaptation to the condition. Some adapt by allowing their interlocutors to believe that they are indeed from the country their accent suggests. This is often much simpler, and more expedient, than having to explain over and over again that their perceived accent results from a subtle and rare form of neurological injury.

There is evidence that, in neurological cases, FAS may emerge as a stage of recovery from nervous system damage and may have been preceded by a more severe speech and language disorder (i.e. aphasia). It is a given that in recovery or decline in neurological conditions the symptomatic picture evolves, not just in overall severity, but in the constellation of which impairments are present or not, prominent or not. This evolving clinical portrait stems partly from direct recovery of initially damaged tissue (or in progressive conditions loss of more cells/capacities). It is also well attested that the evolution arises as an effect of the brain reorganising its pattern of function to compensate for lost centres or pathways. An fMRI study of one individual with FAS from a subcortical (putamen) lesion clearly demonstrated this finding, with increased cortical activity in speech areas representing apparent reorganisational compensation. Individuals may also instigate compensatory tactics themselves to overcome impairments. This opens up the speculation that perceived accent change in neurological conditions may be one manifestation of a stage in recovery representing not just loss of particular aspects of speech programming and control, but also the effects of reorganisational or compensatory mechanisms. One path of future research may be to examine whether the pattern of natural and conscious compensation is different in speakers with FAS compared to other people with other communication disorders from brain damage.

We also note the remarkably greater number of females who contributed to this volume, despite the fact that at least one retrospective study determined a nearly equal incidence by gender. It is certainly tempting to relate this fact to the observation that females recover differently from stroke, although the empirical evidence to back up this claim remains a topic of debate. Are we witnessing some preliminary evidence of a true gender difference here, or is this difference attributable to the more mundane explanation that males are simply more reluctant to share their stories than women? We certainly made our best efforts to solicit stories from everyone willing to share. While we are aware of a few males who did not elect to share their story in this forum, the overwhelming majority of female cases here leads us to speculate that this gender difference is neurologically based, and merits much closer scientific scrutiny. This issue is considered again later on.

One of the important lines of contemporary research into brain function concerns attempts to understand the recovery process better after injury, not only for insight into the function of the human brain *per se*, but for the wealth of information it promises in terms of rehabilitation. FAS offers a fascinating and potentially fruitful forum for gaining greater insights into understanding the human brain and the speech processes that define our species.

All too often the media have focused on the 'circus freak' aspects of FAS, and devoted precious little attention to its scientific basis. It is our fervent hope that this volume will serve to reorient this unfortunate precedence. If the public can better comprehend the predicament of individuals with this bewildering disorder, it is hoped this volume can pave the way to a brighter future where individuals with FAS no longer suffer in isolation and are no longer exposed to the prejudices of miscomprehension.

The internet has provided some previously unavailable opportunities for people with FAS to communicate with fellow speakers. We should again acknowledge the contribution of the private Facebook page devoted to FAS which has been fundamental to communication and which presently numbers more than fifty participants worldwide – and we know of many individual cases who have chosen not to join the Facebook 'FAS Family', as they refer to themselves. The interaction with those who experience this syndrome has been a highly rewarding part of our work in this area. Many people with FAS have commented on the joy of being able to be put in touch directly with others with the condition.

There have been remarkably few published accounts of speech therapy with patients with FAS, and there is no clear evidence of speech therapy techniques that might prove most beneficial to individuals with FAS. Certainly we possess only anecdotal evidence of whether direct work on speech output has any real ameliorative effect. It is not known if very cutting edge and high tech methods such as electromagnetic articulography (which provides visual feedback about the largely invisible movements of the tongue) might assist speakers to achieve their former speech patterns.

This is just one of the variety of questions that remain to be explored. People with FAS sometimes report listening to tape recordings or viewing video recordings of their former accents and attempting to retrain themselves into their old speech patterns. Unfortunately, they typically report such attempts to be extremely frustrating.

It seems worthwhile to point out that often (and again anecdotally, since no one has carried out evidence-based systematic study) those individuals, who reach a point in their lives where they accept their speech changes, seem to make the most satisfactory adjustment. It is not impossible that, unless performed very judiciously, it may turn out that speech therapy may even interfere with this acceptance process. Certainly several personal accounts here have expressed dissatisfaction. But we are not presently equipped with the requisite evidence-based practice to make informed clinical decisions. We simply know too precious little. Before turning to the very special, often amazing and emotional personal testimonies of those individuals who have lived with FAS, we will next turn our attention to definitions, aetiologies, history and differential diagnosis of the syndrome.

Chapter 2

All about Foreign Accent Syndrome

Nick Miller

Definitions, phenomenology

What is Foreign Accent Syndrome? What are its characteristics?

Foreign Accent Syndrome (FAS) has been held up as 'real twilight zone stuff', a 'strange ailment waiting out there to ambush us'. It has been billed as the 'mysterious acquisition of a (foreign) accent'. To some pundits it comes from damage to the 'accent' module in the brain. People have claimed it is a sign of long-dead relatives from a far-off country struggling to communicate across the divide of time and space. It is linked to miraculous reports of people being knocked off their motorbike and suddenly having the power to speak a language they never knew before. The stream of aberrant assertions, misperceptions, sheer theatre, journalistic invention and misguided medicine that has surrounded this syndrome over recent years has meant that people with Foreign Accent Syndrome are typically totally misunderstood, and people who search for serious, accessible and accurate information on it are faced with a wall of distorted or fanciful facts making it difficult or impossible to glean a clear, reliable view.

This book aims to correct this by offering insights into what Foreign Accent Syndrome really is, based on facts rather than fancy. It complements this description with accounts from people who have the condition to bring into focus what it feels like to experience the involuntary acquisition of a foreign accent. The book is written for a general readership, but it aims to introduce some clinical and theoretical issues that will definitely be of interest to clinicians and speech scientists as well as people who experience FAS, their families and friends.

Today is Monday, a week since Juliana's stroke. Medical staff and her family, not to mention Juliana herself, are totally perplexed. On admission she could follow what others were saying to her, at least in general. Over the first few days, though, she had not been able to produce any intelligible speech. Slowly, from Thursday onwards Juliana was able to make attempts at a few words, but they were largely whispered and still difficult to discern. Gradually her voice became louder, the words more easy to understand. By Sunday it was possible for her to conduct a halting conversation. Bafflingly, though, it was not the speech of Juliana from before her stroke, with her soft Scottish lilt.

Nurse Peters, back on the ward that morning after a week's leave, took her to be a new Russian patient who must have married a local man, given her surname was not Russian. Other staff heard a Slavonic accent, some said Polish, others thought maybe Czech. To start with Juliana had not noticed herself that she spoke any differently from before, other than sensing that getting any sounds and words out was a huge effort. It was only at visiting time on Sunday when her family were staring at her nonplussed and asking her why she was 'talking in that weird way' that she realised something else was amiss.

Juliana had never spoken Russian before. She knew no one who spoke it. She had no reason to suddenly start to speak like someone from Eastern Europe. Try as she might she was unable to alter her accent back to her native Scottish. The family were bewildered. Medical staff suspected psychiatric issues. Juliana felt frightened. Experiencing the stroke had been devastating enough, but she had survived and the return of some speech and first signs of movement in her right arm and leg led her to feel progress was under way. Now this, which no one seemed to be able to make any sense of.

This scenario and the varying and conflicting sentiments of all involved are expressed in many of the contributions in Part II. Juliana's and others' observations encapsulate many of the core elements of how Foreign Accent Syndrome presents: the appearance of a foreign accent seemingly out of nowhere after what seems like a routine stroke or similar neurological event; the ensuing diagnostic quandary; the powerlessness of the individual to alter their accent; the feeling on the part of the speaker that it is a life-changing episode, very foreign, literally as well as metaphorically, and not just because of the accent; the total puzzlement, anxiety, even fright of those concerned. These are all themes that we will be revisiting in much more detail throughout this book.

At its most straightforward FAS labels a condition where someone begins speaking with an accent that is not their own, not their habitual one they have spoken all their life. It may be the accent of a foreign language – a French speaker sounds Russian – or it may be a different regional accent of the same language – a New Yorker suddenly sounds like they are from Louisiana or Australia. This occurs in the context of never having lived in the country or region, never having learned the language, and never having associated with people from these places.

This opening vignette hints at some other characteristic phenomena around Foreign Accent Syndrome that add to the puzzlement of all concerned and certainly muddy the waters when it comes to differential diagnosis of what is happening. Listeners do not necessarily all hear the same accent. Indeed, some may not even hear a foreign accent at all – they hear disordered speech or perfectly normal speech – although slow and with some effort maybe, but otherwise normal. Not uncommonly listeners remark that they hear patches of the person's former accent in amongst the foreignness, stoking up suspicions that the person is putting all this on or there is some added aetiology other than simply the underlying neurological changes. This opinion can be reinforced by not only different staff perceiving different accents on the same occasion, but the same listener on different occasions hearing separate accents. In instances where FAS arises in multilingual speakers it can even happen that the speaker has developed FAS in one language but not the other.

The course of FAS is also highly variable. For some it may emerge early in the recovery phase after stroke or head injury; for others it may be weeks or months later. Where FAS is linked to degenerative neurological conditions it can be an early or late accompaniment. For some speakers FAS persists but a few days, whilst others experience it for weeks or months. Lasting, stable FAS with neurological aetiologies is relatively rare, and when it does persist, as will be discussed later under causes and differential diagnosis of FAS, there may be multiple reasons why it is sustained.

As we will see later, why FAS comes about, why people hear a particular accent, why the nature of the accent may change from situation to situation, time to time, why it does or does not resolve over time in different individuals, is a more complex story than the outline definition divulges, a complexity which this book aims to capture and elucidate.

Note, too, we are talking here of accent change, how sounds and words are pronounced. We are not talking of 'language' – the words one uses, the grammar one employs. What Foreign Accent Syndrome is not is the sudden appearance of a foreign language, being suddenly able to speak Spanish when you have never known a single word of Spanish before, or claiming because the person does utter their two words of Japanese they are now a fluent Japanese speaker. Claims along these lines periodically crop up in the popular press. They belong, though, to the annals of science fiction, not science fact. Someone who has never learned or spoken a language before is not invested with the power to speak it by a hit on the head, a stroke or any other neurological condition.

Such stories probably come about not just from total sheer ignorance and journalistic laziness in checking the facts, but in part because in the field of studies of brain damage in people who are or who have been bilingual or multilingual there are a wide variety of well-attested effects of brain damage on a speaker's access to, or use of, different languages. After stroke or head injury or when they have developed a dementia for instance, a speaker may well lose access to their German, but not their Italian. The next day this might be the opposite way round. They may lose their Hindi and their English after their stroke, one gets better the other does not. They may be unable to separate out the grammar and words of the two languages – what comes out is a total mixture of the two. They might still be able to read in French, but no longer in Spanish, but can speak the two equally well. Such cases have been documented at least since the early nineteenth century – Jonathan Osborne (1794–1864, a Dublin physician and surgical pioneer) in the 1830s noted 'several cases are recorded of persons after wounds or apoplectic seizures, ceasing to speak their usual language and resuming the use of some language with which they had been familiar at some former period'.

All this, though, involves people who have learned two or more languages, and has to do with their understanding or expression of the words and grammar of those different languages. Such cases are not the subject matter of this book. We are concerned centrally with instances of people who suddenly seem to be speaking with a different accent of their one language. If they also happen to be bi- or multilingual that is by the by, and not the nub of the matter in relation to FAS. So, what characterises the speech of someone with FAS, other than sounding foreign or from a different region?

What does someone with FAS sound like?

For a listener to hear a different accent it is not necessary for the speaker to present with a full-blown, thick, unmistakable accent. Listeners can detect a different accent even on the basis of hearing millisecond splices of speech. Occasional and subtle deviations from the expected norm are all that is required to form an impression of foreignness.

This may be a slight shift in the pronunciation of certain sounds. 'Lip' sounds like 'leap', or 'ship' like 'sheep'; 'my' sounds like 'ma', or 'chips' and 'cheat' like 'ships' and 'sheet', 'think' and 'faith' like 'sink' and 'face'. Added or omitted sounds may underlie perception of foreignness in other instances. 'Pass me the flask from the rucksack' may be heard as 'pass me e flass from the russa', or 'turn on the television' is produced as what is heard as 'turna ona di teldivision'. For another speaker/listener a tip in the balance of nasalness in their speech may be all that is required to lead listeners to suspect they are foreign.

Furthermore, it does not have to be (just) alterations to individual sounds. Changes to the rhythm of speech that listeners hear as crossing some perceptual boundary between local–not local, native tongue–non-native tongue can suggest foreignness. The speaker may, for example, place the stress in words or phrases in unexpected places – 'a big CROcodile' is heard as 'a big croCOdile'; 'PICnic' is taken as 'picNIC'; 'are YOU COming out toNIGHT?' may be heard as 'ARE you coming out TOnight?' Speakers may have exaggerated rises or falls in the melody of their speech, or the rises and falls occur in what in the local accent would be unanticipated locations in the sentence.

People with FAS may often speak at the same rate as everyone else, without hesitations or constant corrections. More typically people with FAS have a slower than normal speech rate. Their speech may be typified too by breaks – to correct the sounds and words they are saying, to pause whilst they find a word that is eluding them, while they remind themselves of what they were trying to say. These dysfluencies do not have to be accompanied by accent alteration for someone to suspect foreignness rather than having a speech disorder, especially in the absence of other clues (hemiplegia, wheelchair ...) that their struggle has origins elsewhere. Where such dysfluencies in speech occur alongside particular perceived changes to sounds, then their joint appearance can considerably boost the impression of foreignness.

We may label someone as foreign too on the basis of the words they employ or the grammar they use. People with FAS may evidence these characteristics – there are subtly, or not so subtly, wrong choices of word or grammatical structure: '*I am think it is late*'; '*she has a smelling face*'; '*can I have knife [spoon* was intended] *to eat my ice cream?*'. One may gain the impression that the person uses only a limited range of grammatical structures and all their phrases are short.

In other words, the answer to how does someone with FAS sound is simply that their speech contains elements of sound changes, rhythm and intonation changes and word and grammar alterations that we associate with foreign speakers of our language. Of course this begs the questions of why would this kind of picture be provoked by a stroke or similar condition; why do these specific changes arise; why do different listeners hear different accents or no accent; and so forth. Much more is said about these topics in the later section on causes of FAS, when we look at how FAS arises, not simply in the mouth of the speaker but crucially too in the ear of the listener.

How common is FAS?

There is no straightforward answer. No one keeps or has kept a register of cases as they occur, not even for limited geographical regions or institutions. Aronson in 1990 noted thirteen cases on the files at the Mayo clinic in Rochester, New York, but did not state over how long these had accrued nor what proportion this represented of all referrals. If we go by the number of case studies mentioned in the medical, psychology and linguistics journals then over the decades there have been well over 150 cases reported. However, counting literature reports is not a reliable or valid way of estimating how common a condition is.

Some people have carried out limited surveys of speech language pathologists to see how often they come across someone with FAS. Again, this method is subject to all sorts of biases and so we cannot really take the outcomes as firm conclusions. One of those biases is that most people with FAS may never actually be referred to speech language pathology as their speech may be entirely intelligible and from the comprehensibility point of view, there is no disorder. The issues that arise from FAS may mean they are just as likely to be referred to a psychologist, counsellor or psychiatrist. The latter point emphasises that there still exists a considerable amount of uncertainty concerning FAS. Many people, professionals and public alike, despite the periodic mania in the media, have never heard of it. Or they are highly sceptical about its origins and course.

Thus, whether you are diagnosed with FAS and what happens to you can be highly dependent on which hospital and clinic you arrive at, even on which health professional you see.

Another factor that renders arriving at an answer to the incidence conundrum well-nigh impossible is the fact that, for most people, sounding foreign represents only a transitory phase, either in their recovery from head injury or stroke or in the course of deterioration when there is a degenerative neurological cause. This phase may last for a few days or a few months until the constellation of changes to their speech no longer sounds foreign, they are back to their former accent, or the predominant impression now is of 'disorderedness', not foreignness. Relatively few people are left permanently with entirely foreign-sounding speech. That may sound like it makes the counting easier, but that is only true if someone is noting down all the instances in a systematic way free of reporting bias, with evidence to confirm the aetiology, the speech picture, the foreignness status. No one is doing this currently.

Remember too, as will be seen later, that a key element of FAS is the ear of the listener. Different listeners are quite likely to place different labels and descriptions on what they hear, and the cut-off between local and outsider accent or foreign and disordered is different for different listeners. The power of expectation is also at work – if I say 'come and listen to this person who sounds foreign' you are already primed to hear someone foreign. We carried out some research ourselves related to this. We used a set of recordings of people who had been diagnosed with FAS, people who had been diagnosed with a motor speech disorder and no FAS, people who had a foreign accent, but because of where they came from and not for any neurological reason, and a group who had just an ordinary local accent. We asked listeners to rate them on degree of 'foreignness' in their speech on a five-point scale ('definitely local' to 'definitely foreign'). The people with FAS came out as being rated most similar to the people with a 'genuine' foreign accent. When we employed the self-same tracks but asked listeners to rate people for degree of speech disorder, the speakers with FAS were perceived as most similar to the people with a motor speech disorder, not the bona fide foreign accent group.

These are just a few of the barriers to establishing a 'true' estimation of how many people develop FAS over a given time span and how many people are living with it. So, the answer to how many people have FAS as far as we know at the present time is that it is many more than are represented by the number of formal reports in the literature or newspapers. It is certainly an order of magnitude more than the 'only five other cases in the world' and similar claims trumpeted by some journalists chasing a quick sensational story but too lazy to research their facts. At the same time, there is not someone with FAS around every corner, and even those who experience FAS may do so for only a limited time and to a varying degree.

Before leaving the topic of general characteristics of FAS one point should be mentioned, that for some is somewhat of an elephant in the room.

Practically all the cases of FAS reported in specialist journals are female, and anecdotally the same predominance is found clinically. Does this reflect some important facts about brain organisation and functioning, speech motor control, social interaction, assessment and referral; or, is it just an accident, a bias in reporting?

It is likely that the predominance of females stems from a multiplicity of sources, some rather trivial, but others potentially highly important in terms of understanding FAS and the lessons it may hold about brain organisation and speech motor control.

At its most straightforward, the scarcity of male speakers with FAS may simply signify a reporting bias. Alternatively a referral bias may lie behind it, again with numerous possible reasons why that might be so. For instance, males may simply prefer to hide their problems or cope with them in a different fashion. Women may be more ready to discuss their health issues and concerns compared to men. Clinicians' reactions to females using a foreign accent may be different to their reactions to occurrences in men.

Imbalances in prevalence are not unusual in medicine overall or in communication disorders in particular. Recent trends point towards more women being diagnosed with multiple sclerosis than men. Laryngeal cancer is more prevalent in males. There is a more or less equal incidence of skin melanoma across genders, but men are more likely to be diagnosed later and more liable to die from it – the latter fact not fully explained by presenting at clinic at a later stage. The lifetime prevalence of depression is around 1.5–3.0 times more common in women. Many more males are stutterers than females. Conversely, significantly more women present with functional voice disorders than men. Globus pharyngeus (the sensation of having a lump in the throat) seems to be experienced as often by men as women, but women are much more likely to seek help for it. Some of these discrepancies may have their origin in lifestyle dissimilarities, but susceptibility may also be determined by gender differences in body or brain biochemistry. Genetic factors definitely play a part in some instances of gender inequalities in incidence and prevalence. Women may cope with illness and adversity differently to men and this can influence referral patterns, strategies for coming to terms with changes and how these manifest themselves in broader behaviour.

Closer to FAS, there is support for the argument that women have different patterns of aphasia and recovery from aphasia compared to men, which possibly leads back to divergences in brain organisation and functioning. This may apply to speech disorders too, though no one has directly investigated this to our knowledge. It is quite likely that the differing sizes of the vocal cords, the vocal tract and accompanying differences in pitch and loudness exercise some influence on patterns of breakdown and recovery of acquired neurogenic speech disorders – for instance perhaps men are more likely to sound disordered as opposed to having a different accent. Tantalising insights into this possibility exist in research reports. Further, it is well recognised that females' attitudes to accented speech, diction, speech fashions and speech change contrast to men's, adding another dimension to the search for the explanations of female predominance in FAS.

It is certain that in most instances a range of factors will be at play in bringing about gender differences in FAS. Whatever the reasons for the imbalance, this is an area that could turn up some fascinating facts about the mind and even have important implications for rehabilitation.

The last pages have outlined some of the headline features around the presentation and phenomenology of FAS. Later sections elucidate issues around what causes FAS and why speech changes in the way it does. Before proceeding with that, lest we start to think that FAS is perhaps some isolated phenomenon that has only recently entered our thinking, we make a digression to look at the history of FAS reports.

Historical perspective

The World Wide Web, chat rooms, social media sites, newspapers, blogs and even academic journals have evidenced a mushrooming of reports, materials and speculation on FAS in recent years. It is easy to think FAS is a modern-day creation fuelled by a trend in obsession with the bizarre, the creation of urban myths, the invention of a syndrome to explain just about any behaviour. Faced with this, it may come as a surprise to many that there exists a long history of accounts of and debate on accent change. This section takes a tour around some of the more prominent landmarks in the history of FAS scholarship.

Arnold Pick (1851–1924) was a celebrated Czech-German neurologist and psychiatrist working in the Carl's University in Prague. He was deeply interested not just in the neuropathology of brain disease, but also in the behavioural and cognitive (thought process) changes that arose in association with pathological alterations. He is probably best remembered nowadays for being the first person to detail a form of dementia where degeneration commences in the front parts of the brain, which for many years was labelled 'Pick's disease', though now it is more commonly termed frontal (-temporal) dementia. In 1891 he had also been the first to use the term dementia praecox to describe a type of early onset dementia, nowadays subsumed under the label schizophrenia. He worked closely with his Bavarian colleague Alois Alzheimer (1864–1915) on these topics. Pick was also the first to describe and provide a theoretical motivation for the disorder termed ideational apraxia, a problem of action planning and use of objects (the person tries to comb their hair with a toothbrush, stirs their tea using a dunking motion with a fork). In 1903 he was the first doctor in modern times (possible accounts exist from the eighteenth century) to characterise and label the syndrome that for many people surpasses even FAS in terms of challenges to one's belief. That syndrome was 'reduplicative paramnesia,' where an individual believes they are not in the actual place where it looks as if they are, but in a duplication of this site elsewhere. Pick's original description entailed a woman who maintained she was attending not his clinic in the centre of Prague, but a (non-existent, but not for her) replica of this in the suburbs.

However, what will be more interesting for present readers is that in December 1914 Pick was invited by a colleague, Otto Fischer (1861–1917, famous for pioneering work in studying human gait and in the development of prostheses to aid gait disorders) to come and see a patient, Karel. He was a former butcher, who had speech and language difficulties and some right-sided weakness after a stroke two years before. There was nothing noteworthy about that, and nothing exceptional about the grammatical and word-finding difficulties the man was experiencing. Why Fischer had asked Pick over was because of the man's remarkable speech changes. He was born and bred Czech, yet he sounded as if he were Polish.

This Czech man was not the first person to be described as developing what sounded like a foreign accent after brain injury. Indeed, Pick himself had reported on a woman in 1898 who spoke Czech and German and yet, due to the nature of the altered accentuation of syllables, she sounded foreign (she was tending to stress the final syllables, not the first as in Czech or in most German words). The similar picture in both these instances seemed to confirm that Karel sounded foreign due to the effects of his stroke on his speech and not because he had spent some time in the army in Polish speaking areas.

Altered accent was familiar too to the famous French neurologist Pierre Marie (1853–1940). In 1907 he presented four cases of people with speech disorders before a meeting of the Paris Hospitals' Medical Society. The second of his patients was a Parisian with a right hemiplegia who, it was said, had been unable to speak for nine years. Speech had recently re-emerged. His word finding and grammatical usage were impeccable, he wrote perfectly (with his left hand). But there remained vestiges of dysarthric speech which made him sound as if he came from Alsace far to the east where the Germanic Alsatian dialect was spoken, not from his native Paris.

Clinically instances arise where brain damage leaves an individual with intact understanding of others' speech and of written material, they may even be able to write fluently and accurately, but there are marked speech difficulties. Jonathan Osborne, the Dublin professor of medicine and surgery mentioned earlier, was probably the first to graphically describe one such case in 1833. It is of interest here as the attempts of this person to speak succeeded only in production of incomprehensible jargon. To those unaware that he had suffered a stroke, it sounded as if he were talking in a foreign tongue.

Osborne's description concerned a twenty-six-year-old gent of considerable learning (proficient in French, German, Italian, Latin and English and planning to take up medical training) who a year previously had suffered a stroke in the country whilst having breakfast after his morning swim in a nearby lake. Although 'restored to his intellects' after about two weeks, he 'had the mortification of finding himself deprived of the gift of speech'. He had no paralysis, and spoke fluently, with apparent ease. When he came back up to Dublin, though, his extraordinary jargon caused him to be taken as a foreigner. Osborne gave him some sentences to read, and wrote down what he heard – an early endeavour to phonetically transcribe disordered speech after stroke. Although through writing the patient could at the time translate Latin, report on medical tracts in French, play draughts and perform calculations with ease, his speaking remained an impenetrable jargon. His rendition of the sentence 'It shall be in the power of the College to examine or not examine any Licentiate, previously to his admission to a Fellowship as they see fit' was transcribed by Osborne as '*And the be what in the tomother of the trothertodoo to majorum or that emidrate ein einkrastrai mestreit to ketra totombreidei to ra fromtreido asthat kekritest'*.

Osborne speculated that a principal factor associated with this man's jargon was his polyglot status. His speech output apparatus was unable to stably focus on one language, but ranged amongst them all. Although this was certainly a possible ingredient, it is unlikely to have been the prime factor. The gentle-man presented either with what nowadays we might term apraxia of speech, conduction aphasia or phonological jargon (Osborne does not offer sufficient detail to clinch a definitive diagnosis). These do not require that someone speaks more than one language for them to arise. It certainly too is not the case in FAS, where one of the diagnostic markers is that the accent arises *de novo* and is not associated with another language which the person speaks, or has spoken. Osborne's account of how this man was mistaken for a foreigner does, though, illustrate the power of the perceptual impression of the listener to read into a situation a dimension which is, in objective terms, not there.

It was not just in the surgical field that Osborne was an innovator. The patient received the treatment of the day for apoplectic seizures (strokes): repeated applications of leeches, a succession of blisters to the nape (back of the neck) and occiput (back of the head), mercurial purgatives and shower baths every morning. But to no avail. Based on his systematic investigation of what the man was, and was not, able to accomplish by way of speech, Osborne was able to show that these interventions were unlikely to affect the underlying speech problem. Instead he prescribed actual speech therapy – something totally novel at the time. Given the later clearer transcriptions of the College regulation sentence in Osborne's report, the therapy appeared to afford great strides forward. No doubt cessation of the other treatments may have had a hand in progress too!

Reports from previous centuries also record that the perceived altered accent does not necessarily have to be that of a foreign language. An individual may sound as if they have taken on a different regional or social accent of the same language. Recently studies of people with different regional/social accents have appeared of Dutch sounding Flemish, Americans sounding British, southern English sounding Scottish, a Korean woman from Cholla-buk in the southwest sounding like someone from Kangwon in the northeast, people formerly with a marked regional accent sounding as if they now speak a refined standard version. A high-profile example in 2012 was the case of the British pop singer George Michael, whose new West Country regional accent disappeared over a period of weeks as he recovered from a coma.

As ever, if we search earlier works, we find recent reports are not the first. The British neurologist Macdonald Critchley (1900–1997) recorded three instances – coincidentally (or not?) all of English speakers sounding Welsh. Forty-nine-year-old Mrs ME was involved in a car crash in 1956 where she received a compound fracture of the skull and was briefly unconscious. Two years later she still had speech that was dysarthric, slow, hesitant and 'syllabic'. More conspicuous was the excessive range of modulation in pitch of her speech, which was not wholly congruous with the content of her conversations, as Critchley described it. Listeners had the impression she possessed a Welsh accent. She had indeed been born in Wales and was married to a Welshman, but had spent most of her life in Chester, in England. Despite the clear neurological trauma and persisting dysarthric speech, Critchley labelled the woman as 'neurotic'. Her case, in association with the car accident, actually went to the law courts where ME was 'twitted [taunted] as claiming damages on account of the handicap of a Welsh "accent"'. Not for the last time health staff, officials and the press seemed to have grasped the wrong end of the stick.

Three other cases recounted by Critchley entailed one reported to him by Joan van Thal, a speech language therapist in the hospital where he practised and a fifty-six-year-old woman who in 1953 had suffered a stroke and subsequently sounded Welsh. The third, Mrs EL, apart from the fact that she had had what was presumably a stroke involving the right side of her brain, was not dissimilar to Mrs ME, except this time Critchley concluded this was not a case of neurosis but a bona fide neurogenic accent change.

Mrs EL was thirty-nine in 1957 and lived in Bristol, England (just over the border from Wales, but definitely not a Welsh city) when she abruptly experienced a left-sided paralysis and loss of speech. Her former speech patterns eventually returned, but with a staccato, sing-song-like, decidedly Welsh lilt, of which she was fully aware and detested. The other change of note was an alteration to her personality (not uncommon after head injury or with other neurological conditions). She had turned to frequently swearing and believed she had grown old, ugly and fat (the swearing confirmed by others, the appearance changes not).

The cases of ME and EL are illustrative of several points that recur in the reports and words of people with FAS. Alterations to prosody (the stress and intonation aspects of speech) after right brain damage are well attested and, like Astrid L (below), these seem to be the origin of EL's Welsh-sounding speech. Perceptions of an altered personality, as we will see, are a frequent complaint of people with FAS and these perceptions become entwined with issues around the altered accent and its effect on identity. Social and psychological issues may well be detected in the background, which can complicate diagnosis and may colour judgements made by medical staff or friends and relatives. ME seems to have suffered at the hands of a misunderstanding judiciary and may not have been best served by her medical team. EL was stigmatised as a divorcee (in 1957 Britain still seen as a social slur) with the lingering undertones in the report that her new accent was all to do with her divorce from a Welsh husband and that her account might not fully be trusted due to her not being of a 'sufficient cultural level'.

Doubtless, over the centuries there were many more people than these who developed what sounded like a foreign or different regional accent in association with some illness. We have no accounts handed down. What we can be relatively sure of, is that they would not have been received well by their communities. Beliefs surrounding speech changes, theories of why speech changes came about, why people were born with them or acquired them, what it said about their soul, their character, their mind were widely different to the beliefs we hold today. In European scholarship there was scant understanding before the eighteenth century that linked muscles and nerves and brain, that understood speech and its control lying outside the narrow confines of the tongue and voice box. Speech disorders were associated with 'dryness' or 'moisture' or 'hot' or 'cold' conditions of the tongue or vocal cords or of the brain. In the popular view, people with speech 'defects' were eyed with suspicion, with fear, with despising. Afflictions of the tongue, 'visitations' or 'possession' by spirits, were often the cause of persecution, of being ostracised from the community or banishment to an institution. Amongst these unfortunate individuals it is quite probable that there were those with what sounded to their community like an altered accent. It all feels bizarre and inhumane to us nowadays, but is a theme we will be returning to later on.

We probably also have not located earlier reports on altered accent because the cases have been taken as addressing other debates, have been stepping stones in the progress of our understanding of brain and behaviour in general and speech and language in particular, rather than specifically about foreign accents.

For instance, Pick did not label his case with a contemporary equivalent of 'Foreign Accent Syndrome' – he discussed matters within the context of the syndrome of 'infantilism' or 'puerilism', the idea that someone has regressed to talking like a child. Indeed, the case descriptions of the noted Cornish neurologist Bastian, of the great French and German neurologists Charcot, Déjerine, Kussmaul, Lichtheim and Wernicke are replete with mention of people who had regressed to speaking like a child.

Henry Bastian (1837–1915) was famous (some say infamous) in the nineteenth century for his controversial views in favour of archebiosis or abiogenesis (the creation of living organisms from non-living matter). He was also an astute describer of cases he encountered on his neurology rounds. He reasoned for the independence of different 'memories' for words. He distinguished between memories for meaning and memories for sound, with pathways connecting these centres. These are commonplace insights nowadays, but were revolutionary ideas at the time (1868–9), ahead of later similar treatises by Ludwig Lichtheim (1845–1928) and Carl Wernicke (1848–1905), whose fame has overshadowed Bastian's work. Examples of where accent altered but word choice and content did not, or the other way round, were for Bastian strong arguments in favour of this division and his discussions of accent change play out partly in this arena. Similarly, Marie presented his case as part of the contemporary debate over aphasic (language) versus anarthric (speech) disruption to communication, of the debate around anterior and posterior injuries to the brain and possible differences in speech breakdown associated with them.

Critchley set his cases in the context of discussions around upper-class and lower-class (he termed it 'demotic' speech) expression and attitudes to regional accents. Ås and Fromm (see below) introduced their descriptions of the re-emergence of a previous accent/language as contributions to the debate over whether age regression under hypnosis was possible or what the actual nature of the state of mind was in people who appeared to be age-regressed.

A further field where discussions of foreign soundingness have appeared has concerned debates around how the brain controls prosody of speech, i.e. the pattern of stress on different words and syllables (black *bird* versus *black*bird, that's *my* coat versus that's my *coat*), the intonation, rising and falling melody of speech ('you're coming tomorrow' spoken as a command versus questioningly; 'yes' uttered as a definite versus tentative response, happy versus sad judgement). Critchley and his Welsh-sounding speakers are pertinent here, where the perceived other accent stemmed not from alterations to individual speech sounds, but to the lilt of the ladies' speech.

An especially influential report in the history of the understanding of Foreign Accent Syndrome was one which appeared in 1947 written by the Norwegian neurologist Georg Monrad-Krohn (1884–1964). It has caught the imagination and sympathy of people interested in FAS, not just because of its careful account of prosodic changes in speech leading to perception of a foreign accent, but because of the poignancy of the case, how the brain injury had come about and the social reactions the patient subsequently suffered.

On 6 September 1941 in the early years of the Second World War, Astrid L was a thirty-year-old who was tragically caught in the open during a bombing raid on her native Oslo (she was from Nordstrand, then just outside the capital). She was blown down a steep embankment and shrapnel split open the left side (frontal–temporal–parietal regions) of her skull, exposing her brain. She was unconscious for four days and when she came round she could not speak nor move her right side. Over the next two years, despite some epileptic-like seizures and lingering emotional lability, her aphasia had largely recovered, she walked without any sign of a limp and there were few other consequences of her injuries still troubling her. But that did not spell the end of her woes. There were no major after-effects of her brain injury – apart from how she spoke.

When Monrad-Krohn first encountered her in 1943, he took her to be French or German. Her residual speech difficulties rendered it difficult for her to produce the tones or pitch accents of Norwegian speech that help distinguish between certain pairs of words (e.g. between one-syllable 'bönder' (the 'd' is silent) – peasants – and two-syllable 'bönner' – beans or prayers), and overall the amount of stress she gave to syllables was altered and the atypical direction and amount of falling and rising in her speech was noteworthy. For Astrid the complaint was that listeners did not perceive this as a speech difficulty. What they heard was someone speaking with a German accent at the time of the armed occupation of Norway by Nazi forces. She was branded a collaborator or sympathiser and shunned in shops. This is another theme to which we will return in due course. As a happier footnote, one might mention that life took a turn for the better for Astrid with the birth of her son soon after the war.

We have seen then that, until the 1980s, there were numerous reports of people who sounded foreign in association with either neurologically or psychologically altered states. Until the 1980s, though, no one had heard of the label 'Foreign Accent Syndrome'. There had been descriptions of 'infantilism', 'anarthria', 'dysprosody', 'pseudoaccent', and 'unlearned foreign accent'. The common thread was that the individuals had attracted people's attention because their accent did not match the one they had grown up with. The person who is credited with coining the term FAS is Harry Whitaker, an American neurolinguist. In a 1982 report he and colleagues presented an American woman who sounded Spanish. Since then Foreign Accent Syndrome has been the more usual label applied, at least in the Anglophone world. Whether this represents the most apt label is a moot point, but for the time being, we bow to current fashion and retain FAS (or syndromes, given there are a variety of aetiologies).

Before moving on from the historical perspectives, one more important contribution from earlier reports is noteworthy. Several accounts of FAS are notable not solely because they drew our attention to the phenomenon, but because the writers endeavoured to throw light on why their patients sounded foreign. In 1919 Pick published an analysis of the speech of Fischer's patient. He highlighted several aspects of speech that are well in keeping with conclusions arrived at by more recent acoustic and kinematic analyses. There were changes in the length of vowels; alteration to the degree of nasality on some vowels; and sounds like 'sh' and 'ch', though pronounced as 'sh' and 'ch', were nevertheless produced with noticeably different force. A key factor concerned the alteration of where the stress tended to fall in words – the tendency of Karel to emphasise later syllables instead of the expected first syllable for Czech was a prominent signal to listeners that he might be Polish. Pick also pointed out how grammatical slips added to the impression of 'Polishness'.

Monrad-Krohn extended this in his description of the prosody changes in the speech of Astrid L, when he noted that foreignness could be perceived purely on the basis of altered stress and rhythm, and that alterations to individual sounds were not obligatory. The cases of Critchley also underlined this.

Osborne took a two-pronged perspective in his case. On the one hand, he sought to establish why the particular speech patterns had arisen, and settled on the polyglot skills of the man as a source. On the other hand though, he illustrated that the perception of foreignness was also in the ear of the listener. Nielsen and McKeown in 1961 very much emphasised this too in relation to the FAS cases they presented, astutely observing that 'If the examiner did not have acquaintance with any language but his own, he would not see a simulation of some foreign language but only a peculiar form of dysarthria, a disturbance of rhythm'.

The historical descriptions that we have looked at here demonstrate that FAS has been seen and heard for a very long time already. They also illustrate that many of the issues and arguments of today were already ripe in the minds of the pioneers in the field. Their studies have flagged factors that were to become the focus of attention in the literature later in the twentieth century and down to this day. They have noted changes to individual sounds. They have heard alterations to where the stress falls in a word or sentence and to alterations in the melody of speech – there is a rise in intonation where one expects a fall or the rise is far higher or lower than one would expect for the person's native language. Language disturbances have been noted as a common co-occurrence. The person makes grammatical slips. They use inappropriate words, or there is considerable hesitation when searching for the right word.

Further observations point to another frequent finding, that the speech and language difficulties are not an isolated difficulty. The person may also have problems with arm and leg movement. This is not unsurprising as the areas of brain linked to arm and leg movement are very close to the areas involved in speech control. But they may also have other cognitive (thought process) changes, for instance difficulties with calculations previously not present, with reading and writing and spelling, with memory, with attention. Again, this is not incongruous – these other functions rely partly on language and speech processing and/or the nerve pathways and centres in the brain supporting these other cognitive functions are situated close to the areas and pathways involved in speech and language. When it comes to differentially diagnosing neurological from psychological aetiologies of FAS, the picture of accompanying disturbances, as we will see, can be instructive. Finally, in between the lines or as a frank mention, it has been clear from the start that FAS is not just a speech disorder but that it may alter the life of the person; it can, under circumstances, exercise far-reaching effects on the individual's psychological and social life and that of their family and friends.

The fact that the FAS phenomenon has been reported in numerous countries, involving many different languages and has been described by researchers and medical staff from widely differing traditions, is also of note. It underlines that FAS is not a quirk of Anglophone countries – it occurs in a wide variety of languages. It is not the product of misinterpretation of signs in one hospital centre or group of professionals. Despite the range of interpretations regarding the origin of FAS, there is consistency across languages with the kind of alterations to speech that bring about the impression of foreignness. Finally, it is not a freakish phenomenon fuelled by recent journalistic over-fervour to wring a sensational story out of every corner of life's events – though some of the more bizarre claims and misconceptions around FAS can probably be assigned to these ill-informed media sources.

What causes Foreign Accent Syndrome?

FAS is the label assigned when someone has started to speak with an accent not previously their own. From the introduction, and the historical accounts, it is clear there can be a variety of forces behind why speech should suddenly sound foreign or from a different region. One approach to broadly dividing these up is to categorise underlying causes as:

(a) neurological – i.e. associated with damage to the brain by for example a stroke, head injury or changes to the nervous system linked to progressive neurological conditions;

(b) structural-mechanical – i.e. linked to alterations to the topography of the vocal tract from injury to bones or soft tissue – e.g. a broken jaw, dental work, arthritis of the temporal-mandibular joint;

(c) psychological – i.e. not explained on the basis of neurological or mechanical changes and therefore assumed to arise in association with changes in psychological functioning or state of consciousness;

(d) sociological – i.e. the result of conscious or non-conscious sociolinguistic processes such as accent accommodation (see below), social distancing or solidarity. This category does not truly fall within the realm of what researchers normally encompass with the term FAS, but it is mentioned as a dimension that may enter differential diagnostic reckoning, and as an area of study that lends insights into many of the secondary psychosocial effects of FAS.

Of course the above is only a starting point. There still remains the conundrum of why a stroke brings about FAS for one person but not for another. Why does everyone with a fractured mandible not sound foreign? What is it that causes one person to react to life's stresses and strains with a new accent whilst the next person develops a weak leg or tremoring arm?

There is also the thorny issue that real-life personal histories frequently fail to follow textbook notions of neatly divided categories. Everything points to the underlying aetiology being a stroke, but scans fail to indicate central nervous system changes. The scans confirm a head injury, but the site of damage is inconsistent with alterations to speech. The site of damage is compatible with speech changes, but imaging and other investigations over time suggest the speech deficits ought to have long since resolved, but they have not.

Psychological, personality and affective changes can accompany a head injury or other neurological disorder, introducing strands of both neurogenic and functional aetiologies. People with psychiatric problems may suffer a stroke. The same accident that fractured the jaw and dentition may have caused a brain injury. When it comes to clinical presentation there is no shortage of mimics and chameleons. For instance, what looks on the surface like a stroke may in the end be something quite different that only mimics stroke symptoms; what appears decidedly 'unstrokelike' may transpire after much investigation to be just that nevertheless: it was a stroke in disguise.

In other words, one can set up idealised divisions, but often aetiologies may interact. After all we are dealing with complex human beings, not laboratory-bred mice or simple chemical reactions. We will talk more about how one might sift out neurological from psychological or mechanical from neurological when we discuss assessment and diagnosis later. Below we give an overview of conditions with which FAS has been associated in published reports or personal cases we have seen and how it has presented. Before that, however, a few words around notions of causality to bear in mind, for those new to pondering these issues.

In medicine and related fields, there is long-standing debate on what constitutes a description or explanation of a phenomenon. One can describe a condition – whether it is measles, a head injury, effects of electrocution, speech changes – according to what we see or hear with our naked eyes or ears or detect through various instrumental assessments as an observer. The pupils do not react equally to light; there is a raised temperature; the tongue cannot protrude beyond the lips; blood tests show raised antibodies; audiology demonstrates a 20-decibel hearing loss in the left ear.

We can describe FAS as an accent that sounds different to that which the person habitually used; in particular it is a different regional or national accent. Many reports of people with FAS stop at this point, with what in effect is a circular account (the person sounds foreign because their speech sounds German when they are actually English). This level of description is not at all helpful in telling anyone why the accent change has come about, nor even why it is that language X is perceived, or regional accent Y. Going a little further, some studies might add more description, stating that the person with FAS has reduced range of tongue movement, or their /t/ sounds are more like /s/ sounds. These reports may give a description of what someone sees or hears, but they still fail to tell us what has actually caused the foreign-sounding speech to appear.

One way to step beyond this is to search for the underlying cause of the speech changes, or raised temperature, hearing loss, or whatever. Some distinctions can be drawn. The immediate answer might be 'the person has a virus', 'he has glue ear', 'she has had a stroke'. But still these are not fully explanatory accounts, they do not lead to an understanding of why temperature rises in the presence of a viral infection, why a stroke should bring about speech changes, and in particular why a stroke should make someone sound foreign. One needs to delve further to explain how changes associated with infection or stroke lead to the observed phenomena. Therefore clinicians or researchers seek to account for phenomena in terms of the underlying pathology, how body functions are impaired – i.e. why or how changes to body functions and structures have arisen and how these in turn can explain the observed behaviour.

Applied to speech changes after a stroke for instance, this might lead one to state, after further assessment to confirm the suspicion, that the speech changes are linked to alterations in the way an individual's muscles are working. This results in imperfections in the shapes their tongue, lips and vocal cords are assuming for different sounds. On the basis of this, one diagnoses a motor speech disorder, one type of which is neurogenic FAS. However, describing someone as having a motor speech disorder is not an explanation, any more than saying red eyes, raised temperature, greyish-white spots in the mouth and reddish rash spreading in a particular fashion explain what causes measles. It merely shifts the quest for an answer to another stage – why should movements for producing speech be distorted?

A common explanation after stroke would be that disturbed neuromuscular function or/and speech motor programming has led to distortions in the shapes a person's tongue, lips and vocal cords assume. This still would not satisfy in terms of a conclusive explanation. What type of neuromuscular dysfunction (there are many different types depending on which parts of the central and peripheral nervous system are involved and in which ways)? What type of planning disorder – and planning/programming of what? The pursuit of the 'cause' shifts to an account of which neuromuscular or programming disorder.

One senses here the direction of argument – one set of answers only begs a whole new set of questions. The follow-on from explanations for how neuromuscular or speech programming alterations arise might be couched in terms of changes to the electrochemistry of function in the central and peripheral nervous systems, disturbances at the junction between nerves and muscles, or even the biochemistry of muscle contraction and relaxation, as well as changes to patterns of excitation and inhibition of different neural networks within the brain. But then why, for their part, these alterations come about heads off into the realm of cell function and ever finer distinctions, and how the stroke might have brought those changes about.

Such a reductionist model delivers an explanation of sorts, but like analysing every last bit of metal in an aeroplane down to the last atom will tell you a lot about how an aeroplane is constructed and how metal might fatigue, how it oxidises, how it behaves under particular circumstances and so forth, it will never tell you how an aeroplane flies or about the experience of flying. For this, a different perspective is required. One requires perspectives that demonstrate how all the different sub-elements of function (cells, electrochemistry of nerve function/neural transmission and so forth, excitation and inhibition of different neural circuits in the brain) work in concert to produce the movements of speech. One needs insights into how speech relates to closely germane functions such as choosing the right word and putting words into grammatically meaningful sentences, to the listener's perception of sounds as well as the speaker's production of sounds.

Crucially any account of, and experience of, a condition will be incomplete if it ignores how it affects a person's day-to-day activities, their inter-actions with others and the effects this has on their participation in life, how it impacts the individual and their family. These are all different angles from which to describe the same phenomenon. No standpoint is inherently better or worse – it depends on what one's aim is in describing or explaining a phenomenon – but it serves to remind us that no interpretation of FAS will be entire unless such a holistic view is taken.

Returning to the query of 'what causes FAS', simply stating that it represents the appearance of a foreign accent 'out of the blue' denotes a very restricted, non-specific reply. Saying someone has FAS is not a diagnosis; it constitutes a descriptive label. There is no box or gene or pathway in the brain that deter-mines what accent we speak which, when it breaks down, will cause us to produce a different accent. FAS is a symptom, a sign of other changes in the body. In this way it is like the diagnosis 'headache' or 'backache' or 'problems with memory'. These labels tell us something about what the person is experi-encing and are indications that something else is happening in the body to bring these states about, but they themselves are not the primary, underlying problem.

So it is with FAS. It appears in association with changes to how someone speaks. However, speech changes can arise for a whole variety of reasons, encompassing neurological causes, psychological origins or mechanical changes. The role of the medical and psychological team is to determine which of the many possible causes of altered accent is at play in any one particular case. This is not to deny that for the person who experiences the pain of headache or distress of memory problems that they are not very real and very immediate, or that an altered accent is not real and the worries of the person experiencing the appearance of what people hear as a foreign accent is also not very real. What it does say, though, is that simply stating 'you have FAS' is only a very preliminary step in understanding what is happening.

Speech and language changes are a common sequel of brain damage from traumatic brain injury or strokes – for example around a third of people with stroke experience speech and language changes. Many neurological disorders, such as multiple sclerosis, cerebral vasculitis, dystonia and Parkinson's disease, are associated with speech and voice alterations. FAS has been recorded as a sequel to migraines, to atrophy in certain regions of the brain. It has been associated with drug reactions/interactions and with electrocution. There are reports of FAS in youngsters in association with childhood speech disorders, that can be linked to the way that the child's speech is developing or as a result of an accident the child has had that affects brain function.

The common denominator here is that the individual's ability to form sounds and words in the manner that people expect in their particular speech community has been altered by changes to the speed, force, range, sustainability and coordination of contraction of the muscles of articulation (i.e. lips, tongue, soft palate – the soft section at the back of the roof of one's mouth – vocal cords, chest wall). Such behaviours, in neurological aetiologies of FAS, are linked to alterations to the tone, power and timing of movements of muscles due to damage in parts of the brain involved in programming what sets of movements need to be made to produce given sounds and words and/or in actually being able to make those movements. In turn this dysfunction emerges from changes in brain biochemistry, impairment in the transmission of nerve impulses from the brain to muscles and/or problems in the contraction and relaxation of muscles.

There is one massive further ingredient though to FAS that goes beyond the analogy with headache or backache. If deviant speech is part of many neurological disorders, why does everyone who has a neurogenic speech disturbance not sound foreign? We will delve into this more extensively later, but the central hypothesis here revolves around the nature of speech perception, how listeners interpret what they hear. In analysing spoken communication the minimum unit is a speaker and a listener. There are sounds in the mouth of the speaker and we can try and search for the cause of FAS in the mouth of the speaker. But sounds people make are only understood and made real in the ear and brain of the listener. The key ingredient in understanding FAS entails linking changes to the speech of the speaker to how those changes are perceived by the listener.

The view that will be prevalent through this book is that, certainly in relation to neurogenic speech changes, the person with FAS is no different to anyone else who has dysarthria or apraxia of speech or dysprosody (common classes of motor speech disorders). If one analyses the speech of individuals with FAS phonetically, acoustically, physiologically, kinematically (the movements they are making to produce sounds), what emerges is evidence of an underlying motor speech disorder affecting the production of particular sounds, particular combinations/sequences of sounds or maintaining the appropriate (for the local accent) pattern of stress and intonation, the appropriate speech melody. Strokes and other neurological conditions do not cause foreign accents. They bring about motor speech disorders.

Where 'foreignness' enters the equation is not primarily in the mouth of the speaker but in the ear of the listener. When we hear someone speak there are myriad cues that we pick up which deliver all kinds of information that we may exploit to judge or categorise the speaker – their age, gender, mood, social class, geographical provenance or whether we think they have a speech impediment or not. Critically, as regards labelling someone as having FAS, if the cues that the listener hears in terms of speech changes due to the underlying motor speech disorder remind them of a particular foreign or different regional accent, then what they will hear is not a speech disorder, but a different accent. As Nielsen and McKeown, whom we mentioned previously, accurately concluded: if listeners did not know what Swedish (that being the accent that people heard in the two men they report) sounded like, all that they would have heard before them were two people with a speech disorder, not foreign-sounding speech. This is more than likely too the explanation for why we never hear reports of people from Britain sounding like a Basque speaker, Australians sounding like an Inuit, or Americans like a Moldovan. The accents of these languages are simply outside of the experience of listeners. One would speculate though that someone with FAS in Gijon, Reykjavik or Odessa (Ukraine, not Texas) may well be perceived by locals respectively as a speaker of Basque, Inuit or Moldovan.

So, how does this 'in the ear of the listener' mechanism work? Some examples illustrate the possibilities. A sequel of the neurological condition may be weakened lips. In turn this can bring about an apparent difficulty pronouncing labial sounds – p, b, w and other sounds made using the lips. If the predominant impression of someone who has such a difficulty by an English listener is difficulty pronouncing the 'w' sound – e.g. 'water' sounds like 'vater', 'well' like 'vell' – the listener may well conclude they are speaking with a German accent. An alteration to tongue placement may mean that vowels are produced with the tongue placed systematically higher than it should be. Consequently, for an English speaker what should sound like the 'i' as in 'ship' is heard by the listener as 'ee' – 'ship' sounds like 'sheep', 'pen' may be heard as 'pain', 'but' as 'boot'. On this basis a listener may perceive the accent as Italian. The essential point is that although the reasons for altered lip movement and higher placement of the tongue are due to the neuromuscular changes arising from the nervous system damage, the perception of German or Italian accents here arises from the listener's association of 'vater' and 'sheep' with how they believe a German and Italian might pronounce 'water' and 'ship' when speaking English.

Where alterations to the stress and intonation patterns of speech (the melody of speech) have occurred – falls and rises come in the wrong place or in the unexpected direction or to a greater or lesser degree than expected – then it might suggest to a British ear they are listening to a Welsh or Swedish or Chinese speaker. For a variety of well-understood motor control and linguistic reasons people who have neurological motor speech disorders may introduce an 'uh' sound into words – 'stairs' can sound like 'suhtairs', 'cut' like 'ahcut' or 'cutah', 'white shirt' like 'whiteuh shirt'. This alters the perceived structure of the word and rhythm of the sentence. Importantly for English listeners, such changes can trigger the impression that this is someone with an Italian accent trying to speak English.

If, however, what the listener hears are distortions to speech that are outside of their experience of natural languages – there are blocks and repetitions similar to a stutterer, constant excess nasality, altered, gruff, squeaky voice quality, severely distorted sounds – '*magazine*' sounds like '*flimazjin*' – then what they will perceive is a speech disorder. We will see later on that what is typically found in people with FAS due to neurological origins, if one listens or analyses very carefully, is that there are distortions to sounds, alterations to voice quality, changes to how nasal the speech sounds that clearly indicate an underlying speech disorder. However, amongst these there will be speech distortions that listeners may classify as signifying a different regional or foreign accent. So, it is not a question of absolutes – all the sounds sound foreign in someone with FAS versus all the sounds sound disordered in anyone with a different kind of motor speech disorder. Rather it is the relative preponderance of perceived changes. If the salient alterations for the listener fall within the 'natural language' category their brain will ignore the disordered signals and hear a different accent. If the principal derailments they perceive fall into their 'disordered' category they will hear someone with a speech defect.

This is not unusual, not some remarkable phenomenon that happens only in certain rare cases of speech change associated with brain damage. We are exposed to this process every day. When we are listening to someone and we are not sure where they hail from we may latch onto key features of their speech to give us clues, to see if they fit our classification of someone from this or that region or social group. The occasional burred 'r' suggests to us Irish, a rolled 'r' creeping in occasionally leads us to Scotland, a more guttural 'r' excites echoes of French or German. But maybe that burred 'r' means they are from the West Country or are North American, not Irish at all.

We listen then for other clues that point in one direction or the other, we make a judgement based on preponderance of occurrence of given features. The sound change does not have to be there all the time; it can be infrequent and fleeting. Our brain is working on probabilities. The frequency or saliency of one particular change or confluence of two or three particular changes will push our judgements off in one direction or the other. It only takes a slight tip in the balance for us to change our minds – this is a speech disorder after all; no, this is an Italian, not a Spaniard. The same happens when we are sizing up someone for which social group they come from, whether we find them sympathetic, what age or gender they are. We are picking up on nuances of speech that push our perceptions in this direction or that.

These 'ear of the listener' ingredients to the FAS equation immediately put into perspective several commonly attested phenomena around FAS. A feature that often throws professionals and public alike off the trail of a neurological origin to the FAS is the fact that different people listening to the same person and at the same time hear different accents. One person believes they hear French, another Italian, another Chinese and another person wonders what the fuss is about – for them there is no altered accent, they hear a speech disorder, not a difference. What is happening here is that one listener is tuning into one aspect of change – maybe altered rhythm – another focuses on difficulty with certain sounds which they associate with speakers from a different country, whilst for another listener the salient change involves the odd rises in melody at the end of phrases that are not part of the local accent.

Furthermore, if any more proof were needed that the ear of the listener plays a central role here, when placed alongside a speaker with a genuine Italian, Russian or whatever accent, one can immediately discern that the accent of the person with FAS is quite different – a generic accent or 'pseudoaccent' as some (e.g. in Francophone literature or some earlier English writing) have labelled it to signify that it is foreign sounding, but not clearly the accent of one language or another. It has a Scandinavian lilt, an Eastern European quality, or Chinese or Asian rhythm, but not a unique Spanish, Hindi, Icelandic character or the like.

A related phenomenon appears in the field of entertainment. Ventriloquists make their living from manipulating 'ear of the listener' effects. The lips do not move for '*bottle of beer*' but we do not hear '*gottle of geer*', we still hear '*b*' sounds. If we analyse what sounds are actually being produced, though, it is more likely to be '*ottle o eer*'. The missing correct sounds are inserted by our brain's expectations, by suggestive auditory cues elsewhere in the utterance and by priming from the visual and narrative context.

Similarly, the impersonator who mimics other actors, politicians, or public figures can have us totally convinced it is the genuine person speaking. Yet, if one analyses their speech output carefully it is clear most of it still resembles the impersonator's own speech; placed directly alongside the speech of their target of fun, one immediately picks up who is the real Mr(s) X. The impressionist's skill lies not in developing a carbon copy of the speech of the victim of their lampoon, but in identifying salient features, ones that mark them as different to others, their chief mannerisms and idiosyncrasies. The rest of their speech does not need to bear a close resemblance, just sufficient to tip the balance of perception and probability of supposition in a given direction in the ear of listener.

If there are other characteristics, visual mannerisms for instance, then these help to underline the illusion. Similarly, in the case of FAS added features not directly related to speech such as word-finding pauses, using the wrong word, grammatical slips, hesitations, slow deliberate speech, or altered facial and hand gestures during speech, all contrive to reinforce the impression and provide an added illusion that the person is not a native speaker.

Here is a short speech transcript from someone who had FAS after a burst aneurysm (abnormal swelling of a blood vessel). It obviously does not show the sound changes, just the words and grammar that listeners heard. Even without being able to discern the accent, though, chances are if you were asked who is speaking/writing here you may well wager it is a foreign speaker.

I was very well before I go into hospital with these headache. I take eight tablet every day for six week. Still a headaches all of the time. Then I go into hospital ... You know how I came out. The head it began to be better after all this time and all this tablet. And then all of sudden about 2 o'clock the day before yesterday I began to fell myself looking around again and by bedtime I was almost to be demented ... The boy outsides start to shout to he friend up the street and it motivate me to get moving ... I ranned through here ... I rang to my niece. She come to me and she stay with me all night.

Some of the changes are arguably related to the speech output difficulties – such as loss of 's' on '*headache*' and '*tablet*', the perception of '*this*' rather than '*these tablet*', '*his*' heard as '*he friend*', even the '*ranned*' example. It is probably only a phonetician or speech pathologist, though, who would spot these as sound-based slips. Most speakers are likely to hear them as deviations in language rules. Their supposition will be further boosted by hearing the slips that are most probably language based – '*I go*', not '*I went*'; '*I was almost to be demented*'.

An even more extreme example of 'ear of the listener' effects is found in the field of talking animals. Periodically the popular press presents a story about a parrot, a whale, a dolphin, or a dog that has learned to speak like a human. Listening to the culprit recordings, if one closes one's eyes and lets the imagination loose it is sometimes possible to discern what sounds like recognisable human sounds or words. A more objective look or listen at the evidence, though, brings one back to reality – the sounds are still of a whale or dog, they require a stretch of the imagination to pin the human speech label on them, and, as with divergent perceptions of accent and speech in FAS, one person can hear '*pretty Polly*', the next hears '*many potties*', the next hears only a cat meowing or a pigeon cooing.

There are other characteristics of speech output or speech disorders that may enhance the impression of foreignness and at the same time seed doubt in the minds of people not familiar with how motor speech disorders behave concerning the neurological versus functional origins of the speech changes. Some of these other characteristics include, for instance, the well-documented fact that people with speech disorders after neurological insult find words and phrases that require less processing capacity relatively easy to produce. Passing the time of day, producing well-learned phrases and sayings or sequences (reciting the ABC, 'you know how it is', common prayers) count as relatively easy. Talking about everyday topics can be much less taxing than joining in a deep philosophical discussion or explaining a complex concept. Spontaneous speech can be easier than reading, especially if the person was not a frequent reader before their insult. Words with no or few complex syllables (e.g. '*sang*' versus '*sprang*'; '*tick*', '*sit*' versus '*strict*') or words in predictable contexts as opposed to less predictable ('*I want a cup of t*' ... versus '*I hope to see p*' ...) generally prove less error prone. In the easier contexts, with sounds, words, phrases that are more automatic or familiar, one may hear clear instances of the person's old accent;

where the brain has to use up more processing power to retrieve less frequent words or sound combinations or simultaneously programme complex grammatical structures, speech may alter back to foreign or disordered sounding. Such variability is perfectly congruent with well-established and understood features of how the brain controls speech. It is not an immediate cause to suspect a psychological aetiology for the speech changes.

There is another intriguing factor that has been mentioned in passing in some reports and certainly comes through in some individuals' anecdotes about how communication has evolved since the onset of their new accent. People have noted alterations in the hand gestures that they make accompanying speech. Whitty mentioned this for instance in his 1964 account of a London (England) woman with a history of migraines who sounded German after she suffered a cerebral bleed. Apart from the speech changes, she had also started using hand gestures unusual for her. A personal case was also noted by her relatives to be employing exaggerated hand gestures which seemed to underline the impression of her Italian-sounding speech.

Again, this finding fits well with what we know about gestures in people with no neurological condition and changes to movement after brain injury. Hand and arm gestures, head movements, facial expression and speech are intimately yoked to each other in communication. Right from the earliest descriptions of people with neurological injury and speech changes, observers noted altered arm, head and face movement, not just altered speech and language. Gestures change in their range, rate, force; people may be no longer able to produce iconic gestures (e.g. sign of the cross, thumbs-up sign) or mime actions (e.g. how to hammer a nail, put on lipstick). The disruption can extend to no longer comprehending the gestures of others. Couple this with the fact that many gestural conventions are culturally specific (as comedians are wont to portray in their stereotyped imitations of foreigners) and one can envisage how changes to gestures and facial expression may add to the illusion of foreignness.

In feeling that the person with FAS has altered gestures, we may be experiencing here rather than an ear of the listener, an eye of the listener effect. People hear not just the altered accent and the pauses, hesitation and awkward grammar and word choice from language dysfunction. They see manual gestures that are different in range and rhythm to what one associates with local speakers. The accented speech leads one to assume this difference in gesture grows not out of the consequences of brain damage but derives from their foreignness. This represents a speculation waiting to be confirmed, but an intriguing scenario nevertheless.

Why an individual feels they are taking on the non-verbal characteristics of another culture may have an answer elsewhere. Again, the topic is entirely uninvestigated, at least within the field of neurology. What is known, though, is that when people use a foreign language they may also accommodate to the non-verbal characteristics of that language. Sometimes this is a sign of total proficiency. Other times it may be a conscious or subconscious way of signalling affiliation with a group, matching up identities. If someone senses they have taken on a French or Russian or Chinese identity via their accent, it is not a giant stride to conjecture that they may also then express this new identity through their body posture and manual gestures. Another personal case spontaneously admitted to having acquired hand gestures over the years that he never used before, which he linked to his acquired foreign accent.

So, in relation to the question posed at the start of the section, what causes FAS, one account is that neurological damage to certain parts of the brain impairs the tone, power and coordination of movements for speech and/or the programming of movements for speech sounds. These changes in turn are associated with an individual's difficulty in producing sufficient speed, force, range, sustainability and coordination of the target movements for a sound or word, and/or problems controlling the pattern of stress, rate and intonation for a whole phrase. If the constellation of speech changes heard by a listener strongly coincides with their impression of how the speech of particular foreign speakers sounds, then rather than perceiving a speech disorder they pick up a foreign accent. The variability from listener to listener on what accent is heard relates to the variability in what features sound salient for a given listener and to the experience of foreign speech of that listener. The fact that some people with stroke or other underlying medical condition sound foreign when others do not likewise relates to the constellation of perceived changes and their relative predominance.

As remarked earlier, though, this is an unsatisfactory account from a variety of angles. Whilst the interaction of mouth of speaker and ear of listener factor is almost certainly correct, the interplay between the precise nature of speech/movement changes and the probabilistic perceptual processes at work in creating an impression of foreignness invites further elucidation. Although a reductionist 'swallowed a bird to catch the spider, swallowed a cat to catch the bird, swallowed a dog to catch the cat ... ' line of enquiry brings some insights into underlying causes, it entirely misses the holistic, interactive nature of speech production and perception, and crucially the manner in which suddenly developing a new accent impacts on individuals and their families. Hence, below we examine in more detail aspects of the social-psychological impact of FAS and what it means to the individual and family.

It is also an incomplete account of what causes FAS in as much as the account is true of how changes to speech patterns might arise in neurological conditions, but it appears that frequently (we do not know how frequently, since no one has yet carried out the kind of study that would give an accurate answer) FAS arises from other sources. We now turn to look in some more detail at the variety of origins of an altered accent.

Aetiologies of FAS: neurogenic

Speech changes are not an uncommon sequel to changes in the brain from injury or illness. Speech and voice disorders happen when the neurological changes affect areas of brain involved in producing speech. There is no single area of brain uniquely devoted to speech. Producing speech is a highly complex act, there is probably nothing more complex that humans, or any species for that matter, achieve than speaking. Second by second, we control to millisecond timing and millimetre precision the movements of hundreds of muscle contractions and coordination of these contractions across the whole vocal tract – from the abdomen and diaphragm involved in the control of breathing for speech, via the rib cage, the most delicate muscles of the voice box or larynx, the soft palate at the back of the mouth for gaining the right balance of nasality in the voice, through to the tongue, lips and mandible (jawbone). But that's scarcely the half of it.

At the same time we are also retrieving the words we require to convey our ideas and feelings, we are computing what sounds we will need to utter those words. We are placing the words into sentences in a way that will enable others to know exactly what we mean. The right words have to be stressed, the right intonation to the sentence needs to be given to communicate the way in which we intend the phrase to be taken. The loudness, rate and general tone of voice need to be controlled to convey the mood or emotion we wish to project. All this entails multiple areas of brain working in concert to maintain this miracle of evolution. And we accomplish it as adults without having to give barely a thought to it; it runs automatically like clockwork. Until, of course, we suffer some insult.

Distortion to any one of these components unbalances the whole system and opens the door for misunderstandings, misperceptions of what we wish to say, the tone we wish to convey it in and the picture of ourselves we want to portray. Neurological conditions may alter the range, rate, power and coordination of movements. They may modify the ability to plan and programme the movements. They can transform control of the delicate nuancing of pitch, loudness or rate of speech. They may alter our ability to retrieve the words we need or to retrieve them as fast as we need them, as well as disrupt our ability to place words into grammatically clear sentences.

How speech production breaks down when the central nervous system is affected is highly varied. You may not take in enough breath for the utterance you have to say, or you cannot coordinate breathing with speech. Your voice quality alters (e.g. too creaky, too breathy). Control of pitch comes from how well we control tension in the vocal cords – problems there will lead to speech that is too flat, monotonous, or with widely exaggerated rises and falls or speech arrests, sudden silence. Voice loudness and placing the right emphasis on a syllable or word is a delicate balancing act between the pressure of air coming from the lungs and the tightness with which one presses together the vocal cords. Imbalance will alter the control of appropriate loudness or stress – '*canOE*' (stress on second syllable) might sound like '*CANoe*' (stress on first); '*I want that RED one*', ends up sounding like '*I WANT that red one*'. Problems with the soft palate alter the balance between nasal and non-nasal sounds – speech sounds twangy or words like '*we*', '*Dee*' and '*lame*' sound like '*me*', '*knee*' and '*name*'. If the tongue will not travel far enough, fast enough, strongly enough or precisely enough, speech sounds become distorted. '*Tea*' and '*it's*' sound like '*see*' and '*itch*'. Ditto for the lips where '*pea*' and '*bee*' might be perceived by listeners as '*fee*' and '*V*'.

All movements have to be programmed, and every aspect of retrieving and programming the right movements for the sounds one needs may be impaired. This is all, too, without fitting in the computations for the other components – saying the right words in the right order, with the right endings and stress patterns to convey ideas with the appropriate tone of voice and mood (see the excerpt above from the person with FAS who also had difficulties with word finding and grammar). Consider also for instance the following – '*that's a lovely dress you have on*' uttered in an affirming, complimentary fashion, versus with a sarcastic edge. '*Oh you've finally arrived*' called out with a gasp of relief, versus anger. '*You're eating carrots*' intended as an exclamation of surprise versus as an order. '*They're hunting dogs*' spoken with completely different meanings depending on where the stress falls in the phrase.

These all depend on delicate timing and control across the vocal tract. Imbalance does not have to be so extreme that the listener cannot understand any more, as can be the case for many people with neurological speech disorders. A slight disparity between the intended tone of voice, intonation or rate of speech or precision of articulation might not result in unintelligibility, but it certainly might mean being misconstrued, and more pertinently here might mean being perceived as speaking with a different accent.

Disruptions to the operation of different parts of the brain bring about varying changes to speech and voice. The main areas of brain active in speech control are the left side of the brain (the left hemisphere) in most people, in particular regions of the parietal lobe and frontal lobe, the insula and connections between them. The cerebellum and basal ganglia play vital roles, in particular in the initiation, rate, and rhythm of speech. Of course all the messages from the brain have to travel out to the muscles of the trunk, voice box, soft palate, mouth and face, so intactness of the pathways between the brain and the muscles is also vital for normal speech. The right hemisphere appears to play a particular role in the perception of the tone of voice of people one is listening to, and contributes to controlling the appropriate stress and intonation pattern of one's own speech to convey the correct tone of voice and mood.

Where sites of brain damage have been reported in people with FAS, they generally conform to the sites of lesions seen in anyone else with a speech disorder, i.e. certain areas of cortex, the basal ganglia, cerebellum and pathways between them just outlined. When the actual speech changes are put under close scrutiny, again nothing unusual emerges. There are distortions of sounds due to undershooting or overshooting of movements, contacts between tongue and palate or between the lips are less strong, alterations to tongue placement cause vowel sounds to be off-target and some sounds may sound more nasal than usual. All these are in keeping with the kinds of neuromuscular impairments found after brain damage and which lie behind the common speech disorder called dysarthria. Speech apraxia and dysprosodic (distortions to stress, rhythm and intonation) derailments to sounds are common after brain damage, and these too are well attested in people with FAS. In the thirteen cases from the Mayo clinic mentioned by Aronson in 1990, eight appear to have been associated with apraxia of speech.

The majority of published reports of FAS stemming from neurological events are associated with stroke or head injury. This may simply be a reflection of the fact that these conditions are very common compared to other causes; it may reflect too the kinds of facilities that people interested in FAS work in; it may also represent a bias from the fact that many people who conduct research on FAS have previously worked on the much more frequently encountered disorder of aphasia, which tends to be more often associated with strokes and head injury, not other neurological disorders. There are certainly reports of FAS associated with many other underlying conditions, as outlined earlier – multiple sclerosis, dystonia, cerebral vasculitis, electrocution, and brain atrophy in given areas.

It is not uncommon for some neurological conditions to commence as an isolated speech change, just as apparently isolated reading, writing, memory and motor control deficits may be harbingers of some otherwise hidden neurological degeneration, or hint that a central nervous system event has taken place. FAS has been reported as the initial sign of primary progressive aphasia and fronto-temporal dementia.

Some neurological conditions strongly associated with speech changes are conspicuous by their absence in the FAS literature, and this raises an interesting question. Why do we never hear of someone who stutters sounding foreign, or people with motor neurone disease/amyotrophic lateral sclerosis (ALS), or Huntington's having FAS? Why are the speech distortions of people who are or who become deaf not classified as foreign sounding? They can experience the same classes of changes to voice and speech and language that people with FAS show when linked to other conditions. The reason may be this: in Parkinson's, ALS, deafness and the like, the kinds of alterations to voice and speech may be strongly associated with what listeners perceive as disordered speech or voice right from the start. A strong element of voice (contrasted to speech) deterioration right from the start may also mitigate against perceptions of foreignness. Foreign speakers may have altered pronunciation, but in general they do not use a huskier, breathier or more creaky voice, though changes in the habitual pitch level one uses (towards higher or lower) may add to impressions of foreignness. Furthermore, people have very fixed ideas of what someone who stutters or someone who is deaf sounds like; the kind of distortions to speech flow, intonation and voice setting are familiar and categorised in listeners' minds as 'disorder' not 'difference'.

Typically FAS occurs alongside other common sequelae of stroke or head injury or other cause. These may include language problems, memory disturbances, changes in sensation or loss of power in the arm and leg. Occasionally, it has been reported as a sole symptom or only residual symptom after other changes have resolved. The latter cases are often the most problematic when it comes to establishing why the FAS has arisen. When the pattern of speech and non-speech changes ties in with well-recognised patterns of breakdown, one can be relatively confident that the origin may be neurogenic, especially if imaging and other test results likewise concur with changes observed. Isolated speech changes, especially with scant or no support of neurological changes from alternative investigatory sources, require a lot more careful consideration – a topic we return to later under differential diagnosis.

Still on the topic of appearance of an altered accent in association with neurological conditions, there is another way in which this might happen. This concerns instances of what has been labelled re-emergence of a former accent.

Re-emergence of a former accent

The initial characterisation of FAS at the start of the book stated that typically the speaker has never learned or had any association with the language that is now attributed to them. There is one phenomenon, though, where an apparently new accent appears that people who know the speaker have previously never heard, but which is an accent the speaker had in the past. This is the case in re-emergence of a previous foreign accent.

Immigrants to a community can become so proficient at their new 'native' tongue that to all intents and purposes their friends, colleagues and people they encounter in their day to day life take them as a local. Then they suffer a stroke or similar, and the accent of the language they grew up with but have long since left behind, re-emerges.

One of the close colleagues of Bastian, mentioned earlier in the section on historical reports of FAS, was Sir William Broadbent (1835–1907), an English neurologist who worked in St Mary's Hospital, London. He was probably the first person to document re-emergence of a 'lost' accent, even though the phenomenon must have been occurring since humans first wandered off into foreign lands and adopted the speech of their hosts. He relayed to Bastian the case of a thirty-four-year-old German who prior to admission had spoken English particularly well. On 4 February 1870 he was found having fallen off his stool at work with what transpired to be a stroke. He was brought to the hospital with right-sided paralysis on the 8th. For several days he remained speechless. Six days later some words were possible, but highly distorted and with a low monotonous voice. What was remarkable for Broadbent was the thick German accent that now pervaded his whole speech.

The case might have been dismissed as something that was in Broadbent's imagination on account of the man's German name, or perhaps Broadbent was being overgenerous in his intimation of 'particularly good' English before the stoke. But the phenomenon has subsequently been reliably documented many times. The British neurologist Critchley had referred to him in 1960 the case of a forty-eight-year-old bilingual French woman living in London, England who spoke with a perfect English accent. She had been out choosing wall-paper when she experienced what was later assumed to have been a transient ischaemic attack (temporary blockage of blood flow to part of her brain). Initially she could not speak and only seemed to be able to think in French. When words were finally emitted they came out slurred and with a strong French accent. Fearing she would be taken as drunk and create a scandal (we are talking here of 1960s shops for refined clientele) she managed with much difficulty of expression to take a taxi home. As her speech gradually returned the slurring remained (which points to the neurological origin for the changes), but super-imposed on this was her re-emerged strong French accent.

More recent accounts have covered the re-emergence of a Dutch accent and an Irish brogue in immigrants to the USA. A different angle on the issue of re-emergence of a previous accent is furnished in reports by two American psychiatrists whilst practising hypnosis and age regression.

Arvid Ås in 1962 described the case of an eighteen-year-old with an unmistakably American accent who had been born in Finland of Swedish-speaking parents. On the death of his father when S was five years old, he and his mother moved to the USA. His mother remarried twice: first another Swedish Finn who sadly died and then a Finn who spoke no Swedish. Once in the USA they spoke almost exclusively English, and certainly from when S was aged eight Swedish was not used any more. At eighteen he asserted he had absolutely no recollection of Swedish, and a language test seemed to confirm he possessed now only rudimentary knowledge.

Over the course of a fortnight, Ås used hypnosis to induce age regression until S believed he was five years old, shortly after his arrival in the USA. He reported in this state, in English, that he had been in the USA a few months then but could recall some Swedish. A reapplication of the language test under hypnosis, and with significantly higher scores than previously (though still only just under fifty per cent correct), seemed to confirm that he did indeed still have some fluency in a language he felt he had forgotten.

Erika Fromm (1909–2003, a German-American clinical psychologist and specialist in hypnosis) conducted a similar investigation which was reported in 1970. It involved a student, alias Don. His grandparents were from Japan but he and his own parents had been born in the USA. Shortly after Don was born, in December 1941, they had all been interned in a relocation camp for undesirable aliens. He lived there hearing Japanese till the end of the Second World War. Following release, he and his parents used only English. Both parents died while he was an adolescent. At age twenty-eight he attested to remembering only a few fixed phrases of Japanese. However, when brought back under hypnosis to believing he was aged three he commenced in a child-like voice to speak fluent Japanese. After arousal from the trance he held no recollection of this and still maintained he no longer knew Japanese. Fromm's interpretation was that, for whatever reasons, his knowledge or acknowledge-ment of Japanese was repressed and it was only when the repression was lifted or bypassed that the latent knowledge came to light.

Whatever the merits of these two cases and comparison with instances of re-emergence of accents after stroke, they serve to underline the fact that the mind performs some rather amazing things, and the dividing line between psychological and neurological explanations of behaviour can sometimes be very fluid and thin. Unfortunately also, when such cases are taken out of con-text they may cloud the general public's perspectives and beliefs concerning FAS.

One of the explanations for re-emergence of a previous accent centres on the cost (e.g. in terms of processing capacity and power, of attention) to the brain of perfecting and maintaining a new accent later in life which is not the one that comes as the most automatic to the speaker. This is possible so long as the brain is functioning optimally. When a neurological insult robs the brain of some of its processing capacity, the more automatic, not so costly accent, re-emerges.

In the cases presented by Ås and Fromm the explanations they advanced were somewhat different. For S and Don there was definitely no suggestion of neurological damage. The two psychiatrists were arguing that the languages were not so much lost as repressed. The trauma around internment and discrimination in Don's case and the events around the death of his father, uprooting from Finland and the presence of two stepfathers in the space of a few years in S's experience, were reasons to supress associations with their respective childhood languages. It was only when this repression was lifted that they regained access to something reputedly lost.

The latter two cases are unlikely to provide explanations for many, if any, cases of FAS, in as much as the events recounted arose only under highly specific circumstances and not within day-to-day routine. They do start to highlight, though, that forces of the mind and emotions can be powerful ingredients in the origin and maintenance of a new accent. That is the topic to which we turn presently. Before then just some brief words on some instances where alterations to the structure, mechanics or topography of the vocal tract may prompt what sounds like a new accent.

Aetiologies of FAS: structural changes

By structural we mean here alterations to the shape of one's mouth or throat or any part of the vocal tract which causes the ways or the directions in which lips, tongue, vocal cords and jaw travel to be transformed. Probably most people have experienced changes such as this and noticed that for a while their speech had altered – or at least felt it had altered: having a brace fitted as a teenager; at the opposite end of the age range, getting a new set of dentures or having a set that do not fit snugly; the period whilst the anaesthetic wears off after a trip to the dentist; having a sore, enlarged, ulcerated tongue; or after you have just had your tonsils out. These provide a few examples. Less common experiences cover having a fractured jaw, knocked out teeth, or inflammation of the temporal-mandibular joint (the hinges of the jaw just in front of the ears). Accounts of individuals sounding foreign in such circumstances do exist.

Theoretically, such changes should be highly transitory. Anyone who has been subject to braces or dentures knows that one soon adjusts to the altered topography and one learns to compensate for articulatory pain. We are designed as humans to be highly adaptable motorically, in terms of the movements we make to achieve a physical goal. We do not have to learn to walk differently just because the ground beneath our feet alters; the brain automatically adjusts parameters to prevent us from falling over. We can still speak perfectly intelligibly even though we are holding a cigarette between our lips or have a mouth full of hot potato or when we speak propping the chin up with the elbow on the table. People who have part of their tongue removed for cancer soon learn to speak as they did previously; people with severe Bell's palsy (weakness of one side of the face) readily adjust their speech to maintain intelligibility; individuals who have their jaw wired together after a fracture still manage clear speech. As mentioned previously, ventriloquists make a living from speaking with radically altered speech movement patterns.

Given this, it is feasible that someone might develop a different-sounding accent during the period of adjustment in illness or injury. At the same time, given the exquisite capability we have for compensating for even gross mechanical and structural disturbance, one would expect the deviation to be only temporary. If an altered accent persists, one would be left searching for reasons beyond the immediate structural-mechanical aetiology.

One scenario might be that the same trauma that brought about the fractured jaw, lost teeth, or abrased tongue also altered the innervation to the muscles that move the affected parts. The same car crash that resulted in the facial injuries may also have caused damage to the brain, and through that impaired the person's ability to naturally compensate for the changed movement patterns. A third possibility is that a persisting accent change in cases of structural alterations arises for psychological reasons. Surviving a traumatic event where one sustained painful injuries can release anxieties and other emotions that become expressed in a persisting altered accent. Being left with perceived disfigurement in such circumstances might similarly engender deeper seated feelings that manifest themselves in persisting speech changes in the face of lack of any continued physical cause for the altered accent. Psychological aetiologies represent a significant area of consideration in relation to FAS.

Aetiologies of FAS: psychogenic

This section turns to consider instances where a new accent appears to have arisen for no apparent neurological, speech developmental or structural reasons and where the suspicion therefore is that the origins are to be sought more in the workings of the mind of the individual and their interaction with their environment. There are cases reported in specialist medical and psychology journals that indicate psychological factors can be the cause of accent change. From personal clinical experience it is certainly clear. As no one has ever conducted a detailed in-depth survey of large numbers of people with FAS, it is not possible to state how many cases might arise exclusively for psychogenic rather than neurogenic reasons, or what the typical and more unusual patterns of interaction between the two might be. Published reports are a poor guide to numbers here, and without detailed assessments clinical anecdote of prevalence in one direction or the other may also be distorted. What is probably also true is that cases labelled psychogenic in the past may well have been disclosed as neurogenic if the researchers had had at their disposal some of the more sophisticated brain imaging techniques now available. It is true, too, that as it becomes ever more possible to view the detailed workings of the brain, our insights into psychogenic versus neurogenic FAS will become more precise. Likewise, we will be able to study the intricate interplay between neuro- and psychogenic determinants of speech change.

There is nothing new to the notion of speech disorders arising from psychological origins rather than neurological, or of speech symptoms appearing that are quite out of keeping with a recognised neurological event and so psychological overlay must be suspected. There are numerous reports of individuals who developed a new foreign or bizarre accent in association with psychiatric conditions such as bipolar disorder, schizophrenia, psychogenic fugue or conversion disorder. A case is reported of a woman with schizophrenia, who during exacerbations of her psychotic state habitually imitated or echoed the accent of the person she was speaking to – allegedly without recollection of having done this when the exacerbation passed. In these circumstances the accent change is commonly just one part of a much more complex picture of behavioural change in keeping with recognised abnormal states, and the diagnostic direction is generally clear.

Delving into why some people should adopt a foreign accent as part of a psychotic episode moves outside the bounds of this book. The majority of people who arrive in clinic with FAS are unlikely to be described as psychotic or constitute full-blown psychiatric cases. It is quite possible for speech to alter for far lesser reasons. We are all familiar with speech changes (not necessarily growing into FAS) that are linked to altered emotional states – the dry mouth before a major interview, feeling speechless once in the interview, becoming tongue-tied when speaking to the company boss or a celebrity. We talk differently when we are anxious, when we are in a panic, if we suffer from social phobia, or simply when we are tired or bored. There are distinct speech patterns in depression or when we are overexcited or euphoric. It should not be a surprise, then, that speech might change in relation to other emotional states.

This section concentrates on cases where an individual appears otherwise healthy or where attested other conditions (a stroke, a head injury) do not seem to offer a full or plausible explanation for the speech alterations. Under the umbrella of this label one could also number cases of feigning or malingering, of conscious accent mimicry as opposed to the changes in other psychological aetiologies that may be entirely outside the conscious or volitional control of the speaker.

The section is headed 'psychogenic' as this is a label often used to denote speech disorders of no other apparent origin. However, it is not the only label employed and books and articles speak of psychiatric, psychological, functional, somatoform, affective or medically unexplained symptoms and similar to denote the same thing. Psychogenic is chosen here to be as neutral as possible and simply to signify a contrast with neurological or mechanical origins.

It is recognised, though, that all these labels, and others mentioned below, carry a considerable amount of theoretical baggage with them for people who work in the field. Whilst they may give the impression of being overarching and neutral, they do in fact signal different kinds of beliefs and attitudes about the nature, origins and treatment of psychosomatic (another frequently found but theoretically and emotionally charged word) changes to behaviour. The training health workers receive, and the terminology and taxonomies of disorders employed in different countries, mean that labels diverge too, and the evolving views and changing fashions in psychiatry have produced more variation. This book is not the forum to deliberate over which term should be used or what different labels imply. Suffice it to say for the time being, that the non-neutrality of labels should be borne in mind when reading more widely on the topic or in appreciating what clinicians might be meaning when they indicate someone has psychological FAS, or that FAS for them is a medically unexplained symptom.

The labels functional, psychosomatic and so forth carry theoretical baggage. For the person who hears these terms applied to themselves, they can also carry a considerable weight of emotional burden. They can be felt as highly stigmatising; individuals may sense they are being blamed for speaking differently or not being taken seriously in their accounts of what they believe has happened or is happening and why it is happening. These issues embrace more general societal and individual attitudes to mind matters and this book cannot resolve these questions. The position taken here is that suggesting that in psychogenic aetiologies the search for causes is in the mind of the speaker should not be taken to imply that the issues faced by the speaker and their family and the earnestness of the search for ways in which to help the individual are any less real or any less serious than if the altered accent had arisen from neurological changes. It only implies that the search for explanations is in different places, along different routes, and, if a functional, psychogenic origin is established, that the types of support and intervention offered will be different compared to other origins. In applying terms such as 'medically unexplained' and 'psychogenic', healthcare staff are not insinuating that the individual is somehow feigning or putting on the accent or has conscious control over it (well, not in the majority of cases; very occasionally this does happen) or that the concerns they face are any less real than with a new accent from any other aetiology. The symptoms are indeed real to the individual who experiences them.

Searching for explanations for FAS in the mind rather than the mouth of the speaker or ear of the listener is nothing novel. In the wider field of medicine it is not unusual for people to present with symptoms that look decidedly as if they must be due to some neurological disturbance or the result of some injury to the mouth or neck, or that started in association with an infection, but which transpire to have their roots in the psychological sphere.

Anywhere between ten and thirty per cent of cases arriving in neurology departments are estimated to finally be diagnosed as functional disorders, with symptoms not explained by a stroke, tumour, infection or other physical cause. This can include symptoms as extreme as apparently paralysed arms or legs, apparent blindness, deafness, tremors, blackouts, seizures, severe and persisting headaches, alterations to gait and posture, memory loss or inability to understand one's native language any more. In other fields of medicine severe breathlessness and palpitations do not have to signify cardiovascular or respiratory disease. Nausea and vomiting commonly arise for emotional reasons too; they do not automatically indicate some serious pathology in the stomach. Everyone must have experienced the tight chest, racing pulse and butterflies in the stomach on the morning of an exam or important interview. It is easy to see how prolonged tension, stress and apprehension would show themselves in more lasting and more severe symptoms of disturbed breathing or gastro-intestinal dysfunction.

In ear nose and throat clinics, functional, psychogenic voice disorders are a rather common occurrence – instances where someone's tone or quality of voice alters, or they may even be unable to speak at all, but in the absence of any pathological changes to their vocal cords. Irritable larynx syndrome is another condition which invites worries of tumours, neurological disturbance or infection but which has a functional origin. Acquired psychogenic stuttering is likewise a well-recognised entity where someone who previously spoke without effort or disruption to their flow of speech now finds they stumble over sounds and experience speech blocks, facial contortions and irrepressible repetition of syllables and words over which they feel they have no control. It is definitely the case that for some FAS speakers their accent change has roots akin to functional paralysis, acquired psychogenic stuttering or functional voice disorders.

In all the circumstances above there may occasionally be a key recognisable trigger to the onset of symptoms. More typically, exhaustive investigations uncover no immediately discernible single cause. A personal case where there was an obvious event linking cause and effect concerned a woman involved in an incident in which a gunman had held a pistol to her daughter's head. She screamed and grabbed for his arm. The gunman pulled the trigger. At that point she blacked out. When she came to, mercifully the gun had jammed and help had arrived, but the arm that had gone to grab the gun was paralysed and she was mute, incapable of producing any sound. Another personal case was someone who developed a severe stutter after being involved in a bombing. Physically she survived unscathed, but mentally was left with acute anxiety and speech changes. A further personal case where the link between a specific event and onset of symptoms seemed clear concerned someone with FAS. Mrs Y was strongly religious. She had committed what for her was a grievous sin. Discussions disclosed how she had consciously adopted the new accent and whole new persona that went with this, to distance herself from her sinful part and emphasise a new beginning.

Another instance involved the sudden, overnight, out-of-the-blue appearance of a Scottish accent in a fifteen-year-old English girl. She even developed a history for herself as to why she spoke this way – where she lived in Scotland, what school she went to, which exams she took. To explain why her mother spoke quite differently to her she introduced her as her aunt. When she was eighteen she equally suddenly switched her accent to Canadian – specifically, as she maintained, from Toronto. This accent still persists, with her now in her thirties. When asked why she altered her accent, she felt she had no control over it. However, she rationalised that it was probably due to her intense hatred of the particular English accent which she used to have, which in the media and popular culture held negative connotations of 'chavs, thick females dancing round their white handbags' whom everybody ridiculed and reviled. By adopting another accent, she removed herself from being tarred with the same brush and being judged as stupid (she was assessed as having a well above average IQ, though she was diagnosed as having autistic spectrum disorder/Asperger's syndrome). She described her 'new' accent as a joy – it gave her freedom to be more 'herself' and to express herself in more 'colourful' tones than the English accent allowed. She can switch back to the former accent when asked to, but rarely speaks more than a few sentences before it makes her feel strange and uncomfortable. The sense is that it brings back horrible memories of being badly bullied in school because of her autism and being misunderstood by everybody. She also noted that speaking Canadian has given her a fantastic vocabulary and an intense interest in words and how they are used.

Relatively clear-cut cases such as these are probably in the minority. In the initial clinical interview people may express clear beliefs about a direct link between the onset of symptoms and something that happened to them – a bout of laryngitis, a dental operation, a fall off their bike, an epileptic-like seizure. As often as not, however, these prove to be insufficient, improbable or impossible explanations for the observed behaviour. More commonly sources lead back to a whole knot of factors that have grown up over an extended period of time, and assessment entails teasing out where the true lines of causality might lie.

As the case of Mrs Y illustrates, given the multitude of medically unexplained, functional changes that do happen to people, it is not surprising that change of accent should feature amongst the symptoms. Why precisely for some individuals mind matters manifest themselves in an altered accent, whilst for others it is muteness or stuttering or altered posture or tremor, is not at all clear. Just as with other functional disorders like paralysis, tics and seizures, answers are sought in an individual's specific circumstances within their own bio-psychosocial sphere.

There is some speculation that people for whom voice is a central part of their life (e.g. they pride themselves on their clear voice; they are priests or teachers who require a clear, loud voice for their vocation) may be more prone to developing psychogenic voice disorders than other groups. They may be more perfectionist in their standards and feel the effects of (voice) fatigue more keenly than matched companions. In similar vein one might speculate that individuals for whom manner of speaking is important in their lives, or who view speech as a vehicle to present or conceal aspects of their personality or feelings, may be more prone to divulge psychological issues in their accent. No one has conducted any research that confirms or refutes this in relation to FAS, but it could prove a fruitful line of enquiry.

As intimated in the last paragraph, another direction of search for underlying influences may involve issues of personal identity and the role of accent. Below we explain, under the section on sociolinguistic dimensions in accent change, how this can be and how accent is used to manipulate relationships with others, to colour the portrayal of self one wishes to project. Altered accent can be a method to conceal or deny one's true identity or shade certain corners of self. An altered accent may be a means to protect elements of self or deflect listeners' attitudes or beliefs away from other features of personality or behaviour one wishes to hide. It is a means to create a new identity. It is a vehicle for expressing solidarity or dissimilarity, closeness or distance with another person(s), place or group.

Different accents carry different social-psychological profiles – warmer, friendlier, colder, less intelligent, modern, old fashioned and much more. Call-centre managers and TV advertising directors are well aware of this. They subliminally manipulate our reaction to and associations with their product through the accent of the personnel or actors they choose to present their product. Playwrights and comedians have long used accent to signal whether the character they are presenting is meant to be taken as a country bumpkin, a city sophisticate, young and up and coming, behind the times, an insider or outsider.

As intimated in an earlier section, the dividing line between functional and physical disorders is not necessarily as sharp as one would imagine. Individuals with functional issues may have a stroke or develop a degenerative neurological condition. People with the latter conditions can develop psychological issues either as a direct result of or reaction to the primary condition or independently of it. Depression and anxiety, and all the behaviours they may provoke, are well-documented sequels of a host of neurological conditions. Thus for some speakers FAS of functional origin may be entwined with effects of physical changes.

Consider the following scenario, which is unquestionably a likelihood for presentation in clinic. Someone experiences neurological damage. One of the consequences is a motor speech disorder and associated with this is a perceived foreign accent. Other symptoms like hemiplegia, aphasia and attention difficulties resolve. Speech motor assessments suggest the speech changes, too, ought to have at least improved if not have disappeared altogether; yet they have not. In other words, FAS may arise in association with a neurological event, but its persistence cannot be explained given the resolution of the underlying neurological motor speech disorder. This is not some new discovery unique to FAS – persistence of restricted movement or conscious or non-conscious exaggeration of symptoms that ought to have ameliorated is found in numerous clinical situations. What this scenario suggests is that if clinical assessments are conclusive in indicating that there is no reason for persisting dysarthria or apraxia of speech or dysprosody underlying the foreign accent, then the search for explanations and treatments shifts from the physical to the functional.

The reasons are legion why symptoms should persist when physically they should not. There is no fixed list of reasons to check through to determine why any one individual is in this situation. It is entirely down to individual circumstances and reactions. Nevertheless, there are some well-recognised mechanisms. In one way or another, for instance, an individual may accrue secondary gains from having a new accent and there may be greater costs to losing the accent than to retaining it. The person may or may not be consciously aware of the gains. People may fall into a state of learned helplessness and see no way in which they can move beyond their present state. The new mode of speaking may already have become a fixed habit difficult to break.

Experiences from personal cases where there was persistence of FAS illustrate some of the factors that can be at play in extending the existence of an accent when it could have been left behind. One woman felt unsure of herself after her stroke, and had lost all her self-confidence. If she spoke with a foreign accent, though, people would take her as a foreigner and think that was why she was so nervous and hesitant. Another felt she had had to make huge adjustments to come to terms with sounding foreign. She had had to accommodate the new accent as part of this different self. She sensed that making the move back to her former self would entail another huge effort she was not sure she could manage, and she was afraid, having experienced this new self, that she would not be able to rediscover her old self and then would be totally lost. M felt she had always been shy, finding it difficult to gain entry to conversations or maintain people's attention. She saw the new accent as a front, first to attract and maintain people's attention, but second, if she failed and they ignored her, she could always put this down to the fact that they were not interested in foreigners, and that it was nothing to do with her own individual personality.

E, another speaker with FAS, sounded Italian. One of the contributory factors to this was almost definitely the 'uh' sounds she inserted into her sentences (*I watch-ed-uh that uh puh-rog-uh-ramme-uh on-uh the TV*). She knew very well how the words should sound, but when she attempted to say them without the 'uh' sounds they came out highly distorted. For her the persistence with this feature of her accent seemed to be a compensatory tactic to maintain clarity and fluency in her speech.

A further possibility that is well attested in other quarters relates to circumstances where individuals share a symptom or beliefs concerning their symptoms. Through identifying with each other they develop behaviours to the detriment, rather than benefit, of the resolution of their symptoms. This can encompass instances where someone who was previously symptomless (at least as regards sounding foreign) now, for one reason or another, identifies with people who do show FAS and they themselves commence speaking with a foreign accent. It may entail a person with FAS where there is or was every prospect for resolution of symptoms (e.g. recovery from the neurological condition that caused the speech changes; insight into and self-management of a depressive disorder that should have resulted in recovery) but where identification with or unconscious obligation to an unrecovered speaker results in persistence of symptoms. In other words, the contact becomes a vehicle for the instigation or maintenance of the behaviour in question when the original neurological or structural trigger has long since resolved. Contact may hamper rather than assist resolution, or even result in the elaboration of the symptom and extension of the individual's or group's delusional beliefs around the origins and nature of the behaviour. This is somewhat akin to the phenomenon first described in the nineteenth century of *folie à deux*, or *à trois* or *à plusieurs*, or, as sometimes more recently termed, 'shared psychotic disorder' or 'induced delusional disorder' or 'mass psychogenic illness outbreaks'.

The label 'delusional disorder' may be too extreme to characterise all instances of this, but even where there is no frank psychosis, outcomes can be the same. For example, support groups, online chat rooms or blogs can provide invaluable help to some people, especially if well managed and supervised, with good quality information and explanation. However, group dynamics in such situations can be exceedingly complex. On the one hand, members may gain positive and sympathetic advice from others, feel no longer alone with their symptoms and worries, feel themselves a member of a non-threatening group that understands them and does not try to assign labels such as psychogenic speech disorder in the face of their conviction that the origin of their accent must lie elsewhere. On the other hand, when membership and identification with the group becomes an end in itself, when the advice received does not point a way out of and beyond the negative circumstances, when group inter-actions only serve to complicate and obfuscate the true circumstances around an individual's state, then outcomes can be seriously negative or maladaptive. At a minimum, they act as a potent force in maintenance of a behaviour; at worst they compound the problems and misunderstandings.

Whatever the reason(s) for the development of a foreign accent for psychological as opposed to structural or neurological causes, several observations are true. The origins can be just as complex, if not more complex than in non-psychological situations. Uncovering the motivating factors requires as rigorous and systematic an investigation as with neurological cases. One may not move to explore functional aetiology until other possibilities have been exhausted. Simply assigning a label of functional or psychogenic by default, though, is not the end of the search. Diagnosis still needs to proceed to why, in any individual case, the accent has arisen. Finally, simply because a new accent has emerged as a result of psychological factors does not signify that that accent and the issues of identity that it raises are any less real for the individual compared to other origins. Neither does it denote that they necessarily have any more conscious, volitional control over it than people with neurogenic FAS do. This is a point generally misunderstood in such cases; the symptoms are just as real, and the need for resolution and support just as pressing. When it is concluded the aetiology is psychological, though, it does mean that intervention and support must target the underlying psychological issues. Therapies directed at specific aspects of speech output are not only unlikely to succeed (the problem is not in producing particular sounds or sound combinations), but they might even serve as perpetuators of the accent.

Aetiologies of FAS: sociolinguistic

Sociolinguistic factors are not really a cause of FAS as conceptualised in this book. That is, the origin of an altered accent for sociolinguistic reasons does not have its roots in abnormal neurological or emotional functioning. The field of sociolinguistic accent studies is mentioned, however, as several deter-minants of normal accent change are closely germane to processes that may contribute to the neurogenic or functional picture of some individuals. Certainly the branch of sociolinguistics that examines listeners' attitudes to different accents and the implications this may have for acceptance or prejudice, for alienation and discrimination, is highly pertinent to understanding the psychosocial consequences of FAS. There is no room for an exhaustive exposition of issues and findings, but the following observations will give a flavour of the forces that may be at work.

Accent change is all around us. We do not give a second thought to learning that someone grew up in the north and had a northern accent, but since moving south many years ago now speaks like a southerner. We are not usually surprised when this person returns from their holiday 'back home' sounding again more like their former self. One of the authors (NM) used to speak with a strong Belfast accent, but after years living in different parts of Britain has few vestiges of this. However, his wife knows immediately when he is speaking to someone in Belfast on the phone, as his accent switches right back.

This is one aspect of a phenomenon known as accent accommodation. The accents of two people who speak different accents may converge. It may be bilateral – they meet in the middle, or, depending on the dynamics of the social interaction it may be the accent of only one of the participants that accommodates. Sometimes this can take on bizarre proportions. British readers will recall the incident of Steve McClaren, the former English national football team manager who, after he was dismissed, took up a post managing the Dutch team FC Twente. In interviews with British TV and radio, suddenly he was speaking with a Dutch accent and in broken English. The exact same happened to the English footballer Joey Barton when he transferred to the French team Marseilles.

Geographical accent variation is the tip of the iceberg. We all alter our accents on a constant basis. We speak differently in formal versus informal settings. Our accent can be influenced by what we perceive the relative social status of our interlocutor to be. Our speech style may alter according to topic. Our habitual accent is determined not just by our geographical situation but by our age, gender, social class, mood, health, and a host of other factors. Indeed, understanding the role of our accent and learning to vary our accent is an integral component of language acquisition and controlling the highly complex nature of social intercourse.

Accent, as much, and most likely more so, than our clothes, our hairstyle, our facial expression and posture, is a key portrayer to the outside world of who we are or who we wish to be taken to be. Our accent is part of our character, whom we believe we are, as much a part of us as the colour of our eyes or the car we drive. At the same time, the opinion we form of others is instantly and constantly shaped and reshaped by what we perceive their accent to be, and how they vary it. In this way we see that speech is, in many ways, the most complex outward manifestation of the inward workings of the human brain, it is a sensitive barometer of our inner physical and emotional world.

Because control of our accent is so deeply ingrained, most of the time we do not even notice that we vary our speech, it happens subconsciously. We control our accent to express solidarity with others or to underline our differences. We are used to thinking of geographical groups developing distinctive accent characteristics to stamp the identity of place. Equally, though, this happens with social groups, whether it is broad social stratification, occupational groupings, or inclusion or exclusion from the neighbourhood gang. People who do not speak our accent are treated differently, with difference being expressed in myriad forms from genuine curiosity, through to social distancing, to outright prejudice and social suppression.

A question frequently asked of people with FAS runs along the lines of 'So you have a different accent, but otherwise you are healthy, so why all the fuss and depression?' If one ponders how accent is so deeply seated in our psyche and social being one can begin to gain insights into why some people with FAS react in such ways. Core features of who they believe they are have been altered. Inherent ways in how they thought the world operated in terms of their use of accent and reactions to others' impression of their accent have radically shifted. The rules of identity and engagement they have grown up with and may have abided by for fifty, sixty years or more, no longer operate. Such deep-seated emotional feelings come through strongly in many of the personal accounts later in the book.

In summary, sociolinguistic factors are not a cause of FAS, but to gain a full understanding of the impact of FAS recourse to sociolinguistic truisms is a necessity. In people with neurogenic FAS, consideration of these sociolinguistic dimensions assists in the understanding of the complications arising beyond just having a different accent. For people with functional FAS, delving into issues of power and solidarity, identity and alienation may well disclose factors behind the development and maintenance of a different accent, insights into why particular underlying social-psychological matters should have manifested themselves in accent change.

Some other views on the origins of FAS

The sensationalist press (and sometimes reporters in higher quality organs who should know better), online chat room members and the general public occasionally put forward other explanations about why someone starts to use a foreign accent. Journalists (suddenly becoming armchair neuroscientists!) have claimed there is an accent module in the brain containing all the accents one might possibly produce. According to them brain damage disrupts this gene or module and causes one to switch to one of the dormant accents. Another theory ventured has been that people with FAS may be autistic, obsessively internalising different accents they have heard on the television or in the street. Then something triggers a compulsion to suddenly use one of these acquired accents rather than their habitual speech. Others have surmised that the foreign accent comes from a long-departed ancestor from a distant land who is trying to call through their relative. Akin to this, others claim the person with FAS in a former life was a Russian, Chinese or whatever speaker, and now the former self is struggling to communicate to them across the centuries.

Scientific evidence allows us to immediately refute some of these claims as science fiction rather than science fact. Others are unprovable one way or the other. They require a leap of faith to believe or deny, though the sceptic might agree that on balance the likelihood of these accounts representing explanations for even some instances of FAS, let alone all, has to be dismissed or treated with a very large pinch (even shovelful) of salt.

In summary, as regards the aetiology of FAS, like so many matters of the mind, neat divisions between neurology and psychology, mind and body, perception and production, can be misleading. In reality there may be considerable grey areas, with interaction between or overlapping of factors.

There is one fundamental factor we have not drawn out so far regarding FAS. FAS can be described in terms of underlying neurological disturbance, altered acoustic patterns, altered perceived speech sounds. For the majority of people who present with FAS, however, the overriding experience is not of the physical or acoustic changes, but the psychosocial impact on them as a speaker and on their family as a whole. We turn now to some of these issues.

Psychosocial consequences of FAS

Psychosocial aspects are understood here to refer to the ways in which FAS has altered feelings and beliefs about oneself, how it has altered or coloured interactions with or reactions from others. Evaluation of these aspects can constitute an important part of clinical evaluation, including possible differential diagnostic issues in decisions regarding whether the aetiology is neurological or psychological. It certainly constitutes an important ingredient in rehabilitation, in so far as any intervention specifically concerning speech and communication should involve addressing not just the minutiae of speech production but entail discussion and planning around adjustment to the altered communication circumstances, around resuming one's normal life. At the same time it represents a complex knot of issues from the point of view of disentangling the effects of FAS from the consequences of all the other things that might have happened to the person, and is not a straightforward exercise.

People with FAS of neurological origin typically have suffered a stroke or head injury. Sometimes they might have been diagnosed with a degenerative neurological condition. Coming to terms with the very fact that fate has dealt one one of these major events can be life changing in itself for the individual and their family. This is quite aside from any changes to one's physical or mental ability that those involved may have to face up to, quite apart from coming to terms with issues surrounding the accident that brought about the head injury, the impact of the stroke, the implications of prognosis of the condition for employment, finance, life-style and survival, and any one of a host of issues that one can encounter at such major junctions on one's life journey.

These life-changing circumstances may also pose deep, emotionally challenging questions for the individual around issues such as self-worth, self-image, their values in life, who and where they now feel themself to be. How one copes with the challenges is likely to be shaped not just by one's current physical and mental status but by one's whole experience of life so far – how one has dealt with success and adversity in the past; what one felt about oneself as an individual, as a member of the family, as a work colleague, as a member of society in general before all this started; what support networks one could call upon; one's belief systems about how life and the universe works; and so forth. In this fashion, then, what the person with FAS has to confront is no different to anyone else with a sudden or progressive neurological condition. Indeed, many of the issues might be shared too with people with non-neurological conditions, such as heart attack, loss of limbs or facial disfigurement, arthritis, or cancer survival.

Beyond coming to terms with a major event or diagnosis, though, the person with FAS may well face other changes to how they act or feel as a consequence of the neurological changes. FAS, or speech changes more generally, seldom arise in isolation. Physical changes such as arm or leg weakness or paralysis may well be present; there may be debilitating or annoying fatigue. There may be alterations to language – finding the right words, being able to put these into meaningful sentences, being able to understand what others are saying, being able to read and write. The potential for these to influence self-view and social intercourse is immense. Obvious or more subtle alterations to memory and/or to attention and concentration are common sequels to neurological trauma and stroke. These all easily undermine the ability to cope socially; they can sap confidence and compound confusion. The personal accounts which follow in Part II are poignantly adept at sensitising the reader to these issues. Furthermore, the presence of such changes and their effects are not necessarily easily noticed or appreciated by individuals and their families for what they are.

On top of language, physical, memory and other disability, small or more blatant modifications to personality and other behavioural variations are a frequent phenomenon in neurological disorders. Partners (even the person themself) may report the previously happy-go-lucky person, the highly motivated person with energy and drive, has become depressed, introverted, indifferent, apathetic; the formerly reticent individual now is unstoppably loquacious, their conversations even peppered with socially inappropriate innuendo or insinuating observations. The once considerate and listening family member may be perceived now as self-centred, oblivious to the views and feelings of others. The once calm and unflappable person may now be overanxious, uncertain, oversensitive to others' remarks.

In other words, to fully appreciate what is linked to the overall situation and what is specifically tied to the FAS it is necessary to be aware of all the other potential forces that may be at play in shaping an individual's behaviour and feelings. It is into this whirlpool of questions, feelings, issues, trials and tribulations that FAS is cast. Gauging the effects of and coping with FAS needs to be evaluated against this wider backdrop. What are the issues for the individual and family regarding impact from the neurological event in general versus FAS in particular? How far do reactions of others stem from general social attitudes to disability and difference versus specifically attitudes to altered accents? To what extent are matters of adjustment for the individual and family focused on broader concerns and challenges around the overall medical condition; how far, or which ones, are centred on the new accent?

FAS represents essentially a particular set of changes in relation to pronunciation. What is the picture in terms of speaker and listener reactions when we narrow down the focus to just the changes to speech? Again, the task of discerning which changes to communication, reactions and feelings of self and others have their source in speech changes in general rather than FAS in particular is not a transparent process. Many of the 'problems' described in the literature as part of FAS are in fact no different to those experienced by anyone with a (neurological) speech disorder – unsurprising if one keeps in mind that neurogenic FAS represents a specific manifestation of an underlying speech disorder.

On the surface, people with motor speech disorders relate how they may be misunderstood despite apparently viable intelligibility, how people frequently get the wrong end of the stick of what they are trying to explain or misinterpret the sense with which it was conveyed. People with motor speech disorders often report that the words do not come out as they intended – they wish to express humour or irony, love, definiteness, yet the listener mistakes their attitudes as aggression, indifference, hesitancy or not being someone to take seriously. Such confusions are easily traced back to alterations in stress and intonation patterns, to changes in rate and fluency of speech, not just to the more general outlooks on people with speech difficulties or other disabilities.

Alas, there are no shortages either of reports about the general negative attitudes and reactions encountered from others. These may range from acts of outright conscious hostility (hanging up on the phone, verbal abuse, cheating over prices or fares in shops and on public transport and the like) through to less obviously discriminatory behaviours, but behaviours that nevertheless may decisively influence social interaction and the speaker's view of themselves. This may take the form of conscious or unconscious exclusion from conversations, people talking past one, addressing a partner on the assumption that one is no longer capable of providing one's own answer or opinion. They may be expressed through the stated or implied assumption that one is no longer intellectually capable of understanding or providing an answer. At other times the attitudes or misunderstandings are shown in the apparent lack of patience to wait for the person with speech changes to formulate and deliver an opinion or reply, or speaking to them in baby talk or loud speech – as if they were intellectually regressed or even deaf.

Occasionally more humorous scenarios are encountered – the foreign speech directed at people with FAS; the person in the shop who wants to speak to you in your own language, interested enquiries about where you come from and why you emigrated to here, recommendations on what local attractions to visit whilst you are here. Such encounters, on the one hand, can serve as jolly anecdotes, as pleasant interludes. On the other hand, for some individuals they only underscore their sense of not belonging, the deep down sense that, despite being born and bred in the neighbourhood, they are no longer perceived as being a member or part of it. These situations hint at possible dimensions more unique to people with FAS, which we will return to shortly.

Before that, there are deeper reactions assumed in some of the literature to be characteristic of people with FAS that are in fact shared with the more general population of people with acquired speech disorders. For instance, it is not an uncommon feeling amongst people who have experienced loss of speech or language due to a stroke or head injury to suffer a feeling of loss, the sense that part of one's psyche has been stolen, the belief that one is no longer a complete person, not the person one was before it all started. Reactions similar to losing a limb, or even to losing a loved one and the bereavement that follows, are well attested amongst people with aphasia and dysarthria in relation to their speech. Family members may experience comparable responses, pass through similar phases of sense of loss, of anger, of wondering where it all went, why it had to happen. Many quotes from people with FAS later on in this book amply illustrate this.

It is not difficult to understand how such sentiments may come about. Our voice, how we speak, our ability to convey our thoughts and emotions and be understood as we intended by others, is central to expressing who, how and why we are. From a person's voice and accent we can discern their age, their gender, maybe their physical build. We assign them to a social class or to social groups on the basis of their accent, and of course to a geographical region. On the basis of their tone of voice we judge how much they agree with us, us with them; we estimate empathy and sympathy, love or antagonism. The rate of speech and the intonation of someone's voice lend clues to their emotional state: sadness, joy, impatience. We daily use our voices consciously or unconsciously to convey, to manipulate, to emphasise, to conceal all these clues to our feelings, affinities, our belonging, our aspirations. Our speech is the window into our souls for listeners, the channel for them to view our unspoken attitudes, history and feelings. It is also our loudspeaker that broadcasts to others how we wish to be taken, where we wish them to think we stand, to determine who and how they should perceive us.

Each speech community has its own conventions for how these spoken and unspoken messages are transmitted. We are socialised into the conventions from the very first utterances we perceive in the cradle, from the interactions of the very first cooings of mother and child between each other. Our entire upbringing teaches us the workings and nuances of this whole elaborate system – who can say what to whom, when and how; how to signal this or that feeling, intended or implied meaning; how to interpret others' messages for what they truly mean, about what is being spoken about and what they wish us to understand on the surface and between the lines about their pronouncements.

For anyone with an acquired speech disorder, coping with changes to the operation of all these rules and conventions provides a real or potential barrier to communication and identification. Small wonder then that this might be magnified for the person with FAS, that they may feel cast adrift in an alien world. The words are still the same, but the way they emerge, the tone with which they are produced, the understanding with which they are received, are no longer the old and familiar, the intended. The altered tone of voice and accent fail to convey the meaning they wished. Listeners interpret their speech in a way they did not aim for, they build a picture of them that is no longer congruent with the picture they have or had of themselves. The reassuring tone may be taken as annoyance, the endearing tone as indifference. On top of this, for the individual with FAS, the signals that 'I am the same as you', 'I come from here', 'I am one of you', 'this is the same John or Mary you knew before the stroke', all miss their mark, lead to negation of, not affirmation of what they wish to say; denial, not confirmation of who they wish to state they are. Again, accounts of people with FAS are replete with such sentiments – including the personal accounts presented later.

A special hurt is sensed by many people with FAS in relation to press reports and interviews. Someone waking up with a new identity, especially with something so tangible as a new accent, makes good copy. So frequently, though, articles or radio and TV slots totally miss the mark. Instead of seeing the struggle to find one's self, instead of hearing the bereavement or displacement, individuals are mocked and vilified. They are portrayed as freaks, charlatans, as malingerers and attention seekers. There is little or no endeavour to understand where the accent has come from or what it means to the speaker and their family, or even beyond that what it might tell us about the human brain. This sense of injustice is even more acute when it appears that health professionals who should know better adopt similar stances.

This quandary, the tension between who I feel I am, and who others take me to be, engenders diverse reactions in people with FAS and their families. Some reactions may be adaptive, positive moves, others maladaptive ones that themselves may create further difficulties rather than solve them. Responses may entail complete denial of the situation, a striving to uphold the status quo in the face of overwhelming evidence to the contrary that the state of affairs is not as was; through various forms of struggle to come to terms with the situation; to reconciliation with themselves, others and the situation. Happily for some individuals there is no issue – they still feel entirely themselves, they are glad to have survived the stroke or operation, and 'if the price of survival is that I now speak with a different accent, well so what, I'm alive, I am still here for my family and friends'.

The words people with FAS use to describe emotions they have travelled through encompass anger, guilt, denial, disbelief, puzzlement, why-me, resignation, dejection, enmity, alienation, estrangement, bereavement, determination to set things right, relief, optimism that the situation will pass – the whole gamut of sentiments familiar from anyone or any situation where frightening, unexpected, unwanted, uneasy change has been imposed.

The efforts to come to terms with the situation may take many forms. There is unlikely to be one sole strategy that is deployed. The reactions and strategies vary from situation to situation and from interlocutor to interlocutor, for a whole variety of reasons. As with responses to any trauma they also typically evolve over time. Some of the more commonly expressed responses to FAS typically encompass searching, humour, acquiescence, and re-evaluation of self.

Many people with FAS report a sense of loss: of accent, of part of themselves, or of their whole self. The response to loss may be a searching for where this sense of self disappeared. It may remain a metaphysical search, but as the accounts later show, for some the searching realises itself in travel to other parts to find the people who speak with your accent or where your accent will not stand out as different.

'Laughing it off' is a tactic for some. If you cannot beat them, join them. Under some circumstances people with FAS report how they tire of the constant conversations about 'no I'm not a foreigner, I was born here; I've had a stroke, that's why I talk differently'. Instead they create a story of how they emigrated to these parts, why they came, what it was like back home. All very well until one encounters someone who can also speak the language of 'back home', as some people with FAS record.

For some, the path to recovery, or at least understanding, entails a re-evaluation of self. This may be through a realisation that, despite the surface differences, deep down 'I am still the same me'. There are still the same core values, the same aspirations in life and social discourse and feelings for others. It may be through an acceptance of the new situation, encompassing the altered aspects of self. One woman with FAS expressed how at first she did not want to let in the FAS, it was alien, not part of her. In the end she had to adjust, she had to take charge of it, otherwise the FAS would have taken charge of her.

We have written much more on the psychosocial reactions to FAS elsewhere and will not dwell on matters here. However, explicitly and between the lines in the accounts in Part II, there are ample testimonies to the phases in reaction to FAS that people pass through. Whatever the reactions and path of change, almost all people with or who have experienced FAS speak of 'a journey'. A journey back to self. A journey to find a new self. A journey to discover new things about an old self. Understanding the individual's journey must be integral to appreciating the significance of FAS for them.

To the definition and conception of FAS we have then to add psychosocial issues as an integral layer, as a variable that for some represents a minimal disruption to their travels through life, for others a major storm which blows them way off course to a land they know not where, a longing for 'home', a searching for the way back, and if lucky finding it or at least settling in a new environment that is different but ultimately just as good and one they can live with/in. We outlined that many of these sentiments are shared with people with neurological and other conditions independently of FAS.

The one dimension of FAS that one must take as unique to people with a perceived different regional or national accent, as opposed to experiences shared with other people with different kinds of acquired neurological speech disorder, must surely be the dimension of alienation and foreignness. People with FAS sound foreign and may be taken as foreigners, they share the reactions of the public to foreign accent. Yet they are not foreign. They share with others who have chronic medical conditions and the effects of neurological disorders the changes to language and speech. Yet, listeners and observers dwell on the accent and too often deny them the physical origin. People with FAS are at home but people do not treat them thus. They are treated as outsiders, yet they have no other home.

Differential diagnosis

It was stressed early in this chapter that the label FAS is not a diagnosis in itself. To state that someone has FAS is equivalent to concluding someone suffers from headaches, has a skin rash, is limping, or is handicapped by memory problems. The condition is distressing for the individual and poses problems in coping with the consequences, both for the person and their family. However, headaches, memory loss and the like have multiple causes. In order to be able to do anything about them, one has to move beyond the headline labels, to ascertain what the underlying cause is in the particular instance. The same holds true for FAS. There are multiple conditions that lie behind FAS, both in general terms (neurological versus psychological, for instance), as well as divisions within each of the broader categories. Depending on what the primary disturbance is, it will trigger a different pathway in management and support for the speaker.

The aim here is not to detail all the neurological and psychological assessments that are routinely conducted to establish the nature of an underlying condition. These are well documented in many other works. This section concentrates on the role that speech assessment may play in determining the origin and nature of disturbances that lie behind the altered accent. Specifically, it examines possible features to search for and to compare, to weigh up whether the altered accent has a neurological or functional, psychogenic origin or, if there are elements of both, what the proportions might be.

Speech differential diagnosis in cases of FAS

The key strategy entails a close examination of speech output and related neuropsychological functions (i.e. language, attention, pragmatics, the nature of language use in interaction, etc.) to establish whether the profile is consistent with known characteristics of the onset and course of neurogenic motor speech disorders and the pattern of utterance-to-utterance, day-to-day and month-to-month variations one would expect from them. The more the configuration of features corresponds to the well-recognised profile in acquired motor speech disorders, the more one is confident in assigning a neurological aetiology; the less they are in keeping with that profile in terms of features and patterns of variability, the more likely it is that the underlying driver of the altered accent is functional.

There is nothing mystical in accomplishing this. There is no magic formula for making the distinction between neurological and functional aetiologies. The same principles apply as when facing any other differential diagnostic challenge. Decisions are based on an intimate knowledge of the causes, course, range of presenting symptoms and their variation associated with candidate syndromes. Information is gleaned from careful history taking, from the speaker and others who know them, about the nature, onset and development of the symptoms. A precise description of the behaviours is made from structured and informal observations and other assessments targeted at teasing out what might underlie a symptom, or disclose how it varies under different diagnostically relevant conditions. Where the decision remains unclear, diagnostic therapy and other techniques may shed further light.

The tools and techniques to achieve the aims are simply the same as with any other case presenting in clinic with a suspected neurological motor speech disorder. The methods for conducting differential diagnosis of different types of acquired neurogenic motor speech disorders from each other and the assessment procedures that enable this are amply covered in textbooks on motor speech disorders. This section offers some general rule-of-thumb pointers in the pursuit of deciding whether FAS in a given speaker stems from neurological or functional factors.

Of course speech and language examination furnishes only one part of the jigsaw puzzle. Speech evaluation is set in the wider context of neurological, radiological, neuropsychological and case history assessments; it informs these other areas of investigation and is at the same time informed by them. From the narrow speech and voice assessment perspective, the nub of the differentiation concerns whether observed speech behaviours correspond with the pattern of occurrence recognised as characteristic of given neurological motor speech disorders. One seeks to ascertain whether the nature of variation in speech sound production obeys rules and patterns of variability known to typify motor speech disorders. The case history establishes whether the onset and course of the speech changes has followed well-attested neurological lines.

For the initial speech motor examination, one examines control of respiration for speech. Voice production is measured with perceptual rating scales and may also be backed up by acoustic measures. Prolonged vowels and speech tasks are employed. Detailed assessment of prosody is likely to be of central interest. Articulation is evaluated with diadochokinetic (i.e. reiterative) speech tasks to look at variables such as (stability of) voice onset time, ability to sustain range and rate of movement, differential effects of weakness or incoordination at different sites between for instance lips, tongue tip, and tongue back.

Speech sounds are examined in word lists and sentence contexts controlled for length and complexity of utterances, phonotactic predictability (how likely one sound is to follow another), as well as word class (noun, verb, adjective, etc.), frequency (how often a sound or word crops up in a language) and propositionality (roughly, how much thought and concentration has to go into preparing what you have to say). More automatic sequences are contrasted with less predictable ones. Speech elicited via repetition after the examiner is compared to the same sounds and words elicited through naming or reading or spontaneous conversation. Contrasting speech at habitual, slowed and accelerated rates may be instructive. An intelligibility test is desirable. Assessments of activity limitation, participation restriction and impact complement the impairment measures.

Analyses of performance hold a magnifying glass over the pattern and variability of breakdowns. Are the sound deviations seen and heard in keeping with patterns known to characterise different types of dysarthria and apraxia of speech and the dysprosodias associated with them? Are the sites of sound change in well-attested positions in the word and phrase? Does the profile of changes alter in keeping with manipulations of length and complexity and other key word, sentence and elicitation variables in predicted fashion? Are the associated language, speech perception and impact characteristics those one would expect from a diagnosis of neurological motor speech disorder?

The more incongruent the speech and voice picture is with features of motor speech disorders, the stronger the case becomes for a functional origin. By congruence is meant that the sites and severity of disruption to speech output tie in closely with each other – e.g. difficulties with lip sounds can be linked to concomitant deficits in tone, power or coordination of lip movement in speech; flattened melodic contours are associated with corresponding vocal cord control difficulties; stumbling over transitions from <c> to <t>, as in tractor or black tie, can be explained adequately by motor disturbance of the tongue.

Congruence also looks at co-occurring impairments. Specific sites of lesion in the brain bring about certain expected groupings of signs and symptoms. The presence of particular symptoms in the absence of other expected symptoms arouses suspicions of non-neurological origins, even more so when the combination of symptoms is not consistent with patterns of brain damage or would not be explained by them. For instance, the presence of speech output problems in a strongly right-handed speaker with FAS yet apparent left-sided weakness would be unusual. In a monolingual speaker with FAS who has a French accent one would not expect the person for neurological reasons to suddenly start peppering their speech with French words; a monolingual non-Chinese speaker with FAS with a Chinese accent of neurological origin would not start writing in what look like, and what they claim to be, Chinese characters.

Presence of speech and voice changes in the absence of physical changes to tongue and lip movement does not immediately clinch that changes must be functional. Where FAS leads back to alterations in melody and rhythm of speech, there may be no disruption to individual sounds. Also, speech can be affected by disruption at the stage of planning movements required to produce the necessary sounds for a word. This is true in disorders labelled 'apraxia of speech' and 'conduction aphasia', or more generally phonological paraphasias (seemingly meaningless jumbles of sounds). Furthermore, these impairments display behaviours that at first sight appear to point away from neurogenic disturbance. Speech can be highly variable – on one occasion a person can say a sound or word or phrase perfectly clearly but moments later struggles over the same sounds and words. Their speech sounds unremittingly effortful and then out of the blue appears a perfectly enunciated word or island of fluency. Speech language pathologists who work in neurological facilities will be skilled at discerning the features of apraxic or paraphasic speech to establish whether apraxia is in fact the disorder present, or whether the net has to be cast more widely.

Even with known neurological damage, it does not follow automatically that an acquired speech disorder must have (solely) arisen from this, as has been repeated at several points already. Speech disturbances of functional or psychiatric origin may mimic or be confused with neurogenic motor speech disorders; some neurogenic speech disorders can have a deceptively psychiatric flavour to them. Spasmodic dysphonia, apraxia of speech and palilalia might be mentioned in this connection.

Table 2.1 offers some general guidelines to help distinguish psychological from neurological factors. It is not a definitive differential diagnostic key. No factor on its own provides unequivocal confirmation of psychogenic versus neurogenic aetiology. It is only in the accumulation of clinical indicators on one side of the table or another that the overall direction of search becomes clearer. Neither should the table lead one to believe that diagnosis can proceed in a simple either/or fashion. The distinctions drawn are not always watertight and diagnosis is not always as straightforward as presented.

An example of the speech picture not tying in with the overall behaviour might be: a person reports extreme difficulty with saying words containing /s/ and /t/, but experiences no problems on /d, z, n/, sounds made in the same place and practically the same manner; someone presents with severely hypernasal speech but palatal tone, power, reflexes and sensation appear normal and they can suck and blow quite adequately through a straw; the client claims

Table 2.1 General guidelines to help distinguish psychological from neurological factors

Points to psychogenic	Points to neurogenic
Sudden onset associated with significant life event (loss of partner; non-neurological accident; loss of job . . .)	Sudden onset associated with head injury, vascular episode, infection known to compromise peripheral/central nervous system, head or neck surgery
Gradual onset associated with build-up of negative life events or other stressful situation(s)	Gradual onset independent of other life events and follows pattern of known neurological illnesses
Presenting symptoms do not fit known neurological syndromes	Presenting symptoms fall into familiar neurological clusters
Speech characteristics not in keeping with the presenting physical picture	Close tie between severity and loci of physical changes and speech profile
Speech presentation varies markedly according to person, place, topic, especially where any of these is linked to emotionally loaded factors	Speech varies according to fatigue, recognised drug effects, well-known linguistic parameters (e.g. automatic-propositional effect, word class and frequency effects)
Apparently random, unexplainable variation in severity or symptoms, even on a minute to minute basis; symptoms that are described as linked vary independently of one another	Variation follows lawful patterns linked to known physiological, language and speech production/perception effects
Co-occurring disorders atypical for the alleged neurological diagnosis	Co-occurring disorders fit with typical pictures – e.g. aprosodia and visual spatial dysfunction from right cerebral lesions
May be manipulable in assessment and performance	Not responsive to suggestion, unable to modify symptoms to voluntary control beyond familiar effects such as attention to effort, rate control

or feigns severe lip weakness but has no difficulties with retention of saliva or drinking.

Apraxia of speech has often been misdiagnosed as a functional disturbance because of the absence of physical signs and symptoms and the apparently random and variable nature of breakdown. Key behaviours to look out for here are the nature of the speech 'errors', which should fit the pattern of perceived distortions, substitutions, additions and omissions described for the disorder; be associated with the characteristic trial-and-error attempts to home in on targets; be apparent on repeated trials tasks (geared to the severity level of the presenting picture); and vary along dimensions of propositional, grammatical and articulatory complexity.

Absence of physical, biochemical and radiological signs and symptoms may tempt one to opt immediately for a psychiatric basis, but this absence is not necessarily confirmatory of psychiatric aetiology. Speech can be a sensitive barometer to nervous system changes such as subclinical hypoperfusion in certain cortical areas or early changes in cell density or integrity, that are manifest in disruptions to speech production before they are apparent upon neurological assessment. Once more, the key factors to observe are whether the pattern of changes and course of deterioration fit known patterns of speech language breakdown, or whether the picture and reported course of speech decline and pattern of concurrent behaviours are incongruent with recognised onsets and courses for candidate explanations.

Neurogenic speech disorders can also vary situationally according to setting, interlocutor and topic. In neurogenic aetiologies the variability, though, tends to be linked to situational demands (listener with hearing impairment, interfering background noise, rate pressure, propositionality, time of day for fatigue, etc.), while the time, person, place, topic fluctuations in functional disturbances are more likely to parallel variations in emotional associations of the situation – e.g. place where something bad has happened; speaking with a person the speaker is afraid of; broaching a topic the speaker does not want to or cannot face.

Secondary gain and indifference can also be difficult factors to judge. The reaction of some speakers to a neurogenic disturbance may be to ignore it, try to play it down, to battle through regardless. Careful questioning about coping strategies, deeper feelings about the situation and cross reference to other factors often help unravel this knot. Speakers with a genuine neurological condition may also consciously or subconsciously exaggerate symptoms or sabotage improvement when they discover positive gains can accrue from being a person with a problem. Again, careful questioning and observation about interaction and relationships affords insight for solving this conundrum.

Changes of psychiatric origin can sometimes be uncovered through their response to various manipulations of speech known to influence it in particular ways – e.g. use of delayed auditory feedback, white noise masking (to induce a Lombard effect, involuntary raising of voice intensity against background noise), speech rate control, use of bite block (see below). Typically problems of purely psychogenic origin either fail to respond to these interventions as expected or the reactions are totally out of keeping with predicted modifications to speech – unless the speaker is well-rehearsed in practical phonetics and familiar with the motor speech disorder literature – a fact that must not be overlooked in some highly skilled, consciously intentional feigners.

Speakers' performance can also be highly influenced by what the clinician suggests might happen. The therapist might mention that a bite block (piece of acrylic held between the teeth) is being tried as it has been suggested that it shows up trouble with voice production, hypernasality or some other presenting speech behaviour *un*likely to be altered by a bite block. In highly suggestible subjects the bite block or other modification may indeed ameliorate the symptom, supporting the functional nature of its origin.

Some researchers have recommended using delayed (DAF) or frequency-shifted auditory feedback (FAF) conditions (the speaker wears a device where they hear their own speech delivered a fraction of a second later, or at a higher/lower pitch) to disclose deliberate misleading evidence about speech symptoms. If the person is consciously maintaining altered speech, this becomes much more difficult or impossible under DAF or FAF. But it is not a reliable method. Responsiveness to these manipulations is highly variable, even in healthy individuals; people can develop strategies to counteract the effects; and some genuinely dysarthric speakers may show improvement with them.

Why does the person sound foreign?

There is one added aspect of differential diagnosis pertinent in persistent neurological FAS. What changes are causing people to think the speech is foreign rather than disordered and might therefore be targets of therapy to ameliorate the foreign aspect of speech?

One method to achieve this is as follows. A speech language pathologist creates an audio recorded list of words and phrases spoken by the person in question. It is important to include phrases in order to pick up potential prosodic changes. The items in the list are played one by one to several (the more the better) listeners familiar with the local accent. For each item, they rate it on a scale of say 1–5, where 1 is 'definitely local accent' and 5 'definitely foreign'. Additionally, for those rated as 4 or 5, one might request they state what it is in particular that led them to assign a foreign rating.

The next step is to analyse what speech, voice or language features are in common across all the items consistently rated with high foreignness, focusing on phonetic characteristics that do not occur amongst the 'local' rated items. This should deliver firm insights into what aspects of speech lie behind the foreign perception.

The follow-up stage would be to use results from speech motor assessments, or further motor speech evaluation guided by the listener ratings, to determine why the particular phonetic modifications have come about. Does it, for instance, relate to incoordination between articulators, under- or over-shooting? Does it concern particular classes of sound, either by place or manner of articulation? Are highly rated items characterised by particular syllable structures, maybe with deletion of cluster components (*fled* sounds like *fed* or *led*) or difficulties with transitions between consonants? Do non-segmental features play a role – altered stress or intonation, altered rate or balance of nasality? Answers to these queries should deliver targets for therapy. The reasons for why the changes have taken place should indicate methods of therapy, whether they should be methods suited to different forms of dysarthria or apraxia of speech, segmental or suprasegmental (e.g. rate, intonation) features.

There have been no detailed, systematic and controlled investigations of intervention for neurological FAS speech changes. Thus claims that working according to the above signposts, in terms of targets and methods, is the direction to proceed await final confirmation. It should be recalled too that FAS is a motor speech disorder. Focusing intervention on speech characteristics linked to perceptions of foreignness may ameliorate impressions of foreignness. However, other therapy will still need to be conducted to deal with aspects of activity limitation, participation restriction and impact.

Where functional elements are determinants of accent change, direct work on phonetic output is unlikely to exercise any effect. In these cases pharmacological treatment, talking therapies or behaviour modification approaches, or some combination of these, are likely to come to the fore. Evaluation will have explored the affective, biopsychcosocial variables at play that need to be modified to bring about lasting change. Again, detailed studies of therapy for functional FAS are lacking. From germane fields such as functional voice and movement disorders, positive prognosis appears to be linked to factors such as strong physical health, positive perception of social life, perception of effective treatment by a doctor, elimination of stressors, and maybe even treatment with a specific medication.

Conclusions

The preceding sections have endeavoured to offer an overview of the nature, presentation and origins of altered accents. We have attempted to give explanations for the characteristics of FAS that have been so often misunderstood or distorted. We have aimed to place FAS in a proper neurological and psychosocial context, away from the sensationalist, bizarre and misinformed framework in which it is too often portrayed. Whilst our explanations have furnished some insights into the true nature of FAS, there is nothing more insightful than the experiences of people with FAS themselves. We now turn our attention to individual personal accounts of FAS.

From the bookshelf

For readers wanting to follow up on some of the topics or facts and figures mentioned in the text, here are some suggestions. This is not a balanced or exhaustive list by any means. The references are to works that give an overview of different fields related to Foreign Accent Syndrome and will give a lead into more specialist literature. Also included are some of the more hard to find historical references.

Selected works on aspects of FAS

Blumstein SE, Alexander MP, Ryalls JH, Katz W and Dworetzky B. On the nature of Foreign Accent Syndrome: a case study. *Brain and Language* 1987;31(2):215–44.

Dankovičová J, Gurd JM, Marshall JC, MacMahon MKC, Stuart-Smith J, Coleman JS and Slater A. Aspects of non-native pronunciation in a case of altered accent following stroke. *Clin Linguist Phon* 2001;15(3):195–218.

Fridriksson J, Ryalls J, Rorden C, Morgan PS, George MS and Baylis GC. Brain damage and cortical compensation in Foreign Accent Syndrome. *Neurocase* 2005;11(5): 319–24.

Gurd JM, Bessell NJ, Bladon RAW and Bamford JM. A case of Foreign Accent Syndrome, with follow-up clinical, neuropsychological and phonetic descriptions. *Neuropsychologia* 1988;26(2):237–51.

Gurd JM, Coleman JS, Costello A and Marshall JC. Organic or functional? A new case of Foreign Accent Syndrome. *Cortex* 2001;37(5):715–18.

Haley KL, Roth HL, Helm-Estabrooks N and Thiessen A. Foreign Accent Syndrome due to conversion disorder: phonetic analyses and clinical course. *Journal Neurolinguistics* 2010;23(1):28–43 DOI: 10.1016/j.jneuroling.2009.08.001.

Katz WF, Garst DM, Briggs RW, Cheshkov S, Ringe W, Gopinath KS, Goyal A and Allen G. Neural bases of Foreign Accent Syndrome: a functional magnetic resonance imaging case study. *Neurocase* 2011:1–13 DOI: 10.1080/13554794.2011.588173.

Kuschmann A, Lowit A, Miller N and Mennen I. Intonation in neurogenic Foreign Accent Syndrome. *Journal Communication Disorders* 2012;45(1):1–11.

Lowit A and Kuschmann A. Characterizing intonation deficit in motor speech disorders: an autosegmental-metrical analysis of spontaneous speech in hypokinetic dysarthria, ataxic dysarthria, and FAS. *J Speech Lang Hear Res* 2012;55(5):1472–84 DOI: 10.1044/1092-4388(2012/11-0263.

Miller N. The merry vibes of Wintzer: the tale of Foreign Accent Syndrome. In: Della-Sala S, ed. *Tall tales about the mind and brain.* Oxford: Oxford University Press, 2007:204–17.

Miller N. Foreign Accent Syndrome: between two worlds, at home in neither. In: Watt D and Llamas C, eds. *Language and identities.* Edinburgh: Edinburgh University Press, 2010: 67–75.

Miller N, Lowit A and O'Sullivan H. What makes acquired Foreign Accent Syndrome foreign? *Journal Neurolinguistics* 2006;19(5):385–409.

Miller N, Taylor J, Howe C and Read J. Living with Foreign Accent Syndrome: insider perspectives. *Aphasiology* 2011;25(9):1053–68 DOI: 10.1080/02687038.2011.573857.

Perkins RA, Ryalls JH, Carson CK and Whiteside JD. Acoustic analyses of two recovered cases of FAS. *Aphasiology* 2010;24(10):1132–54 DOI: 10.1080/02687030 903022211.

Reeves RR, Burke RS and Parker JD. Characteristics of psychotic patients with Foreign Accent Syndrome. *J Neuropsychiatry Clin Neurosci* 2007;19(1):70–76 DOI: 10.1176/appi.neuropsych.19.1.70.

Seliger GM, Abrams GM and Horton A. Irish brogue after stroke. *Stroke* 1992; 23(11):1655–56.

Selected works from the history of FAS

Ås A. The recovery of forgotten language knowledge through hypnotic age regression: a case report. *American Journal Clinical Hypnosis* 1962;5(1):24–29 DOI: 10.1080/0002 9157.1962.10401924.

Bastian H. *A treatise on aphasia and other speech defects*. London: HK Lewis, 1898.

Critchley M. Regional 'accent', demotic speech and aphasia (reprinted from Livre Jubilaire de Ludo van Bogaert 1962, 182–91, Antwerp). In: Critchley M, ed. *Aphasiology and other aspects of language*. London: Arnold, 1970:240–47.

Fromm E. Age regression with unexpected reappearance of repressed childhood language. *International Journal Clinical Experimental Hypnosis* 1970;18:79–88.

Marie M. Presentation de malades atteints d'anarthrie par lesion de l'hemisphere gauche du cerveau. *Bulletins et Mémoires de la Société Médicale des Hôpitaux de Paris* 1907(19 July):864–65.

Monrad-Krohn G. Dysprosody or altered melody of language. *Brain* 1947;70:405–15.

Nielsen J and McKeown M. Dysprosody: report of two cases. *Bulletin of the Los Angeles Neurological Society* 1961;26:157–59.

Pick A. Über Änderungen des Sprachcharakters als Begleiterscheinung aphasicher Störungen. *Zeitschrift für die gesamte Neurologie und Psychiatrie* 1919;45:230–41.

Whitty C. Cortical dysarthria and dysprosody of speech. *J Neurol Neurosurg Psychiatry* 1964;27:507–10.

General works about motor speech disorders

Duffy J. *Motor speech disorders*. 3rd edn. St Louis MO: Elsevier, 2013.

Hixon T, Weismer G and Hoit J. *Prelinical speech science*. San Diego CA: Plural, 2008.

McNeil M, ed. *Clinical management of sensorimotor speech disorders*. New York: Thieme, 2008.

Miller N. Dysarthria. In: Stone J and Blouin M, eds. *International encyclopedia of rehabilitation*. Buffalo NY: Center for International Rehabilitation Research Information and Exchange (CIRRIE), 2010. http://cirrie.buffalo.edu/encyclopedia/article.php?id=242&language=en

Miller N. Motor speech disorders. In: Gurd J, Kischka U and Marshall J, eds. *Handbook of clinical neuropsychology*. Oxford: Oxford University Press, 2010.

Papathanasiou I, Coppens P and Potagas C, eds. *Aphasia and related neurogenic communication disorders*. Boston: Jones Bartlett, 2013.

Personal accounts of recovery from brain damage and communication difficulties

Douglas K. *My stroke of luck*. London: Little, Brown, 2002.

Hale S. *The man who lost his language*. London: Penguin, 2003.

Luria AR. *The man with the shattered world*. London: Penguin, 1972.

Maxwell G. *Falling and laughing: the restoration of Edwyn Collins*. London: Ebury/Random House, 2009.

Wilson B, Winegardner J and Ashworth F. *Life after brain injury: survivors' stories*. Hove: Psychology Press, 2014.

www.aphasia.org/aphasia_community/in_their_own_words.html

www.aphasia.org.au/aphasia/about-section/aphasia-day/

www.utdallas.edu/research/FAS/about-us/

Selected works about functional, psychogenic voice disorders

Aronson A and Bless D. *Clinical voice disorders*. 4th edn. New York: Thieme, 2009.

Deary V and Miller T. Reconsidering the role of psychosocial factors in functional dysphonia. *Current Opinion in Otolaryngology and Head and Neck Surgery* 2011; 19(3):150–54 DOI: 10.1097/MOO.0b013e328346494d.

O'Hara J, Miller T, Carding P, Wilson J and Deary V. Relationship between fatigue, perfectionism, and functional dysphonia. *Otolaryngol Head Neck Surg* 2011; 144(6): 921–26 DOI: 10.1177/0194599811401236.

General works about language and identity

Llamas C and Watt D, eds. *Language and identities*. Edinburgh: Edinburgh University Press, 2010.

Wodak R, Johnstone B and Kerswill P, eds. *Handbook of sociolinguistics*. London: Sage, 2010.

General works about brain damage and the mind

Purves D, Brannon EM, Cabeza R, Huettel SA, LaBar KS, Platt ML and Woldorff M. *Principles of cognitive neuroscience*. Sunderland MA: Sinauer Associates, 2008.

Ward J. *Student's guide to cognitive neuroscience*. 2nd edn. Hove: Psychology Press, 2010.

Some works about functional neurological disorders

Gelauff J, Stone J, Edwards M and Carson A. The prognosis of functional (psychogenic) motor symptoms: a systematic review. *J Neurol Neurosurg Psychiatry* 2013 DOI: 10.1136/jnnp-2013–305321.

Kranick S, Ekanayake V, Martinez V, Ameli R, Hallett M and Voon V. Psychopathology and psychogenic movement disorders. *Mov Disord* 2011;26(10):1844–50 DOI: 10.1002/mds.23830.

Reuber M, Mitchell AJ, Howlett SJ, Crimlisk HL and Grunewald RA. Functional symptoms in neurology: questions and answers. *J Neurol Neurosurg Psychiatry* 2005;76(3):307–14.

Schwingenschuh P, Pont-Sunyer C, Surtees R, Edwards M and Bhatia K. Psychogenic movement disorders in children: a report of 15 cases and a review of the literature. *Mov Disord* 2008;23(13):1882–88.

Stone J, Reuber M and Carson A. Functional symptoms in neurology: mimics and chameleons. *Practical Neurology* 2013;13(2):104–13 DOI: 10.1136/practneurol-2012–000422.

Thomas M, Dat Vuong K and Jankovic J. Long-term prognosis of patients with psychogenic movement disorders. *Parkinsonism and Related Disorders* 2006; 12(6):382–87.

Short glossary of some more specialised terms used in the text

Acoustic   To do with sound signals. Acoustic analyses typically use computer software to measure the exact nature of the sound waves of speech.

Aphasia   A problem after brain damage that affects a person's ability to understand (hear or read) or produce (spoken or written) words and sentences. The person may hear '*cake*' but it means no more to them than '*ilikhekhe*'; they can say *cake, I, want*, but cannot fit them into a sentence to express they want some cake.

Apraxia   A disorder of programming movements for actions. You can make the necessary movements (so there is no weakness or altered tone in your muscles), but the brain cannot organise all the separate movements together to carry out a particular action. In speech apraxia, the problem is producing speech and voice because the brain cannot coordinate the timing and spatial control of the tongue, lips, vocal cords, etc., necessary to produce speech, even though a person can still move their articulators perfectly well individually.

Articulation, articulators   Pronunciation and the parts of the body involved in the production of what we hear as speech sounds – from lungs, via vocal cords and soft palate (the soft part at the back of the roof of the mouth) to the tongue, lips and jaw.

Central nervous system   The brain and spinal cord (see **peripheral nervous system**).

Cognitive   To do with thought, reasoning, mental processing – of language, vision, memories, attention and so forth. Often contrasted with affective, pertaining to emotions.

Conduction aphasia   A kind of aphasia characterised by difficulty producing the correct sounds or the correct sounds in the right order. In mild cases it may sound like an occasional spoonerism, in severe cases speech sounds like a fluent, incomprehensible babble of sounds.

Dysarthria   Neuromuscular (see below) problem with speech due to changes in how strongly, fast or sustained muscles contract due to changes in the nerve messages getting (or not getting) to them from the central nervous system and across the peripheral nervous system.

Dysprosody   Problems in producing the right stress and intonation patterns on words and sentences or the right rhythm of speech. Speech sounds lacking in melody or fluency; or there are over-exaggerated swings in how much a word is stressed or not or how high the voice rises and falls over the length of a sentence (not just at the end). The rises and falls may come in the wrong place for the language you are speaking (and hence you might be perceived as a foreigner). See also **prosody** and **suprasegmental**.

Functional   Used to contrast with neurogenic/neurological. Label used for disorders (functional voice disorder, etc.) when the underlying origin of the problem is in the psychological sphere rather than due to neurological or other physical damage.

Motor   To do with movement and control of movements. A motor speech disorder is where the underlying problem affects the ability to move the tongue, lips, etc. Typically associated with neurological/neuromuscular damage.

Neurogenic   To do with neurological (central and peripheral nervous system damage) origins.

Neuromuscular   To do with the nerve supply to muscles and their response to nerve impulses. A neuromuscular disorder arises when the strength or patterns of nerve impulses from the nervous system leads to impaired patterns of contraction and relaxation of muscles.

Perceptual, perceived   To do with what you hear or see with the naked ear or eye. Contrasts in this book with instrumental assessments that may be able to detect changes that the naked ear or eye cannot perceive or accurately detect.

Peripheral nervous system   The nerve fibres that branch off from the brain and spinal cord to run out to muscles, organs and glands, and that convey messages back from these to the central nervous system.

Phonological   To do with sound systems of languages, the perception and production of the inventory of sounds and the sound contrasts a language uses.

Prosody   To do with the stress, rhythm and intonation patterns of a language. The difference between *black bird* and *blackbird*, and between *you're coming* spoken as a question versus a command, entail differences in prosody (see **dysprosody** and **suprasegmental**).

Psychogenic   Of psychological origin. Used here to contrast with **neurogenic**.

Segmental sounds   Individual sounds of a language – in English, p, a, th, ch, z, etc.

Speech disorder   Problem with pronunciation of sounds due to difficulties with moving the lips, jaw, tongue or soft palate. Contrasts with **voice disorder** or **aphasic**/language disorder.

Stroke   Damage to the nervous system from blockage of or bleeding from a blood vessel in the brain. Sometimes called 'brain attack' to emphasise that it is a medical condition which requires immediate attention. The loss of blood supply causes the affected area to no longer function or to dysfunction. This may lead to problems such as arm weakness, loss of sensation, memory loss, speech disorders and so forth.

Suprasegmental sounds   Aspects of sounds above (supra) the level of individual sounds, taken to include here features such as tone of voice, rate of speech, intonation pattern and so forth (see also **prosody**).

Voice disorder   Difficulty with spoken communication because of problems with the vocal cords. May arise from direct problems with the (muscles of the) cords themselves or balancing vocal cord movements with breath support for speaking. Contrasts with **speech disorder**.

Part II

Personal testimonies

The accounts in this section all come from people who have directly experienced an altered accent, or from their family members. There was no prescribed format or remit given to contributors, other than just to 'tell us about your experience of developing the altered accent and how things have been since'. Accounts appear largely unedited. We made no distinction as regards aetiology. There are instances where the onset is clearly neurological and others where the trigger is not clear. In between there are stories where the onset was almost certainly neurological but where psychological factors have shaped the course and development of the accent; there are examples where individuals point to a seemingly definite neurological or physical event associated with the onset, but where other features indicate that the deeper cause and course are almost certainly not linked to these. Some threads might be discerned running through all or many accounts – a searching, a journey, pain, fatigue, discovery of the true worth of family and friends, of inner strengths and depths. We were not looking for common themes, though, other than the genuine experience of finding oneself, against one's will, with a new accent. We have not sought to structure the chapters; they are organised in alphabetical order by country and by author surname. The accounts are as varied as the individuals all are. We leave the writers to speak for themselves.

Chapter 3

Personal testimonies

AUSTRALIA

Anonymous from **Australia** reminds us just how profoundly FAS affects the entire family unit, and of the profound, essential medical questions that go unanswered and, the reader cannot help but feel, not even understood. One can hardly believe that modern medicine is not able to provide better answers. We feel the struggle of a remarkably intelligent woman to break through to her former self and break free of the bonds of the debilitations of her condition, with incredible perseverance and resolve.

Starting over . . .

ANONYMOUS, *Australia*

May 2012

After months of attending medical consultations between my General Practitioner, three specialist neurologists, two neuropsychologists, a speech and language practitioner, and second opinions from a range of consultant specialists and technicians for various reasons, we were provided with an explanation that came as a major shock, but did provide a sense of relief and a way forward.

It was day four of a week of neuropsychological assessments, specialist consultations and continuous EEG monitoring for seizure activity. The words "Acquired Brain Injury" "Executive Function Deficits" and "Foreign Accent Syndrome (FAS)" are all I can remember . . . the rest of the initial explanation provided by the Doctor on that day is a blur. Only snippets remain entrenched in my memory.

At the time, these three terms used to describe my condition repeated over and over again in my mind. It was as time had stood still. Then, the questions started to race through my head. What does this mean? How did this happen? Will I recover? How long will it take? What can be done? Is there a cure? So many questions . . .

At last after six months of what now seems like being on an endless roller coaster ride of medical consultations, neurological assessments, pathology tests, CT, MRI and PET scans I had some answers – but was this the answer I really wanted to hear? My eyes welled up; I bit my lip, and swallowed hard to stop the tears. My mind was racing; I struggled to force out a sound and find the right words. I said to myself "keep it together – at last someone knows what is going on and perhaps they can tell us more."

After what seemed an eternity, but in reality was only seconds I gathered composure and asked the questions I'd longed to ask. Dr. 'Z' was so kind and sincere in her responses. She told us she had seen this condition three times before in her career. The sense of relief was overwhelming.

I drew a deep breath and asked, "In your experience have the people you've seen with this condition recover their speech the way it used to be?" Dr. Z's answer was unexpectedly brief. "No" she said. She then went on to explain that in the research she had found published about this condition, for the majority of cases, people with Foreign Accent Syndrome do not return to the way they used to be.

Immediately I felt intense anger. How could this happen to me? My mind was racing again. I could see my partner was trying to stay calm. We'd heard of this condition once before this visit with specialists. An earlier assessment a fortnight before by a Speech and Language Practitioner in our local area suggested "Dysprosody". We had looked up the definition of this term the week before so I knew that this term was also referred to as "Pseudo Foreign Accent Syndrome". I also knew that it was extremely rare, not much was known about it and not a lot could be done to treat it other than speech therapy.

Dr. Z did her best to try and explain more about the condition, its origins and how brain injury has been linked to FAS. I listened, still in disbelief that a simple change to prescription medication could lead to this. The urge was too strong – I had to ask "So why then for someone with my history of epilepsy which originates on the left side, and a brain tumor also on the left side, would I have been prescribed a medication that is known also to affect the left side of the brain?" Dr. Z's answer confirmed everything we'd suspected from when my speech started to become affected until that day.

Three months later

I am coming to terms with the fact that I have an Acquired Brain Injury and FAS. I can only describe the last fourteen months as an experience I would not wish upon another human being. I have progressed from a person that was extremely happy with my life, being financially independent, self-sufficient with a thriving career services practice I'd built from the ground up over seven years from nothing, to now having to live on a restricted budget, unable to work in my business to support my clients, and reliant on my partner to take care of me and our youngest child.

In retrospect, before becoming ill in 2011 life was hectic and lived at a very fast pace running my own private practice whilst juggling parenting and family life. There were never enough hours in the day and tiredness and fatigue had become the norm. But I loved my work, built a successful national career services practice, raised three children, been in a loving relationship for 14 or so years where we had built a life together and achieved many of our goals.

Yes we'd had our ups and downs. Everyday life for us was demanding, but at the same time enjoyable, and satisfying, where each day brought new challenges. I looked forward to getting out of bed every day. I had the freedom to work and live independently. We had worked extremely hard to put ourselves into a position where we were working towards financial security, providing for our family's needs and living with a relatively simple yet comfortable lifestyle.

Our life journey so far had been one of many good times and not so good times to get to where we were fourteen months ago when life changed irreversibly. At the time, where we had come from was nothing compared to what was to come next.

June 2011

I can now refer to the fourth day of this month, which was a Saturday, as "the day my life changed – again!" What was so different about this day was that this was the third time in my life I'd faced major life change as a result of health condition.

Since this day I've had so many people ask what happened. My story is quite complex. So rather than go into great detail, I'll explain briefly what had preceded this day . . .

I have managed a minor form of epilepsy referred to as "Temporal Lobe Epilepsy" since onset at the age of 21, with the help of medication. The only time Epilepsy was an issue for me was when I took on too much in my work, or didn't get enough sleep or missed a dose of medication. I could usually manage my epileptic condition and with the help of anticonvulsants, and therefore lived a relatively 'normal' life. That was until 2006.

During 2006 over an eight-month period I experienced break through seizures and a number of other symptoms that led to further investigations. The CT scan showed a small brain tumor in the left temporal region of my brain. Seven weeks later I was admitted to a major metropolitan hospital under the care of a top surgeon and his team to have the tumor surgically removed.

After 10 days in Intensive Care and one day on the general ward I came home to recover. Thankfully this procedure went well with minimal post-operative side effects other than having to re-train my brain gradually to improve reading comprehension, as well as memory and recall functionality. I achieved this over six months and was back to full capacity in my own practice as a private career practitioner and in my home life with my partner raising three children. At the time our youngest was only three.

The only other remarkable event that should be mentioned in sharing my story is that some ten years prior to having the brain tumor removed I did sustain serious neck and back injuries from a work-related car accident that took many years to recover from physically and learn to live with emotionally. This event brought about major change in my life, which I did eventually cope with and recover from to lead a fulfilling life, may I say with some fairly significant adjustments in the way I was able to live, work and function.

So with a major motor vehicle accident and a brain tumor behind me I was in the midst of yet another serious medical event, which is now believed to be the return of a series of "break- through" epileptic seizures. This first event and following seizures over the next few months were quite different to any other seizures I'd experienced in duration, presentation and impact on my body.

During these seizures I was immobilized with weakness in my arms and unable to speak. I could hear what was happening and being said around me, but couldn't respond. These episodes also lasted up to an hour and half, rather than a few minutes. The after effects also lasted much longer. I found I was a little slower in being able to analyze/synthesize information, and I was left with severe headache, neck soreness and sensitivity to light that lasted days rather than a few hours. I hadn't experienced these signs to this degree before with any other seizures.

With the first occurrence I was hospitalized within 48 hours to investigate the possibility of a Transient Ischemic Attack, also known as a Mini Stroke; TIA; or Little Stroke. A TIA was eliminated. This initiated the long search for an answer. After a numerous tests, scans and consultations with specialist neurologists over three months, a further possible explanation of "Sagittal Sinus Thrombosis," which had appeared on an MRI scan with a dye contrast, was also ruled out. At this time speech was intact with no sign of an accent.

Prescribed medications at this time were Epilum (Sodium Valproate) and Tegretol (Carbamazepine). The Epilum dosage was increased, to try and control suspected seizure activity, which as I described above, had become more severe in length and frequency. I'd been taking these two medications at different times in various doses most of my life and more recently simultaneously to successfully control epilepsy.

The next action by Doctors was to change the anticonvulsant medication. A plan was devised by one of the specialist neurologists to wean me off Epilum and replace it with Topamax (Topiramate) gradually over a few months. Tegretol remained a part of my treatment regime.

The first seven days of the 'reduction/introduction' process went well. By week two, something was wrong. I started to feel increasingly unwell with nausea and dizziness, sleep patterns were disrupted, and my ability to talk was noticeably different, where speech was becoming more labored, interrupted and difficult to get words out. Within 15 days and over the following week, my condition worsened. At this time it was determined by Doctors that I had experienced a rare, but 'severe adverse reaction' to Topamax.

I was experiencing a range of side effects to this particular medication, which worsened as the dosage increased as per the plan recommended by the consultant neurologist. Signs included: severe tiredness and fatigue; loss of appetite; nausea; dizziness; taste change; diarrhea and stomach cramps; confusion and trouble thinking clearly; problems with concentration, attention span, recall and memory; difficulty finding the right words; changes to sleep patterns and insomnia.

I also experienced numbness and tingling (like pins and needles) in my arms/hands and legs/feet (known as 'paresthesia'), as well as rapid weight loss. I'd also progressed to the point where I struggled significantly to speak and be understood in everyday conversation.

With this reaction to Topamax, the doctors slowly weaned me off this medication and introduced another anticonvulsant, Lamictal (Lamotrigine), at the same time. With the introduction of this medication I also developed an itch, to the point where my skin felt like it was on fire and I was scratching myself to pieces. I was then being monitored for possible Stevens – Johnson syndrome. The itch did settle as Topamax was removed from my treatment plan, and as Lamictal was tolerated. At this time the diagnosis was "Refractory Epilepsy post Astrocytoma".

Lamictal was eventually ceased at a later date by another neurologist because of its potential to affect speech. Throughout this entire process life became a blur. I was incapable of being able to function at the level I was used to. I was taking four anticonvulsants each day in different dosages depending where the reduction/introduction process was up to. Throughout this process my life had slipped away into nothingness, where each day seemed to take forever to pass. My body had started to survive on stored fat and my weight was rapidly dropping.

With these changes to medications I was left severely debilitated with significant limitations in my ability to take care of myself. I needed constant supervision and assistance from my husband and our youngest child, who was only eight, going on nine years old, at the time. I couldn't drive, cook a meal or do simple chores around the house. I struggled to talk to anyone and watched my practice, a business I'd put so much hard work into slip away from me. Our financial situation was grim; the bank wouldn't consider that we were in hardship.

Each day blended into the next from my vantage point on the world in my recliner chair staring at the television or out the window. Nights were terribly long. I was awake from 1–2am and then all day until I finally fell asleep between 10 and 11pm of an evening. A few hours' sleep and I was awake again, lifeless and struggling with the pain of severe headaches.

My brain and body wouldn't let me sleep or eat. My digestive system was out of whack and my head felt heavy and dull. Each day greeted me within minutes of awakening with a headache that felt like my brain was trying to explode from the inside out. To top it off, it became harder and harder to communicate and be understood – eventually I gave up trying to talk, existing in a world of silence.

January 2013

Today is the beginning of a new year. I found myself asking "Why Me?" and "Why Now?" again. I thought I'd passed this stage of learning to live with FAS. After all, I'd survived a serious motor vehicle accident that impacted on my physical capacity to work, and led to losing my job and career. I'd survived and overcome psychological effects that that took four years, with intensive counseling, to climb out of what seemed a deep dark black hole. I'd survived a brain tumor, which also took a great deal of energy and self-work to come out the other side. I'd also survived a number of other significant life changing events as a child and young adult, which I will not go into detail for this story. Now faced with yet another, forced and unplanned change in my life, I was struggling to come to terms with having to start over again.

I know that life is full of challenges and change is the norm. On this day, a year and half since becoming sick I reflected on what had happened. I feel that a part of me is lost forever. Everything I'd work so hard to achieve to lead a fulfilled life as a parent, partner and professional in a career I had chosen was gone.

Acquired Brain Injury – these words still resonate in my mind in moments of sadness and when my resilience is low. I keep telling myself "you've done it before, you can do it again". I also remind myself that there are so many other people in the world worse off than me.

I know what is ahead of me. Do I have the strength and the courage to get up and keep going? Of course I do. Quitting is not an option. It's never been a part of my vocabulary – only challenges and problems to solve. This is just another challenge to be endured and overcome.

On the other side, I have just spent two days with my new best friend, my recliner chair, unable to function, racked with headache, and extremely unwell. These two days then extended to a 14-day period of nothingness.

So after one and half years this relapse was a stark reminder that I am unable to function at the level I once could and that my journey will be one day at a time.

The hardest part of coming to terms with this condition is letting go of what I once could do in my personal and professional life.

The second hardest has been accepting that what was will no longer be. For me anything less than all is not good enough. I am a "Type A Personality" so this adjustment and changing innate behaviors that is part of my makeup and the person I am is so very painful.

In my professional life as a career practitioner, I assisted clients to "Get the Life They Love". I was also a living example of the theory, principles and practice behind what I did to help people and make a difference to their lives over the eight years of this chapter of my life.

Somehow "Get the Life You Love" has lost its meaning to me, as a result of having a brain injury and Foreign Accent Syndrome. I was living the dream – doing work that was my passion and making a different to lives of others. To have this taken away from me now just doesn't make sense nor seem fair.

On the other side, "change is constant" and is a natural part of our lives. Perhaps this most recent forced unplanned change in my life is the next step towards a higher purpose?

Now, whilst writing for you I cannot answer that question. Right now I don't know where I am heading – what I do know is that I feel so very blessed that am alive breathing and am loved and that I have been able to recover some level of speech and the ability to write, although it's of a lesser standard, to the point where I can, with a great deal of effort, share my story with you.

Living with FAS

In the early days of FAS we found our lives changed considerably in so many ways. It wasn't just the changes to our home and work life. Living in a regional area we also needed to make many trips to large hospitals and clinics in metropolitan centres for numerous medical appointments for assessments, scans, tests and consultations. This too took its toll both emotionally and financially.

I recall one instance where our youngest child appeared withdrawn and angry in the lead up to another trip away to see Doctors. When asked what was wrong she responded with "I hate it that Mummy is sick". With her life disrupted, she was having trouble understanding what was going on around her. On another occasion she told me to "stop speaking like a baby".

The hardest adjustment for our youngest child was trying to understand what I was saying. She also found it difficult to adjust to the change of roles between my partner and I. Additional issues she also struggled with included: getting used to Mummy and Daddy being away often; the reaction of her friends parents who didn't know what was going at home, and the fact that I was unable to attend school events, parent-teacher meetings and school assemblies.

She also had to get used to sitting in on Doctors' appointments made outside of school hours or over school holidays when we couldn't get a sitter – this too was hard on her – imagine hearing people talk about your Mummy and not really understanding what they are talking about. Often she would see me crying and extremely upset.

My partner's life changed over this time as well. His days now revolved around answering the question "How is she?" He stepped in and kept my family in the loop as to what was going on. He also had to change his role in our relationship to being primary carer for me and our youngest child. He'd gone from having a wife to share his life with to a person that had become totally dependent on him for simple necessities and communication with the outside world.

I couldn't go anywhere unassisted, and on the few occasions when I did try, my delayed and restricted speech combined with a very strong accent significantly affected how I was able to interact with people.

My older children also found adjusting to what had happened quite difficult at first. Mainly because it was so very hard for them to understand me over the phone, and they didn't really know what was going on. Both these children are living independently, so phone contact was our usual way of staying in touch. I reverted to text messaging and personal messaging through Facebook as a way to stay in contact.

One of the most amazing reactions I experienced publically was discrimination. I was and am still constantly astounded at the way in which I'm treated particularly when meeting people for the first time or when having to deal with something over the telephone through a call center or receptionist.

As soon as they hear my voice I see or hear a change in tone to the listener's voice. I've been hung up on, spoken down to, laughed at, and treated as if I am unable to understand English. I've had people jump in an try and finish a sentence for me, substitute words when I couldn't quite get out what I wanted to say as well as spoken to in a way where the other person speaks slower because they think I am unable to understand.

I now have to spell my name as well as other words used in a sentence two and three times. I also resort to using substitutes, and the phonetic alphabet when I can remember, to spell out a word, eg A as in 'Alpha' or 'Apple', E as in 'Echo' or 'Elephant,' D as in 'Delta,' V as in 'Victor' etc. I'd learnt the standard Phonetic Alphabet very early on in my career in radio communications as a volunteer with the State Emergency Service. I'm surprised I can still remember some of it today.

When out shopping I also find retail assistants change the way they interact with me –- it's like I'm a tourist, and sometimes it's like I'm not welcome in their store.

The other distressing situation is when making a phone call and the person I am calling thinks I'm a telemarketer or having a lend of them, i.e., joking or just clowning around. These are the hardest to deal with. I usually have to get my partner to call back for me and then pass me the phone.

Because of these difficulties out in public, shopping or talking over the telephone I withdrew from the public, and stopped talking to family and friends. I also was forced to cease my business operations and withdraw from client contact. I enlisted the help of a few very kind colleagues to take care of clients and answer my business line. My partner took over talking to family and friends.

As a result of brain injury and FAS I had become incapacitated and isolated. Any attempt at having to talk, even in short periods affected my ability to function. The more I tried to talk the more exhausted I become. This then made speech and word finding even harder. It was like being stuck in a downward spiral, each day harder to get through than the one before.

I was fortunate enough to eventually find a team of Doctors who were genuinely interested in my condition and willing to be upfront and honest with us to shed some light on what had happened. This team of medical professionals also provided much needed support and connections to resources, as they were able with limited knowledge about FAS and funding. This led to becoming connected with the wider global FAS community and the editors of this book, Jack Ryalls and Nick Miller.

But I have to say, whilst finally gaining support and access to information and resources was a welcome relief for us, it did take almost one year from when I initially became sick with break through epileptic seizures to have a confirmed diagnosis of acquired brain injury, and FAS as a direct result of a severe adverse reaction to medication, and begin a treatment/management plan for speech therapy.

Now over a year and half later I am supported by a caring General Practitioner and Speech and Language Practitioner (SLP), who also liaise with the Neurological Team in a major metropolitan hospital as needed.

Moving Forward with FAS

There is no denying that living with an Acquired Brain Injury has been life changing. In the early days speech sounded disjointed, slow and at times incoherent. I found it easier to leave out words just to reduce the length of time it was taking me to communicate with people.

Even then each word was still difficult to say. In my mind I knew exactly what I wanted to say or ask. I could see it and hear it in my mind. When it came to what actually came out of my mouth – that was different. Each word was an effort. My husband and children had to wait for me to try to get the message across.

After a few weeks I stopped speaking unless absolutely essential. I withdrew from family and friends because it was just simply so hard to talk at any level and make sense. I found at times I also resorted to drawing a simple diagram to demonstrate what I was trying to convey.

As the medication that caused this severe change to my speech and general health was reduced, another was introduced, which was tolerated better. During this "washout" phase a strong accent emerged as I forced myself to resume communicating with my immediate family, selected close friends and colleagues, as well as outsiders I needed to communicate to.

Many commented on the difference in sound, at first comparing it to Asian, Mexican and traditional Australian Aboriginal. Over time the way I sounded when speaking was also compared to Italian, French and lastly Russian. Whilst I worked very hard to improve fluency and the speed at which I was able to say words, pronunciation, rhythm, pitch were still very much different to the way I was before reacting to medication. Grammatical construction of a sentence, word selection and word finding were still also quite difficult.

Depending on when this book is published it will be almost two years or more since speech, language and health were compromised. Whilst I remain seizure free and find life is now a blend of good and not so good days, cognition, speech and language are a constant challenge.

The harder I have to work to speak or the longer I need to speak for – the more tired I become, which then makes talking harder and listening ever harder for people, to the point where I am quite difficult to understand. Periods requiring concentration and higher order cognitive functionality are also demanding. I find that I become quite unwell with severe headache, nausea, loss of appetite, combined with a sensation of being off balance and dullness or unresponsiveness of the brain. When this happens, which is often, I rely heavily on my partner for supervision and to take care of our child and me.

In these periods of sickness, the worse I become and the longer the episode lasts my family suffers also. I become irritable, withdrawn, drained and non-communicative. I also have trouble doing basic things. These periods of being 'not good' can last a few days up to a few weeks at a time.

When I am forced to take a stronger prescription medication for pain and to try and control the severity of headache, I then also become sleepy, and have trouble with functionality for very simple things related to self-care and around the house. This is one of the many changes we've become used to and accept as part of our lives living with FAS. On the whole I awake each day and appreciate simple things. I have accepted having an Acquired Brain Injury and FAS. I now choose to make the most of good days and make sure I rest and take care of myself on the 'not so good days'.

Even now, I am asked often, "Where are you from?" when meeting people for the first time or speaking over the phone, or comments are made about my accent. I find it easier to say to strangers that I have a speech impairment or neurological condition that affects my speech. This is mainly because my story is not easy or simple to tell quickly and concisely. It is easier now to bypass explaining FAS to strangers because of the reaction of shock, or disbelief, or awkwardness.

Living with FAS has become easier through connecting with other people with this condition around the world. This is where synchronicity and happenstance has played an important part in adjusting to living with a brain injury and FAS.

Once I had access to a number of online resources and through the persistence of one the team of specialists taking care of me I was able to connect with Jack Ryalls. Through the magic of the Internet and Facebook, I was then able to connect with the global FAS community, many who have also shared their story in this book. Connecting with other people in the world with this condition has been a blessing.

I know I am not alone anymore. I never really was alone because I have the love and support of family and some very special friends who have stuck by me. But having a condition so rare that affects daily life can be a burden for family and friends. Being a part of the FAS community means that we are able to support each other in good times and not so good times. One thing that has become apparent is that rehabilitation and recovery from brain injury will take a long time, and that it's up to me to work at it every day.

Starting Over . . .

Most of my story has been about the negatives of living with FAS. It's been asked of me has anything good come from having FAS? Now this far along in my journey I can say looking from the other side as a person that see's life 'as a glass half full and not half empty', yes – there is an upside to what has happened to me.

- I listen to music more often, which is now part of ongoing speech therapy.
- I've recovered my sense of humor, and try to laugh more often.
- I've really slow down and try very hard not to multitask or have too higher expectations to the point where I'm too busy for the important things, such as family, relationships, health and wellbeing.
- I lost over 17kgs (without trying) and dropped one to two clothing sizes. I now have less weight to carry around, which is always a good thing.

- I am slowly making new friends in different circles and now put aside time to build these relationships, and
- I am rediscovering longstanding friendships.

When I look at it, I am appreciating some of the more simple things in life. Life was once focused on having to juggle a busy work life, whilst making sure I made quality time for my partner and children. Being forced to make this major life change, I am appreciating more being outdoors feeling the warmth of sunshine on my skin; the pleasant and varied melody of birdsong in the early morning; the smell in the air after rain; the crunch of sand between my toes, and the soothing rhythmic sounds of the ocean at our local beach.

Whilst I did appreciate these simple things before Brain Injury and FAS, when forced to do absolutely nothing, it's amazing at how attuned I've become to the environment around me and finding ways to occupy myself, as well as find solace and inner peace over very long periods of being unwell.

I must say that I am so very grateful that I can still walk and communicate, albeit it at a different level than the way I used to. I do have great empathy now for people who have suffered stroke, have a brain injury or have neurological conditions that have debilitated them to the point where their brain or body are unable to function at all.

I recall a comment from someone who pointed out: "What's her problem?, it's only an accent." FAS is far more than sounding different or having an accent. FAS is a condition that has so many other cognitive and functional effects. For me having FAS is yet another challenge in my life – I've risen above and overcome so many that have come before now – I will endure this one too – it will just take time.

It been said that we shouldn't count time – we should make time count. Now living with FAS as a result of acquired brain injury I intend to do the best I can with the functionality I still have to lead a fulfilling life.

For me now I have to be content with achieving my goals slower than what I intended! And my journey will be different to what I'd envisaged. Now that we know what we are dealing with it's time for the next chapter. Life for me now will be another journey of discovery. Starting over and taking that first step is the hardest part. After the first step, the rest will follow.

I've also come to realize that there is no use looking back on what was or what I've lost – for now it's about making the best of today and looking forward to tomorrow. Any life change is difficult – it's how a person chooses to respond to change that determines the outcome. Out of adversity does come opportunity – It's up to me to make the most of what I can do and let go of what was.

During the initial diagnostic stage of this latest health related event, my life and my family's life was in limbo and at times an uphill struggle. Once we knew what we were dealing with the next step was acceptance. This stage took time coming to terms with what had happened and what it all meant. I still struggle occasionally with acceptance. Now it's about getting on with life. Every day is a new day.

Yes, some days are harder than others, particularly when I have periods of regression and limited function. On the good days I strive to do just one thing that brings me joy or makes me feel good. The next step is to have more good days than not so good and reduce the length of periods of regression.

Another reality is that the life I loved is gone – it's up to me to create a new life that I will love whilst living with a disability.

This quotation by Vivian Green recently attracted my attention.

"Life is not about waiting for the storms to pass . . .
It's about learning to dance in the rain!"

One thing I have learnt from life experience is that we all face adversity in our lives. As I said above, I choose to consider times of adversity as challenges and opportunities. In my years as a career practitioner I had many clients who came to me find it easier to feel sorry for themselves, considering themselves as victims and looking to blame others for their situation.

Instead of expending energy looking outward, the way forward in tough times is to look inward and change your attitude. It's how one reacts that determines our ability to find joy and happiness in life. The secret is to choose to be grateful for what is abundant and choose not to focus on what is missing.

For me I am grateful for today and what is. I work very hard every day to let go of the past and what was. It's truly up to me to recognize what abilities I still do have and take control of my own future. That is until the next life change, then, I'll do it all again!

I draw inspiration from the words of Vivian Green . . . I choose to start over and I'm not waiting anymore for the storm to pass; I am learning to dance in the rain!

CANADA

Kelly Kochut's loving husband Ron takes the metaphor of the athlete to explain his wife's story and the struggle to continue her athletic life in the face of grave physical and mental challenges. The reader feels the love and compassion of a life-long spouse who often wishes that they could take on the illness of their loved one rather than the worse fate of having to observe their loved one suffer.

Kelly's Vancouver Sun Run 2012

RON KOCHUT

I am writing this story about Kelly and how she deals with her efforts to lead a normal life. The Foreign Accent Syndrome is only part of the changes in life she has to endure. After Kelly's injury in 2010, part of her rehabilitation was to get involved with small groups of people. With the help of her best friend Sue, she advanced from going to spin classes, pilates and yoga. Kelly by herself signed up to trying running with the Steveston Community Centre. Her personality makes her apply herself fully to any adventure. One instructor that worked with victims of strokes teaches pilates, yoga and spin classes and the rest of the staff at the local community centre got to know her and her mental problems and took Kelly under their wing so to speak. They found her to be a great motivator for other runners. The training for the 2011 Vancouver Sun Run lasted 13 weeks and immersed Kelly into a clinic of 40 totally new people. Her routine was to get there early and take the same seat near the back for the day's instructions before going out on the run. One lady that was doing marathons befriended Kelly to help her feel welcomed and deal with all the new people. During this time she was asked to be a helper for the team leader. At the end of the training, I would not allow Kelly to go to the run as there wasn't anyone that would take full responsibility for her getting there, being with her throughout the run and returning her home. There would be more then 40,000 runners. Kelly still had problems dealing with crowds and would almost go into a panic state without moving from the spot when left alone.

The community centre asked Kelly to be a team leader for the 2012 Sun Run. She had to go for first-aid training to learn CPR. This turned out to be a bigger challenge than what she was prepared for. First of all she was in a class without anyone she knew. Kelly's inability to count to 10 would be a problem if she ever had to administer CPR. Kelly wasn't going to give up. So right in front of everyone (about 40 in the class) she said that she had had a head injury and was it important to count to 30. The instructors stopped for a moment and said no, the fact that you do something is better than not trying. They said that she could get someone else to count out for her while performing CPR. She was scared and no one wanted to be partnered with her. She was finally teamed up with two others for a test scenario of an accident. One victim, one first aider and one to mark everything down that each person did. This required reading and writing, which added to the stress level as Kelly could not read very well nor write. The instructors paid close attention to everything Kelly did to make sure she would be able to administer first aid or CPR in a real situation. At the end of the day, Kelly cried all the way home. She didn't know what to do but she had made a commitment and she would see it through. She was just overwhelmed by all the pressures of the day.

Again the training was for 13 weeks and Kelly was a leader for the learn to run group. Kelly had to stand up in front of everyone at the clinic and give a short introduction about herself. Kelly said she was an exercise nut. She went on to say light heartedly that she had a brain injury with an ever changing accent and they will never know who will be coming out for the run with them. To assist Kelly with her new role as team leader, I purchased a runner's GPS watch. I had to set it up for each week's activity so Kelly could hear the beeps. Kelly went to every class. She applied the rules for runners to advance to make it through the clinic. She offered her time for anyone in her group to meet for the homework run between training days. It turns out that of all the team leaders for the community centre, Kelly was the only one that was successful and had a small run group meeting on a regular basis. She also worked with one lady (Heidi) from the run faster group and as it turned out she was able to reduce her own time by 5 minutes on race day.

At the end of the training, three ladies offered to take Kelly to the Sun Run. They told her they would pick her up, run with her and make sure she got home. They felt that Kelly had worked too hard to miss out and wanted her to succeed as well as the team she had worked with. They made plans for the just-in-case problems by having their cell phones on and a meet area after the run. I was a little unsure about the whole thing but I let her go. I know I said that if anything happened, I wasn't able to come on a moment's notice to get her and I was going to take out my anger on all of the women that let it happen.

April 15, 2012: the big day came. Kelly met with the ladies and they took her to the train station for the trip downtown. She was one of almost 49,000 runners to run the 10 kilometres of the Vancouver city streets. What better way to start your day than a 25-minute wait to use the washroom? Then using back streets to avoid the crowds, they jogged 3 blocks to get into position for the run, only to wait in the big start line-ups. Kelly was running with the Steveston Community Centre fitness coordinator, Donna. After the run started and about 1 kilometre out, there was a big pile-up as a girl had fallen. They weren't involved and quickly got past. With the pace of their running, they weren't in the masses of people so there was room to run. Near the 4-kilometre mark, Donna had a problem with her foot falling asleep and so they slowed to a walk to get it going again. The whole time Kelly was sticking to Donna like glue. Donna told Kelly to run her race but she wouldn't leave her side. Donna tried to motivate Kelly by telling her she was handling the crowds perfectly, that they had their cell phones in case: Just run the race!

They continued to run until about 7 kilometres when they were caught up in the crowd again. From here Kelly doesn't recall what happened but Donna said that Kelly was pushed ahead and that Kelly was always looking back for Donna yet continued to go forward. Kelly remembers being scared and questioning herself as to if she was running the best she could or not and didn't believe she was. At the finish, Kelly went to the meeting area, pulled out her cell phone and waited for the others. Donna called and they met up. Kelly's time was 1 hour 5 minutes 15.9 seconds, finishing 16386 out of 48904 runners. Donna was so proud of Kelly facing her fears, and complimented her on a well done run.

They all went to the finish line party and then out for something to eat. Kelly was a chatter box when she arrived at home, relaying everything to her father that she remembered. By dinner time she couldn't recall it, only stories that others told her about the race, but she can't remember being there.

Kelly's foreign accent syndrome has not affected her determination or the admiration of those around her. Every day seems to be a different accent and not always understood the first time. She doesn't know it's a problem for others until they say, Pardon? Pardon? Donna is so impressed with Kelly that she wished Kelly had been able to complete her goal to be a personal trainer. She offered to help Kelly in any way should Kelly's reading and comprehension improve. She offered personal tutoring for Kelly to get her training certificates. But at this time it is an impossibility. The community centre uses Kelly's energy as a motivator for all the classes she attends. She has been asked to come back again for the 2013 Sun Run as a team leader. The instructors do not mind Kelly talking to others and offering encouragement in the class. At times she has been able to show them different ways to do various exercises based on the degree of difficulty. Kelly's personal goal is to help others reach their own. Kelly has wanted to be a personal trainer – but who would hire someone that can't remember the exercises or be able to count? Well, at least now she can run.

Since that race, Kelly has done two smaller runs. She improved on her time, but more importantly, on dealing with the crowds.

COSTA RICA

Jeffrey Barquero's story resonates with the love of a son for his mother. He relates his mother's struggle to recover from the debilitating effects of meningitis. There are humorous details which set the story firmly within the cultural matrix of his home country of Costa Rica. We see how his mother's plight has given him a career direction in life – truly a case of taking life's lemons and turning them into lemonade.

My mother and her foreign accent (*Mi madre y su acento extranjero*)

JEFFREY BARQUERO SALAZAR

Ten years ago my mother was in an unconscious state for a month in the hospital in the province of Limon, Costa Rica. Doctors diagnosed her with meningitis. A month later she came to, and reacted slowly but she was never the same. She had lost much short term memory, and her muscles had atrophied. She had trouble eating; bringing a spoon to her mouth, the spoon often missed her mouth, spilling food. But one of the consequences which had the biggest impact on her life was the muscle atrophy. She said that her tongue felt 'heavy' when she spoke. While she knew what she wanted to say and what she meant, she could not say the word she wanted to, and had speech fluency problems. She also had difficulty making mathematical calculations. The doctors diagnosed her with the consequences of a stroke.

She was referred to interdisciplinary therapy, attending physical therapy, speech therapy and other types of therapy to correct the problems of muscle tone and articulation of speech. She improved over time, but still had failing memory. While her language continued to improve, her speech eventually began to have a foreign accent. My aunts began to notice it first of all, and made comments about it. She began to have a Cuban accent in her speech, which my family first thought was because of the close relationship she had with our Cuban neighbors and friends. But then we noticed that when she spoke, her Cuban accent changed over time. Sometimes it would sound like the accent of Costa Rica and then at other times it would sound like a North American English accent.

People who did not know her thought she was trying to be humorous by the way she was speaking. But of course our family knew it was not her normal speech at all.

My mother says that she often did not realize that she was speaking in this strange manner. But eventually she became accustomed to this bizarre way of speaking, although she often experienced difficulties initiating conversations, because people thought she was attempting a joke.

Through my mother's neurological difficulties, I started to become interested in the field of speech-language pathology. I eventually went to Santa Paula University and graduated in speech-language pathology. I then had clinical experience working in a school system with autistic children, children with Down's syndrome and children with hearing impairment. This is difficult but rewarding work. Then I started work in a home for the elderly where I worked with patients who had suffered strokes and were aphasic.

It was during this work that I discovered my true passion in speech-language pathology, which is working with feeding and swallowing problems. I worked closely with the nutritionist at the nursing home to improve the health of elderly patients. Eventually I gained such expertise that I was invited to give workshops on improving the posture, feeding and nutrition of the elderly. Most of the time the general public is not even aware that speech-language pathologists have specialized training in feeding and swallowing and can offer specialized therapeutic techniques to improve dysphasia (swallowing problems) and deglutition.

Presently, my mother has fewer problems with atrophied muscles. She continues to do physical and speech therapy, but she still has a foreign accent. Sometimes it sounds like people from Cuba, sometimes like a person from the United States who is just learning to speak Spanish with a thick 'gringo' accent. Often, when my mother's friends phone they don't recognize her voice, and they think we have visitors or that they have dialed the wrong number. So she tells them 'Noooo! It's me, Laura!'

When she visited her doctor recently, he told her she has to practice her memory exercises more, because she complains that she forgets things sometimes. For example, in Costa Rica it is usually so easy to find your car in the parking lot, because there are relatively few automobiles. But almost every time she has problems finding her car. One day, my mother opened the door of another similar car and climbed in. When she got inside she felt bad when she saw other people already there!

In any case, it is an interesting story that through my mother's difficulties and as a result of meningitis, she helped me to find a way of giving back the love and nurturing she had given me as a child. People who do this work have to have a lot of patience. I just always have to remember just how much I tested her own patience as a child.

GERMANY

Martina Bodeck is the loving and anxious mother of a teenage daughter who cannot find satisfactory medical answers to what is at the base of her daughter's suffering. The reader feels her frustration and the pain of encountering medical authorities who only offer superficial, apparently preconceived notions. One cannot help but think of the Hippocratic Oath which states that physicians should, above all, do no harm. And yet by refusing to listen carefully, to carefully consider the wisdom of a mother's intuition, this is exactly what they are doing.

Lena Bodeck FAS 5.1.2011

MARTINA BODECK

From that day on many things were different . . .

Our then 17-year-old daughter was in her second year of work and had just put the Christmas break behind her when she called me from work on the morning of 5 January 2011, and told me that her right arm had just cramped. I thought nothing of it. Later, she called me again. Could I pick her up from work, she said, because she was too weak to walk back home – about 1km. I told her she should run – it would be great weather – and I talked happily to her. She was brought home by a colleague in his car. At home we had a normal lunch and after lunch they went to my computer, and suddenly she said she could no longer see properly, she could not see anything. Then she became dizzy and felt ill, and she just lay down on the sofa. She got one hell of a headache, and no tablets helped. After about 1 hour she got up slowly, wanting to tell me something, but no words would come out. Fearfully, she began to cry with tears in her eyes. She was fully responsive, but she could not speak. I immediately thought of a stroke, and since she was obviously getting worse, I drove her immediately to the hospital in Lüdenscheid with a suspected stroke . . .

Once there, she could hardly walk, had to be moved in a wheelchair and, because of her age, they brought her to the stroke unit on the children's ward! There, we had to wait 1 1/2 hours for a doctor for an MRI. He had been called away again. The MRI was OK and the next day the doctors were confronted with a mystery. The next day her voice slowly returned, but she had to think deliberately about every word, and how to express it. She rolled her eyes in a very peculiar way when speaking sometimes. The following day, suddenly, overnight, she had developed a very strong foreign accent; no one would have thought that she was German. This French accent didn't stop over the next weeks and months, and later transformed into a Dutch accent.

Back to the hospital . . . for a few days of confusion. A laboratory value of D-dimer was again increased to 2.6 (normally <0.5), and a blood sample was not quite right; but the MRI showed nothing remarkable . . . so the doctors diagnosed that it must surely be psychological! Although, two years earlier, she had already had a sudden facial paralysis on the right and speech disorders, severe headaches, and general weakness. She was treated by the same random doctors who had concluded for no reason that it was a mycoplasma infection. Now they wanted to keep her in for weeks, maybe months, as outlined by psychiatry, but we refused, preferring to see our family doctor. He had known Lena since she was a baby and he did not believe that all this could be psychosomatic. (At this point, I must express our appreciation to our family doctor; he has always supported us and given us the courage to continue searching.)

We then took her back home, and then we visited various other hospitals. Most doctors had never seen this foreign accent syndrome speech before, and therefore could not do anything for it. Since the first clinic in Lüdenscheid declared that it was psychosomatic, the other doctors have assumed this diagnosis without having to worry themselves or listen to Lena's history. The physicians spoke once about problems with her boyfriend, from whom she had since moved on. For our part, we objected that it could not have anything to do with the boyfriend, because she had experienced different neurological problems four years earlier, such as blurred vision, or vision loss at 30–50 per cent, according to a polyp-op at the same Lüdenscheid hospital where she landed up again in 2011. Maybe it was surgical damage from the polyp surgery, maybe it was an unstable cervical vertebra, perhaps migraines? We do not know.

Since this shock on January 5, she always gets recurring spasms, for about 15 minutes, sometimes in the legs or in the left arm, but almost always the right arm. Facial paralysis to the right side has also resulted. On top of this, the language blocks came and went, and then for the next few days they were very bad and her vision was blurry and she was slow. Whenever she was tired and had just woken up, then her language was very bad. She had a total of 8 months illness. It went uphill and downhill again.

I must give a huge thanks to her company. They have always been a great help, and supported us, and we could always talk very openly to Lena's bosses. For this we are very grateful. She started to work again in August, and then she had to repeat the entire second year of training. And the worst thing was that she could not leave because she was on sick leave; she was doubly isolated. She would have also liked to have gone to meetings, despite the FAS, but it was always: 'you are on sick leave'. It was in that year that she turned 18 years old. She was very strongly opposed because she finally became an adult and could decide things for herself and drive. Getting her driver's license took much longer then, because she was staying in the clinic for so long. But this worked out in the autumn of 2011. Moreover, it was not nice for her to finally be 18 but to then have her parents issued with a 'patient proxy' so that they could decide on things just in case. The natural tendency is for youth to find their own way once they turn 18, but this was not always possible due to her illness. But in another way, it has brought us close again after the years of puberty.

Most of Lena's acquaintances are not bothered by her accent, but find it appealing. She is very fun-loving, outgoing and lovable. Over the course of time her language began to get better, even though her teacher still thought we had come from the Netherlands. But she is not the same as before.

Recently the seizures became more frequent. So I got in touch with Kay Russell from England and joined the FAS group on Facebook to possibly get valuable tips from others. At this point – Thank you Kay! I've found you at the right time. The whole FAS family gives Lena and myself so much strength and courage that I cannot describe it! Thank you all!

On the 18th of January 2013 she was again at the office when she suddenly got a cramp in her right arm, and once more could not speak. A stroke was suspected and an ambulance was called. Lena's boss called us, and my husband and I drove straight to the office. She understood everything but could not speak, as in a stroke. She was then taken to the hospital in Lüdenscheid where she had been treated previously. It was Friday afternoon. Because it was the weekend, they couldn't perform the EEG that the emergency physician had ordered. Instead, the doctor just stood around bored, not knowing what to do with us. She took a blood sample and told us to wait for an MRI. LDH was increased two hours after the cramp to 350 (normally 120–220), which was not considered further. She sent us to the MRI with Lena's notes file and while we waited we looked in the briefcase – and saw the discharge report. Lena's symptoms had been diagnosed as psychosomatic! Incredible! I'd never known anything like it: we had seen the doctor, and even before an examination had been made the diagnosis was psychosomatic! This was so incredible! The hospital wasn't helping her, and it was treating us like fools.

In the evening, Lena's speech returned again, though it was very slow and sluggish. Since then she has been speaking with a Dutch accent: the FAS is back. Depending on how she is doing, her speech is better or worse, but often very slow and faint. She has also had two more seizures, is very forgetful, often feels dizzy, weak, and has headaches. Her heart was examined using an ultrasonic echogram, but it is also okay – there is no hole in the heart. A week after the spasm, her homocysteine had increased to 18.5 (normally 10–15), which was not further evaluated.

We do not complain, but refuse to give up our search and hope to find someone who can help us. We know our daughter; her problems must have some cause; it is not psychological. We can live with this illness, Lena is also very self-conscious and admirable about it, but we need to know why it is happening. The concern that she has some condition and is not getting help for it is not doing any of us any good. Had it been a stroke, it would have been dealt with immediately, and she would have got rehabilitation. Lena has the symptoms of a stroke, but the doctors say she could not have had one, and therefore she gets no treatment, despite her serious ailments. Her brother, her friends – nobody who knows her can understand why she can't be helped, and they know the real Lena.

The worst thing is to have to fight against the ignorance and arrogance of the doctors and to always have to prove that she was and is a normal girl. And she has never had such psychological problems that would cause something like this. If it were so then we would all have some such ailment. I feel bad as a mother . . . to feel that there is something which no one has found . . . but I know for sure that I won't stop searching, and one day we'll find someone who can help us, and we'll know what it is. And to everyone else: don't let anything convince you that it's the psyche, because if the doctors can't work it out right away, that's what they say: it must be all in the mind!

I particularly liked the comment of a neurologist and FAS member, which I paraphrase below. This is what he said of the MRI scan from which no FAS diagnosis was made:

> When you look out of an airplane to the ground, you can see exactly where each street and each house is located. If a house has been on fire or collapsed, you can see it right away, but what happens in the houses and in what condition the houses are inside, you cannot see from the plane.

And I think that is the very best explanation of why FAS is not seen in the MRI. It is not the mind, but the research that has not yet gone far enough.

Martina Bodeck, 42 years

UNITED KINGDOM

The link from neurological episode to the onset of FAS is incontrovertible. The emergence of FAS from more general, more severe speech and language problems represents a common picture. **Annabel**, with her deep insights into the workings of the brain from her scientific education and intimate understanding of voice and speech production from her musical training, offers us valuable reflections on the whole breakdown and recovery process. Here, though, is someone who far from resenting her new accent has built a friendship with it. Far from it provoking alienation, so often the case, for her it has prompted a quest for where this accent is from, a new relationship with self.

FAS, my friend

ANNABEL

I cannot imagine myself without FAS. Language suddenly stopped for me when I had a stroke eight years ago (2004), but it was the FAS, a consequence of the stroke, which brought back my capacity to communicate. I am different from before: my stroke imposed limitations (not many now,) FAS opened new doors. FAS is part of my being and I think it always will be.

My speech is now 'normal' far more often than not. Nonetheless, FAS is my shield when I am uncertain or tired and words will not emerge from my mouth, like the period after the stroke when every utterance was an effort. If I am anxious, particularly when I am with strangers, I make grammatical mistakes and people instinctively articulate more slowly. They do this because they think that I am French. I am immensely, secretly, grateful because it gives me time to process their language. If I have a conversation with someone whose first language is not English, it can take less than a sentence before I am straying back to the spectrum of my language, which generally exists along a geographical line between France and the Balkans. This had disastrous, if entertaining, consequences when a person from Greece was helping me to set up Dragon Dictate last year; the programme now only recognises my speech when I am talking in the presence of someone who is Greek. If I talk about FAS, my accent will gradually emerge. If I am feeling uncertain, I do not know what my words will sound like until they issue from my mouth. Each one of these phenomena has occurred during the last week.

In this account, I shall explain my experience of FAS in three segments. A fundamental component of my FAS is what it saved me from, so I shall start by explaining what my life was like between the stroke and the emergence of FAS. [I think it might be very hard to understand my experience of FAS unless you know what things were like before it started.] Then I shall describe the extraordinary transformation brought about by the FAS. After that, I will tell you about my existence as a person with FAS who has had a stroke, both at the time when the FAS was constantly apparent, and now when it is frequently not in my speech but still always inside me. Finally I shall show how I have been reintegrated into a way of life which is, in some ways, more satisfying than it was before the stroke. The evolution of this new life has been highly dependent on FAS.

Before

Imagine that suddenly you cannot talk. In addition, you can only hear slowly; if someone says more than a short sentence or talks quickly, you don't even know that the words have existed. In fact, it was for me a strangely unemotional experience and this is because I was concentrating so profoundly on things inside my head. Everything was completely different from before, utterly nonverbal. Thoughts were like lights in my brain, spatial and, even if I could have talked, I couldn't have made them into a conversation because there was no linear progression – like a string of beads – from one to the next.

The stroke happened out of the blue, first thing one Thursday morning. I reached my hands out towards the coffee machine and I saw that my arms had crossed over. I wondered if something was wrong with the electricity and then I couldn't manage to think any more. I sat down at the kitchen table and it felt as if a very tightly-fitting, heavy metal cap had been put on my head. My husband, P, called my mother who came round (my parents live next door) and he took my daughters, H and E, to school. E told me subsequently that when she had come to say goodbye that morning the sentences I said made sense, but they were not the answers to the questions she had asked. My mother rang her doctor who said, "Take her temperature and if it is normal, get an ambulance."

The paramedics arrived. One asked, "How are you?" "Fine" I said, because that was the only word I could say (which has to be viewed as funny.) I could think other things. I knew that we were not following our normal way to the hospital in Y; as I lay on the bed in the ambulance, I could see the leaves of the trees either side of the road and those trees were on the way to B – not the usual route.

When we arrived at the hospital the doctor who assessed me asked me to perform a series of actions with my arms. My mother tells me that I simply didn't do some of them. Another doctor came and told me that I'd had a stroke. I understood what he had said, but I did not feel connected with it. A few days later, I was waiting for a scan and I looked at my notes. They said: 'severe receptive and expressive aphasia'. The scan showed that my stroke was in the left-hemisphere, in the frontal and parietal lobes. None of this seemed very important to me.

I decided on the first day in hospital that I needed to speak. I would have liked speech therapy during the six days I spent in the hospital, but I think that the doctors said it wasn't possible to arrange to see anyone, so I had to be my own speech therapist. Because I was a specialist teacher of children with severe dyslexia I knew all about phonemes, the smallest distinguishable units of speech sound, and graphemes, the units of writing associated with individual phonemes; I think that this professional knowledge was a godsend. I could manage about five words by the first evening, including 'will', 'had' and 'man'. 'Man' remained very important for some while because I didn't have any pronouns and said 'man' when I meant 'I'.

The other people in my ward were all elderly women. H and E had been brought in to see me on the first two days, and I thought that the patients would like to know their names. I managed 'H' on the evening of the second day. 'E' was rather harder and I couldn't manage till day three. I know why it was difficult; I had written down the alphabet and had no idea how to pronounce almost all of the letters because I just could not think in phonemes. 'E' is hard because the sound /ĕ/ is part of the name 'm'. I remembered that the letter 'e' came first but since I could not think in sounds, all that I was aware of was that what I was trying to say started with the letter name 'm'. It is odd that I could manage H, which sounds harder, but I must have known that the first letter was 'h', and the next two letters are uncomplicated. Later on, from the moment that the FAS started, it was as if a switch had been flicked in my brain and I knew that letters had both names and sounds and that they were different. Gradually I learned to think in phonemes again – in fact I still sometimes manage bits of words which I cannot say or spell by dividing them into phonemes or syllables.

P came to the hospital every day both before and after work in his motor-bike kit, which made the other patients smile. P has a rare gift for making things happen, for example managing to rearrange H's and E's separate skiing holidays at two days' notice so they could both go away with my sister, a wonderful gesture by her. I had no idea what had gone on, but I liked it when they rang me from France. P is also very practical. He brought me a huge bag of brazil nuts because it is hard to explain that you don't eat cereals or potatoes if you cannot say those words. He tells me that 'man' was the only word he can remember me saying all the time that I was in the hospital. He asked me if I wanted to have a shower, and I said, "manamanamanaman."

Written words behaved very remarkably. I was reading a biography of Dante at the time of the stroke and P brought it into the hospital. I continued reading about Dante, but I only understood each individual word when I had looked through to its final letter. This is how I must have read 'severe receptive and expressive aphasia' – logographic reading (each word being a single visual symbol bearing no relationship with the sounds within that word). There was a total absence of phonological awareness (understanding how sounds work within words.) The whole process worked provided I didn't think at all about those sounds. If I did, comprehension completely evaporated. I probably didn't remember much from one page to another; apart from anything else it required a great deal of concentration to avoid thinking about sounds. FAS was, however, going to save my reading.

My mother came to the hospital in the middle of each day. She brought in 'Ten Apples up on Top' by Dr Seuss (a great idea) so that I could try to read it to her. I could recognise the shape of some concrete content words, like 'apple'. What I couldn't manage were function words, like 'that'. I also tried spelling. I was almost completely unable to spell; I tried really hard and could just about cope with a very few consonant-vowel-consonant words by the time I left hospital (I think managed the word 'but' fairly soon). FAS was to become a crucial factor in spelling because it enabled me to hear the components of words, though it must be said that my spelling is still 'wobbly' (to quote Winnie the Pooh) and has been completely hilarious. Because of my work I take notes in seminars, using a laptop, and there is no time to think about spellings. Revisiting notes I have made during even the last two years, I have found: incldugnin (including) legitibmae (legitimate) cognitiionive (cognitive) oterhpeoes (other people) bepopel (people) likleyu or liekkly (likely) adgantafed (advantaged) rleaitonihsp (relationship) throughough (thorough), and plenty more besides. Some phrases are completely incomprehensible even in context; I have no idea what the phrases 'snalke tey' and 'conromtiy hugheley dropeed' meant. These errors would be magical for a dyslexia specialist.

I listened when the doctors came but could not ask questions. My specialist (whom I liked) understood, and he drew a diagram showing the spread of damage out of the focal point of a stroke. He had spotted another book of mine which is called 'Left Brain, Right Brain', laughed, and told me that I knew too much about brains. He also sent a couple of students to have a chat (well, in a manner of speaking) and I enjoyed that. Some months afterwards he told me that I had been "politely interested" in what he had to tell me, but no more.

I have written this account so far from a rather factual viewpoint because I remember almost no sense of strong emotion while I was in hospital. When one of the patients in my ward asked, "Do you have early dementia?" I didn't mind. My specialist told me that I would probably not be able to work again. I was neither sad nor angry. I just knew that he was wrong. I was mildly irritated when it was time to go home and a doctor whom I had not met before told me to get on with things like cooking; I have extremely little interest in cooking and I thought he was being patronising. H tells me that she sat on the end of my bed and wept on the first afternoon, but I cannot remember her tears. I cried just once, silently, on my own. I was not thinking of the future; I did not understand the present.

This is how I was, emotionally almost entirely void, except that I was lonely even before I left hospital six days after my stroke. I know that I had plenty of visitors, both in hospital and once I was at home, but I could not have a conversation and the loneliness relentlessly increased.

I sing semi-professionally. P took me to see my teacher (a kind of third grand-mother) a day after I came home. We found that I could sing rather more words than I could say, and my sense of pitch was very good. In contrast, it became clear over the next few weeks that my understanding of rhythm was profoundly damaged. I simply couldn't count notes lasting for more than one beat, and long notes tied over the bar line were a mystery. I wonder if this rhythmic problem was associated with FAS and prosody. I had some sessions with a National Health Service speech therapist around five months after the stroke. She asked me to repeat sentences and told me that I was not reproducing the emphases which she had used to accentuate important nouns. Certainly, for several years I could not tie up stresses in lyrics with musical structure.

It was so hard not being able to talk. There was a singing master class my first weekend at home. I knew most of the people there. They have told me subsequently that they were staggered that I could sing anything because I was completely unable to have a chat. Conversations went like this: "How are you feeling?" "Fine," another question, embarrassed silence. I felt encased in a shell of being alone. It was even worse with strangers I met around that time (including after the FAS had started) because they treated me as if I were intellectually completely incapable. Conversations were mirrors; people reflected my linguistic simplicity back to me. Their sentences were made of one-syllable words – like the ones I used. Their grammar was simple – mine was simple and incorrect. I could not remember what they had said – they had to repeat it. Their faces were almost always pleasant, but pitying. They had placed me in a box and, at that time, I had no ladder to climb out, but FAS turned out to be my means of escape. I feel profoundly sorry for people who find it hard to articulate speech.

One thing was wonderful. The girls returned from skiing over the weekend of the master class and they have been, ever since, unfailing guiding lights on my journey to liberty. At that time they were still at school, and subsequently they are always there in person or on the end of a telephone. I will never forget what they have done for me, not only in terms of teaching me to cope with language again, but also their love and acceptance of what I was about to become.

FAS and the transition

P had also arranged for me to see a private speech therapist, starting straight after I came out of hospital. One evening, fourteen days after the stroke, I had this feeling that I sounded a bit French. The next day there was a speech therapy session. The therapist's face after my first two words was unforgettable and she gasped: "Where did that come from?" I was Russian (more accurately Balkan, as I later discovered in a phonetics lab) complete with highly accented phoneme endings, wonderful consonants, a 'xh' sound in the back of the throat at the beginning of a significant proportion of the words (a voiceless velar fricative, like the 'ch' in Scottish 'loch', or German 'nach'), spectacular rolled 'r's and the complete disappearance of /ɪ/ which was replaced by /i/ ('preety' instead of 'pretty'.) The sounds were deeper, produced further back, dark purple velvet, the cheek muscles more taut. I wanted to sing Russian songs because I could hear that quality of voice and instinctively knew how to make the back of my mouth and throat the right shape.

Perhaps the most amazing thing was that my spoken vocabulary dramatically increased from the moment that the FAS began. The day after the Russian started I went to an opera rehearsal. Several people from the master-class were there and they were astonished, not only because of the accent, but also because I could actually have conversations. I had no concept of how to speak with an English accent but everyone laughed and I laughed too. The words made me exhausted, but at least I could talk. It was wonderful that they let me continue with the opera, and this is because of my accompanist and friend, who fought for me. Like my teacher he has spent hours helping me to sing the right number of beats, spotting which words I have missed out, and coping highly imaginatively when I make totally unpredictable rhythmic errors in performances.

I also found that I could understand other people's speech noticeably better. I think I translated it into my accent, and then I knew so much more accurately when phonemes and syllables began and ended. This is not widely reflected in the literature about FAS. Perhaps it is just a manifestation of my FAS, but maybe there are some other people like me. I do not think that it fits in with current models of FAS, and I feel a little frustrated by this.

I went on a whirlwind tour of the FAS research community. I have never minded meeting researchers because I'd love to know about how FAS reflects what has happened in the brain. I was taken by my speech therapist to see a neuropsychologist at a different hospital, and she gave me some psychological tests (for example, how many words can you say which start with the sound /s/ – not a great success in my case!). Shortly afterwards she and I met a research phonetician. He measured every contour of my speech, and asked me which words I liked most, and they were 'creature', 'bizarre' and 'beautiful'. They made me feel so happy. Several years later they organised a FAS forum, and I met some other people like me. E came with me, partly for moral support and partly because she was applying to read psychology at university. There was not much time to have a conversation with other people with FAS because I went to sing in a recital at lunchtime. It is odd; I have not felt that I needed to try to stay in touch with them. I feel a bit guilty about this as my experience of FAS seems to have been much more positive than that of most others. Writing an account for this book is perhaps my first attempt at trying to help.

Where did the FAS come from? Why were there suddenly words? It has been hypothesised that the right-hemisphere has some language processing ability – unsophisticated in terms of vocabulary, highly limited, but sometimes identified after brain injury or surgery. I know that this is highly controversial. It is complicated by the fact that whilst language is largely based in the left side of the brain for the great majority of right-handers, a minority of left-handed people have language lateralized in the right hemisphere or their language is bilateral. Although I am definitely right handed, I do some tasks with either hand, for example taking lids off bottles, and I have left-handed relatives. Despite this, I think that before the stroke my speech processing was typical for right handed people (ie largely in the left hemisphere, where the stroke was) but I believe deeply, albeit subjectively, that I had been using right-hemisphere speech between the stroke and the FAS, imprisoned in a tiny corral of overwhelming limitations. I do not know what plasticity in my brain suddenly allowed a slightly different part of the left hemisphere to take over speech, but the extraordinary coincidence of the FAS-onset with so many more words, conversation, feeling included, was magical. It did not take away being worn out by finding or saying words (I used to see it as a jug of words for each day; when they were all poured out there was nothing left). Sometimes I said exactly the opposite of what I had intended ('up' instead of 'down') and there were wonderful made-up and portmanteau words, but that fortnight of loneliness was dramatically ended.

Having FAS and recovering from a stroke

There are so many things to say about FAS and for me they are inevitably tied up with the stroke after-effects. I am trying to focus here on a series of particular themes. First is how I felt about FAS, how my family coped with it and me, and their huge help. Then I shall compare my family's reactions to FAS to that of friends and strangers. Like some other people with FAS, I have become rather consumed by a quest for my origins and I shall try to explain what I am searching for, although this is rather elusive. Finally I will try to show how positive FAS has been in my re-joining and expanding my life trajectory – as a different person.

As I remember it, FAS was the least problematic element of getting over the stroke, although it has been the most apparent manifestation. FAS gave me such a gift when it first emerged and, as I see it now, it has been my friend and protector ever since. My memory, however, turns out to be incomplete. H tells me that I hated the FAS early on and that I cried about it several times, because the accent was completely surreal. She says that none of the family spoke about it for two years because it made me extremely upset. I can remember P asking me whether I wanted him to tell me when there was a word which was normal; I told him that I did not. I think that it was probably emotionally good for him to hear me as I was, but it seemed to me that everyone wanted the old me back again. I knew I was different – inevitable if you have had a bolt through the brain (this is an expression I have used for many years but, bizarrely, it is only while I have been writing this account that I have realised that it is a product of learning about Phineas Gage – look at Google.)

For several years after my stroke I had terrible nightmares almost every night, usually because I could not speak or understand things. Very often I was alone, though probably in a crowd of strangers, but I do remember having spoken in some of my dreams, and I knew, even in the dream, that I was using my foreign accent.

I wonder if FAS and what I felt about noise were associated; I do not remember sound being overwhelming before the accent first appeared. Once FAS was there, I felt that sound assaulted me all of the time, crashing in from all sides, so I made myself a little study, a haven of peace. I was very afraid of having people on both sides of me, or behind me, because they would inevitably make noises and that made me jump. At the same time, I also found that sounds were extremely interesting – if I could control my exposure to them. I found my own foreign accent intensely much more fascinating than normal speech, and I am clearly far more affected by the sound of the voices of other people around me than I was before the stroke, especially if they speak a language from Eastern Europe.

I have a much stronger memory of the after-effects of aphasia. Even now sometimes I cannot hear quickly enough, and this has been a nightmare; P has endlessly listened to answer-machine messages which include telephone numbers because I just cannot hear all the digits. Finding words can be difficult; probably this is not obvious to others but it costs me effort because I have to think mid-sentence about analysing the syllables I want to say. Sometimes words try to get out of my head and they explode against the inside of the bridge of my nose. I am totally dependent on a wonderful crossword dictionary which I use as a thesaurus when I am writing, especially in the evenings. It is the best present that my mother has ever given me.

I have been so lucky to have my family. H, E and P have understood deep down over the years what it is like for me to have FAS. They, and also my mother and father, parents-in-law and my brother's and my sister's families, have had to cope with the fact that my accent was completely different from theirs and how to explain the situation. I do not ever remember Dad referring to my accent; it is just how I am for him. E's boyfriend told me recently that he had been totally puzzled by my accent when he first met me, because he knew that my parents were native speakers of English, and my surname, which was French (several hundred years ago) belongs to P's family not mine. For a long time after the stroke, talking made me anxious, partly because I could not make the words come out, and partly because the accent. P, H and E often supported me when words would not organise themselves in my head. If they were not there, the sole helping hand was the accent, but the FAS itself was sometimes the problem. Even now, E and H tend to deal with complicated verbal transactions if we are out doing things together – I just stand there with the credit card.

In a simplistic way, you could say that H and E have helped me in rather different ways. E has made me laugh, a holiday from the depression which relentlessly targeted itself on me during the months after the stroke, approaching me like a slow-moving Exocet missile. She organised expeditions – I remember going to sleep on the grass in Kew midway through a lovely walk, with her just sitting by me. H, who read Philosophy and Italian literature, helped me to discover who I am now, post-stroke, and also understanding the experience of FAS, just nudging gently at the edge of my comfort zone, making me braver.

E, H and P have taught me how to write first sentences and then paragraphs and essays, patient and encouraging. It is impossible to explain just how much their help meant and means to me. Phrases and words were repeated (which is still sometimes a problem) and for a while, there was a multiplication of syllables in the middle of words, the same one two or three times, and I just couldn't see them. The FAS has been such an invaluable tool for spelling. When I was proof-reading I could work out so much more easily when one sound finished and another started, because when I articulated the letters in sequence I could hear the end of each one.

There was another very important person. I had originally met K, my psychologist, nine months after the stroke. She worked with stroke patients and was curious about FAS. I had masses of IQ and memory tests after our first meeting, but by the time that I came back for the results three weeks later I had finally tipped over an emotional edge. That was the start of a two year relationship. Before I knew that my accent was Balkan (rather than Russian) K, who is herself quarter Russian, told me that it was not like anyone that she had heard before. I could accept that from her because she knew how to tell me without upsetting me. It was because of her help that I came to believe that I could go back to university to do a further degree. She wrote a brief summary about me, explaining first of all the FAS, and stating that I had made an "extraordinary recovery in cognitive terms" although with "clear evidence of residual aphasia." That summary was a small symbol of being worthwhile when I needed it.

FAS has been so much more difficult with some of my friends, although I am sure that they did not mean to upset me. They just could not leave accent alone. It was terrible when I had made a huge effort to articulate a long sentence during the time when it was still so hard to speak, and they just exclaimed at the end that I had said a word in English (which tended to be something rather automatic like 'hello' at the very beginning) and that the FAS had gone away. I knew that it hadn't because I checked afterwards with my family. That single English-sounding word was, apparently, the only thing which had been interesting and the friends did not seem to be able to listen properly any more. If they were listening, they said that I was doing it because we were talking about it, a supposition that I had a degree of autonomy over my language – but I just didn't. I can see now that they may have thought that I would be delighted to find myself going back to whom I had previously been, but that was a huge assumption. To me, their reaction felt like a kind of triumphalism; they were trying to prove to me that I was wrong about my FAS. I was, and even now am, very protective about the accent because it had meant that I could speak, and it still is an important part of me, even if it is no longer there with people I know.

There is a moment of choice when I meet new people. Sometimes I have to clarify who and what I am, because I may see them on other occasions. Other times I do not, especially if I am never likely to meet them again, because it means saying that I have been ill. If they persist in asking about my geographic origins, I say that I am a bit of a mixture and have relations in England, the French-speaking part of Switzerland, Scotland, Ireland and California (all of which is true.) Usually this is sufficient, though some still ask where I was brought up, and whether I have a British passport, which can lead to bureaucratic problems (in the end K gave me a letter stating that both I and my parents are British and that we had all been born in the UK.)

A positive factor in my FAS is that people have always found the accent attractive, both when it was Balkan and in its French form. Friends and some relations say that they are disappointed that my FAS has gone away. They do not understand that it still happens, that I value it, and I find it upsetting that they assume that what they hear is representative of everything that I say to other people. They do not see me when I am anxious – shopping and worrying in case I cannot find the words or answer quickly enough, or when I am abroad, especially at multinational conferences when there is such a magnificent array of language. Other people will probably not have heard me reading aloud, but out comes the Balkan, especially if

I have to read faster than I easily can. They will not have heard when we read prayers in church at Christmas, even last year, about which my children still smile. In fact H called a couple of months ago and almost put the phone down because she heard a Czechoslovak person speaking not very good English – which happened because I had just been talking about FAS to someone I did not know. (H, also a singer, has received coaching for singing in Czech.)

Since the day that my FAS first appeared, I have looked for where I came from. For a long time it was as if I had no first language, and sometimes this is still how it feels; it is so exhausting speaking in another language, even if you do become very fluent. Lack of a mother tongue makes me feel unfinished, not only linguistically, but also geographically and culturally, hence the search. I love huge rivers like the Danube and want to see deltas which are far too enormous for Britain. Whilst I had read some Tolstoy before the stroke, I wanted to read Pushkin because he was the first major Russian novelist who wrote in his own native language (not that I can read the originals) and his novels are often deeply rooted in isolated Russian rural communities, in such an enormous hinterland. I love Bartok, Chopin sends shivers down my spine and Smetana's 'Má Vlast' makes me want to cry.

For a long time I thought that I was from a kingdom between Poland and Belorussia. I called it 'Byelorus' because it did not occur to me to say it any other way. It is still 'Byelorus' to me because it sounds so beautiful that way. H, E, P and I go on a four-night holiday together each year. They have been endlessly patient about going to Eastern European walled-cities (my weakness for medieval history) with not a murmur of dissent. We went to Estonia before the stroke and I knew I did not come from there. A trip to Kraków after the stroke made it clear that Poland was not right, because the speech seemed to be produced further forward in the mouth, like Italian. Then we went to Dubrovnik and there it was. I checked by going to Budapest – alluring but not right. I very much want to go to Romania; I also want to try Bulgaria and Moldova. I want to take the trans-Siberian express. I heard an interview from Samarkand and that was so entrancing. Even now, if I go to any other country my grammar collapses if I spend time with people who are not English, and I am Eastern European once again.

My accent has become a great deal more French over the years. Because of my French surname, there is this general assumption that I am French. Generally, French people know that I am not, although that is not always the case. When I went to a proms concert this year, I bought the interval drinks. Shopping in new places always makes me a little anxious in case I cannot find the words, so I had automatically reverted to my accent. The man behind the bar (dark hair, tan, slight build, not Anglo-Saxon English) said, "Do I hear a French accent?" I replied, "Oh, Swiss-French." His face lit up, "I lived in Lausanne and Geneva for several years, etc." – all in what I am pretty sure was native French. I understood his sentences pretty easily but it was completely impossible for me to formulate a reply in French. It took me years to relearn how to speak fluently in English, let alone make any attempt in French, and my last French lesson was when I was fifteen. The only other language which I have spoken is German, which was at about the same standard as my French before the stroke, and is currently totally unusable. (I can sing with a rather dodgy French accent and in passable German, but that is with the lyrics in front of me, and, as I shall explain, FAS is not evident in my singing.) I smiled at the man in the bar but kept on speaking English, as if it were slightly impolite to use another language in a public place. Except for times like this, I have found it intensely relaxing to be a person who just seems to be French. People are always kind and patient, they do not speak too quickly and no-one questions why the odd word is particularly well pronounced in English.

Reintegration

At the time of my stroke I was working at a specialist school for children with dyslexia. I was welcomed back by the head teacher, after the end of the Easter holidays (having had the stroke just two days before the end of the Spring Term). My particular friends at the school at that time, especially J and F, took away as much pressure as was possible. As an example, I can remember crying because there was a parents evening coming up that term and I did not know how to say the things which were necessary, or how to explain about the accent, and J stood in for me. I taught just two pupils, each for half an hour every day. Interestingly, they never mentioned the accent and, I think three or four years later, it was with the children whom I taught that my spoken accent first reverted to 'normal'. Soon after, it started to become English with my family, although H tells me that it is not quite like it was before the stroke.

Interestingly, I have never had an inappropriate accent when I am singing – very fortunate as for a while I would have been limited to Eastern European repertoire (disappointing if you do not speak or understand any of the languages). Despite this absence of accent, FAS has had a revolutionary effect on my sung diction because I have become much more aware of the ends of syllables which have become hugely fascinating. The: "I can't hear the words" comment, the bane of those learning to sing, disappeared almost overnight. The only problem has been in French when I tend to roll 'r's at the end of words, which is ironic considering how my accent has evolved. I wonder if people with FAS would be helped by having singing lessons. For singers, there is a prolonged period of developing awareness of how projection and diction are intimately associated with every part of the body, especially the mouth and throat. Gradually you become able to express on the outside what you feel inside and, if things are going well, you are in charge of your voice. It's also good fun.

I am back at university (many years after my first degree.) When I applied for a place to do a certificate and then graduate diploma in psychology, I used K's summary of me so they knew what I could and could not do, and about the FAS. Now am doing a PhD, still at the same university, and E is just starting hers in London, also in psychology. I cannot overstate the importance of the understanding and encouragement of my supervisors and lecturers and nobody has baulked when

I could not find words or fell back into French or Balkan. An interesting feature of the PhD is that I shall need to do presentations at conferences; I predict that the FAS will be back in force once I have listened to speakers from other countries; I don't mind about the accent, but I must retrain myself to use English grammar alongside the FAS-speech. Since the stroke I have also completed a part-time MEd at another university. My favourite tutor there and dissertation supervisor has stood steadfastly by me through all my gradual recovery of my capacity to write, and read aloud – albeit haltingly and in Balkan. During last year, H and E were respectively doing an MA and an MSc while I was completing my MEd, and I felt real again.

Conclusion

Re-reading this account, several strands about FAS stand out. The first is the loneliness of not being able to talk until the miraculous intervention of FAS. The second is the need of people I know for me to be the person whom I was previously, and my over-sensitivity to the perhaps unthinking words of those who could only tell me about the 'normal' words I had said. I can no longer be that person. Thirdly is how FAS protects me when it is hard to talk, and how easy it is if the outside world just assumes you are French. Fourthly is my unending (I suspect) search for the place I have come from. Most important, however, are those around me who haven't needed to tell me constantly about how I sound, but have instead helped me to learn to read aloud, spell and write, and protected me when handling words has defeated me and I need to sleep. I know that I have not thanked them enough in this account, but there is not space here – sorry. They believed in my future and helped me to believe in it as well.

I do not mind having FAS because I see it as my friend. Now I am very happy telling people about it, though it still upsets me if they treat it as solely part of my past. I do not feel singled out by fate to have FAS, though just sometimes I did feel that way about the stroke. I am so relieved that I did not have any speech therapy to 'cure' my FAS. Strangely, I am pretty certain that I am only doing a PhD because of having had a stroke; the stroke made me a different person. I am different because the stroke broke part of my brain and also because of the extra dimensions introduced into my life as a result of FAS; new threads have appeared in my tapestry of life. Ultimately, the possibility of going to university was entirely dependent on FAS since it helped me to learn to speak again. Without FAS, I am pretty sure that I would be jobless, as predicted at hospital and, from my perspective, useless.

Claire Coleman describes a situation familiar to many who face the stresses of caring for a slowly dying family member and the subsequent loss – the onset of distressing symptoms, first her speech, then gradually all kinds of other aspects of daily living. The search for support and explanation outside of the family is arduous. The speech changes from being a reaction to stress to becoming the source of stress. Slowly one is faced with 'How will I cope with this intruder into my life?'

'Relax, but how do I relax when I am so worried about my speech?'

CLAIRE COLEMAN

Claire is confused

14/07/2012

Imagine you have been asked to tell someone your name – and when you reply it's not your voice. Imagine trying to ask your children if they have had a good day but when you say their name it sounds like someone else has said it.

As I type this I have no idea what is wrong with me or why it has happened, all I know for sure is that I have not spoken with my own voice for over 6 weeks now. It's been extremely frustrating, upsetting and confusing and while I am trying to come to terms with this person speaking for me I search for answers as to what is going on and why has it happened.

History

Two months ago my dear Mum passed away. It was awful to watch her deteriate before my eyes, but having been diagnosed with Motor Neurone disease in November 2010 I knew this day would come. I had been Mum's main carer through-out this time and devoted myself in creating precious fun memories for us to treasure for years to come. I won't shy away from the fact that it was exhausting but how could I grumble – I didn't know how much time we had. I continued to work full time and care for Mum until March 2012 when I had to admit enough was enough and I couldn't manage to do it all. Mum and her time was my priority so I adjusted to part time hours at work and popped into Mum twice a day to do what I needed to do.

The day before Mum celebrated her 71st birthday in 2012 I was aware she wasn't right, hoping it was just a bad day again. We soon realised on her actual birthday that she may be needed to get checked over and it was suggested she go into the hospice. Mum spent the next -5 days clinging on to her life, until she finally slipped away.

During her stay I hardly slept – I couldn't take my eyes off her and wanted to support her till the very end. And I recall mentioning to my Husband that I felt quite strange with my breathing – a little faint and that I wasn't breathing in my normal pattern. I was shattered and thought some rest after a traumatic few days I would feel ok.

The days following Mum's death I noticed I was developing a strange way to talk. As I started my sentences it was like I was catching my breath – my sister was concerned and took me to see her GP. He said he wasn't concerned but that I needed to rest and try to do things I enjoyed doing. He arranged to see me the following week. The following week I couldn't speak – when I tried to say the words I was twitching and stuttering and it was much easier to write things down. Again he said he wasn't concerned and that it was probably going to return to normal after the funeral. Which was a 3 week wait!!!!

The struggle to speak lasted 2 weeks and slowly it began to return and everyone was fully aware that it sounded French – alarming -YES!! I would miss out key words that linked sentences together. And sometimes miss letters off the ends of my words, and even some words would be said in the wrong order. This felt very worrying and frightening, I got odd looks whenever I spoke and was much easier to stay quiet or go out with my close family who would talk for me.

I found that it took away the fact that I was trying to grieve for losing my wonderful Mum; instead I was being gawped at for talking with a different voice.

A few days before the funeral I was able to have a full blown conversation – and the comments I got were asking if I was South African or from Australia. I tried my best to ignore how it made me feel and concentrated on the fact that I was actually able to speak, and that my sentences were fluent. I admit I shared a few giggles with close friends and family and we remarked on how strange it all was but tried our upmost to ignore it and to carry on as normal.

The morning of the funeral I was struggling slightly but was able to get most words out with the French sounding voice. By the end of the day I was back to Aussie. And stayed that way for a whole week. However during that week a few comments and laughs sent me right back to not being able to get the words out again. And I started to stay indoors a lot in the comfort and safety of my own home. Away from people judging me and the only way I was able to talk. Again once I was relaxed the Australian accent returned.

Returning to the doctors he looked bemused, prescribed antidepressant and suggested a referral to a neurologist. At this time I had not heard my voice in just over a month, and I think he even was admitting that it wasn't quite right but kept telling me that he wasn't at all worried about me and that I should remain relaxed and perhaps have a holiday away somewhere nice if I was able to.

Holiday booked for a few weeks time I tried to settle into this voice, and did a bit of my own research and found information on FAS. It was making a lot of sense but I was not convinced, however I made contact with a group I found to see if they could help me with my concerns. It was such a relief to read other people's stories and to realise that I was not alone – to explain to someone else how you feel is impossible yet there was a small group of people who knew exactly how I felt without me having to say a single word in whatever accent my voice was using. To know I was not alone was a great comfort to me.

Reading other people's symptoms and stories I quickly realised how rare all of this is and that it would be a good idea to keep a note of what happens on a daily basis – so I have been keeping a diary – through doing this I have had to admit to having a fuzzy head almost constantly and on occasions when it is really bad I have blurred vision and it often leads to me being sick. As it stands I have been this way for the last 7 days. I think they are migraines – having never had these before I had to research to see exactly what they were like and yes it seems I have them too.

I have contacted a speech and language therapist who used to work with Mum and she spoke with me via the phone and admitted it doesn't sound at all like me and definitely an Australian voice. We are hoping to meet up soon to discuss things further. And I await an appointment with a neurologist and I shall update as and when I know more.

How does it feel

How does this make me feel?

Awful . . . . . . like someone has kidnapped my voice, my eldest daughter is struggling as she wants to hear her Mum speak. As a family we are trying to come to terms with the death of a dearly loved important member of the family yet we are faced with this speech thing that confuses us and alters everyday life.

If I do a lot of talking it leaves me almost exhausted and I am aware that I need to rest quite a lot now. I have not been able to return to work. And get quite anxious to go out on my own – the times that I have I avoided eye contact with people so as not to have to talk.

At times I struggle to say double figures and prefer to say them singly. I will say one five instead of fifteen. And very often I will say "be to the go" randomly in a sentence for no reason what so ever. My brain just wants me to say it.

Sometimes words come out of my mouth that are not in my usual vocabulary – feels so strange for them to come out. I was explaining to friends that the teachers at my daughter's Prom had been drinking. I would normally have said that they were drunk but I said they were "smashed". This is not a word I would have used in this context.

When I am tired the speech gets worse and I forget to say the words I would normally say to make a sentence. If I am typing sometimes I put letters around the wrong way and I find when someone reads it back that I have typed how I speak with words in the wrong place. But to me as I am doing this it all makes complete sense to me – I would be saying in my head the sentence but reading it back it's not what it should be.

I seem to have migraines every day which always result in me being sick and having fuzzy vision.

Right now I am advised to relax, stay calm and not worry – how can I do this when I have clearly got something wrong with me?

The worry of what has happened to me probably doesn't help my speech at all so I am in a vicious circle. They say because I am stressed this has happened, to make it better I have to not worry, yet my speech makes me worry.

I am keeping everything crossed that my upcoming holiday will find my voice. But for me I am still very keen to find out what has happened to me and why . . . .

To add to my experience of what seems to be FAS it would only be right to explain what happened to my sister.

2 years ago my sister was under immense pressure at work, as a family we were all very worried about what was wrong with our Mum as we had not had a diagnosis, but her speech was very slurred and her swallow was awful, watching our Mum choke happened on a daily basis.

I remember getting a call to explain my sister was admitted to hospital as she couldn't speak – confused and extremely worried I rushed to see her. Where I found her with a stutter and she was unable to get her words out – we played charades and a guessing game to determine what she was saying, and wrote things down. During her 3 day stay in hospital she saw a neurologist and had a CT scan and an MRI, these as far as I am aware ruled out a stroke.

On doctor's orders she was to relax and have a holiday, and as she worked in a school having the summer holiday and a place in France it was simple for her to do just this. On her return at the end of the summer she spoke with a French accent – we joked that she had spent too much time in France and had picked up the accent. Knowing nothing else we carried on as normal and her normal speech returned. From start to finish with my sister's problem it was 2 to 3 months.

What I notice is that when she gets tired the stutter wants to return, this is hardly at all I need to add, but she recognizes this so rests immediately and it returns to normal. I believe she had anti depressants and is still taking them which obviously help her to stay calm. For me I feel yes this stops the speech issues but I want to know what is it that is happening or has happened. Mum had a neurological illness, and is this related?

The Doctor that I have so far been seeing is the one who saw my sister, and he is very relaxed about it all – he is happy that it will return. But for me I want some answers. Some friends are telling me that although we are similar stories, I am quite different to her as my sister's speech returned it was her voice, mine is mostly Australian. FAS was never mentioned.

I am at the beginning of my journey, and am happy to share the outcomes for anyone who is interested. It's certainly the weirdest thing myself, my family and my friends have ever experienced. And although distressing and frustrating I am intrigued to learn more about it.

A stroke; dysarthria; resolving into FAS; and eventually all but clearing. Not the life-path **Wendy**, a special needs teacher, had chosen, but one that provided great lessons. People cope with major illness in myriad ways. Here we view a reappraisal of life's priorities that led to positive outcomes.

'1999 . . . I used to become distraught, when the wiring on the hoover became quite loose . . . '

WENDY HASNIP

1999 . . . My Yorkshire lilt replaced with a French accent . . . life could have been SO much worse!

In 1999, I was teaching children with severe special needs full-time in London, commuting daily from Kent. A job, which I simply loved with all my heart, and earlier that year, had been awarded the first Teaching Award for Special Needs for the South East Region. (Though it was only because it was such an EXCELLENT school I taught in, as the team I worked with were ALL highly skilled!). I was divorced, and had to work full-time, commute daily to London from Otford in Kent, and somehow bring up 5 of my 6 sons (the eldest had left home at this point to live with his girlfriend, now his wife); all were still in full-time education so daily life was a fine balancing act!

But the boys were coping, despite great difficulties financially, they just got on with life. It was a bit like living with a rugby team, and I was very outnumbered when it came to differences of opinion! I had no option but to downsize, given financial difficulties since the divorce, so the 6 of us squashed in somehow, to a 1960s semi with 3 bedrooms (one so small that we had to cut the end of the bunk bed off to fit it in the room). Jack claimed this room, but as he was tall, slept with his feet up on the wall until he left home! The people who I bought it from had 2 children, and were selling, because the house was too small! Fortunately, they never asked me how many children I had! We also had a lovely but HUGE collie cross dog Bertie, and my mother lived in the same road.

Life was jogging along; somehow we all got by, the boys gained a respectful amount of school leaving grades too. I remember working on resources for the children at school, planning lessons, writing policies etc till the early hours of most mornings, but in September, 1999, the hours it took seemed to get longer and longer. I felt tired that term, October half-term came and went, and I returned to school feeling exceptionally tired despite the break. One day, I was working on the computer at lunch time trying to make cards from photos of our morning's activities to use that afternoon. I had the mother of all headaches, but carried on, went back to class for the afternoon session. As I announced the symbol timetable we used, I was stopped in my tracks, by my observant classroom assistant M., who told me to be quiet and sit still. My speech had become very slow and slurred. I was taken to the local hospital, but refused to stay in (wanted to get back to my sons). By this time all speech had disappeared and I was very slowly doing Makaton signing, which Ma, our school nurse who was with me interpreted for me. I just kept signing 'home'. I had had a stroke, little did I realise that that day would be the last time ever I taught a class of the children whom I so loved teaching. My world, as I knew it, had gone completely upside down!

I had a couple of hospital stays, a couple more minor Transient Ischaemic Attacks (T.I.As), but, somehow we all lived through it and learnt to appreciate how lucky I was simply to be here to tell the tale. I suffered with terrible fatigue, my walking became affected, I lurched as if I was drunk, never knowing where my feet would land. The boys, became young men overnight, and it is with great pride that I can say they too lived and survived this rollercoaster ride that life had thrown at all of us. It is due to the AMAZING special needs children I taught, that I escaped falling into a depressive state. Those little ones and their equally amazing families had to cope with so very much more and did just that. So if they could, I could!

Then a little while later, my speech became far quicker, and the accent sounded as if I was a native French person speaking English. I even used expressions I had never used, like calling things 'bizarre'. It was very strange, yet I knew and thankfully my very supportive family and friends knew too, that despite, the difficult gait, the French accent etc I was still the SAME person underneath. I knew, psychologically, I was still ME! Also, that in this same area I must be ok, otherwise my very kind family and friends would have insisted on me getting psychological help. I took mum to a hospital appointment, and the mother of one of the children that I had taught was there who looked suitably horrified when she heard me talk! So I went to the Hospital Friends and Advice Shop and told them my tale and, one very knowledgeable volunteer said she had heard of this happening to someone else after a stroke and looked it all up on their computer and found a Professor who had researched this syndrome. So I phoned the professor and then was researched by her and other colleagues, and beyond all doubt it was proved by recording my speech patterns etc on different occasions that I had actually got Foreign Accent Syndrome.

Yippee, a label at long last, which gave me a huge sense of relief! At the time I was told there were only 13 cases in the world recorded, so maybe I should be more forgiving of some members of the medical profession, who patently knew nothing about it and, therefore the empathy on a few occasions was sadly zilch. One neurologist, in a top London Teaching hospital, in front of no less than 12 of his students, when he asked what was wrong with me and I told him I had FAS. He became angry and threw my hospital file across the desk at me and shouted 'I have never heard of it, read about it, or seen it'. So, in my French accent I told him to contact X University and the hospital there, as they were researching my case of FAS. I left this terrible consultation, in floods of tears. My friend who sat with me, and saw it all was horrified. That day was my worst day ever with FAS. It was only when I next saw the consultant at the university hospital that I was reassured re my diagnosis.

In day to day life it had its moments, a French child came up to me and spoke in French, expecting me to respond, as did her mother. I had been dropped from French before my school leaving exams as I was simply HOPELESS at languages! I began to pick my life up, resigned to the sad fact that I had to take early retirement on health grounds from a job which I loved. I did things around my levels of fatigue, I became used to my lurching walk, but oh did I miss teaching! My school was brilliant and let me go in voluntary for a day a week, just tidying up the art cupboard, doing the odd display etc. They were my lifeline to adapting to how I had become. My displays were a little down on one side at times, as spatially I found it difficult to produce a straight line since the strokes. I loved being with the children in the playground and laughing with them too. One little girl, who was profoundly handi-capped including being blind, was in her standing frame I went over to her, stroked her hand and sang a class song I had sung to her on many occasions, she became totally still and very, very unsure as of course, she couldn't see me and my voice was now that of a stranger to her. This brought a huge lump to my throat and I have to confess to sobbing for the greater part of the train journey home. I didn't care what other people thought of me, my family and friends were always supportive ... but to be unable to be recognized by this dear little child, seemed so sad. A couple of years later lovely J sadly died, but at least I can remember the happy times we shared together before my strokes.

I applied to The Open University to do a BSc Hons in Psychology. They were brilliant they would provide a voice synthesizer etc. But, in the end, I had to be realistic about my levels of fatigue, and as the saying goes, realised this may well have been a 'bridge too far', so decided against doing this. I did a voluntary morn-ing a week in a Neuro Rehabilitation Unit, doing art activities with patients and realised how far I had come to reach this level, even if full-time paid work was a distant memory. It also made me realise how many people are far more badly afflicted than me. At this time also, my 2 very dear friends both lost sons, one 14 and one 26. To me these were both incredible tragedies, I had 6 sons healthy and happy, so ok I spoke as if I was from France ... well ... that is hardly a problem in life's scheme of things is it? About 18 months/2 years afterwards my different accent slowly faded; but when tired my speech would slow down and taxi drivers would ask me if I was from Ireland or Birmingham etc.

So here I am in 2012, 6 sons, 5 partners and wives and 10 gorgeous grandchildren from a few months to 17. How much more blessed can I be? My ambition when I retired was to work voluntarily with disabled street children in India, sadly that could never be, BUT (having been advised never to fly because of strokes etc but always being of a determined nature!) November 2011 saw me in India and Nepal realising an ambition of a lifetime to at least visit India and Nepal.

Life's SIMPLY too short and too precious, not to grab and fill as best we can. Mind you, I took the wise precaution of leaving my will in the kitchen and telling my sons, if anything did happen to me they were under no circumstances to bring me home. If a burning ghat on the Ganges was good enough for Gandhi, it was certainly more than good enough for me . . . and so much more exciting than ending up at the local crematorium! Fortunately, the will is back in the cupboard as I returned home safely . . . BUT I so would like to go camping on the edges of the Gobi Desert in Mongolia next! Must get the will out again then! The motto of my story being there is always life to be lived either, with or without FAS . . . and I am definitely going to!

31.03.2012

'Dysfunctional wiring'

I used to become distraught, when the wiring on the Hoover became
    quite loose,
It took so long to clean the carpet,
Stop, go, stop, go, stop, go,
Patience is a virtue, so they tell me!

I used to be distraught, when the wiring in the washing machine became
    quite loose,
It took so long to wash the clothes,
Stop, go, stop, go, stop, go.
Patience is a virtue, so they tell me!

I am now distraught, because the wires in my brain have become loose
    also.
It takes so very long to talk now,
My voice goes up and down in all the wrong places,
Stop, go, stop, go, stop, go.
Patience is a virtue, so they tell me!

They tell me I may have a higher brain dysfunction, and I will be tested
    for lots of different things.
C.J.D. (known as 'mad cow' disease) may be in this category,
But as my son said, "There's no need for them to test you for that
    Mum, as we all know you have been a mad cow for years!"
My mother has an extremely infected leg ulcer and is finding it hard to
    walk.
I said we should tie ourselves together, and we could conquer the
    world as long as she was the one to talk and I was the one to walk!
Stop, go, stop, go, stop, go.
Patience is a virtue, so they tell me!
And, I really know now, that that is just so!

December 1999

A 'stroke of luck'

Headache, but brain fully working.
Voice disappearing.
Three words, two words, one word and gone!
Right leg trailing.
Colleagues, friends and family taking over.
Doctors discussing me,
Don't they know I am here?

Look at me, look into my eyes and far beyond.
Return to me my dignity.
Respect me.
I am still here, still thinking, still fully aware.
Don't you realise, of course, I know I've had a stroke?
My body is letting me down, but, don't let it persuade you that my brain
    is malfunctioning also.

Stay in hospital? No!
Please take me home to where I belong.
The boys worried. My friend sobbing.
Mum, your eyes say it all, but, look at your daughter's eyes,
I'm still here!
The daughter,
The mother,
The teacher and the friend.
I love you all as you love me, please, please don't be sad.
I write jokes to try and ease your pain away.
I concentrate so hard that my head hurts, but,
I carry on, I won't let this beat me.
I have no choice, but, simply to recover completely to be,
The daughter,
The mother,
The teacher and the friend to love you all too.

One word, two words, three words, four words, five words.

Brain and body reuniting in scrambled egg fashion.
My head aches, but, it's not going to beat me.
Six words, seven words, eight words, nine words, ten words.
Liquid egg becoming jelly-like and solidifying.
Eight hours later, and I return, brain and body in harmony.

Fifteen days in hospital.
The boys alone at home.
My dear friend's young son's tragic death.
Now the perspective is suddenly clear.

Must get home, put C.T. and M.R.I. scans,
Heparin intravenous drips, all behind me now.
Family, friends, flowers and cards continually arriving.

Under the crisp, white sheets, I sob alone.
Sobs of happiness to have been so very lucky to experience, return, and
    yet, to be so relatively undamaged.
Under the crisp, white sheets, I sob alone.
Sobs of despair and terrible sadness, as I share the pain of my dear
    friend's sad loss.
I send flowers and letters, but I so desperately want to hug her tightly,
    and, take her pain away.
I become used to daily episodes of no movement and no speech.
But, I lay and think how lucky I am, as nothing can match my friend's
    suffering at this time.

Then suddenly discharged.
Suitably heparin, warfarin and aspirin loaded.
Goodbye, but not farewell, to a dear companion who encouraged me to
    regain my confidence, and shared laughter.
As I danced, in an ungainly fashion, with my intravenous drip for nine
    days.
No surgery, no stitches, no pain, just simply home again to be,
The daughter,
The mother,
The teacher and the friend.

As a daughter, I must learn to do as the doctors direct, to lessen my
    mother's worry.
As a mother, I must be so proud of my young boys, now simply
    transformed into young men, who can manage my cash card
    without becoming overdrawn!
Who can cook, clean, feed the rabbit and the cats and still find the time
    to visit me as well.
As a teacher, I must learn to be patient so I can recover slowly and
    fully, to teach my very special children once again.
As a friend, to realise the depths of my friendships and to return the
    love so freely given.
To share and try to ease my dear friend's pain, in the tragic loss of her
    dear son.
A stroke, yes, it was and yet hear how very much I have learnt as a
    result!
Certainly, I am truly blessed and now I know the true meaning of a
    'stroke of luck!'

November, 1999

Marbles

Thinking processes functioning,
And yet ~
Legs flailing, stopping, starting and randomly striking,
And yet ~
Arms and body counteracting the continual misplacement of my legs,
And yet ~
Head and neck frantically following,
In order to seek out a safe landing place for the body that they find
    themselves, so unfortunately attached to.

What have I become?
Suddenly, uncoordinated and extremely concerned,
Perpetually awaiting intervention from the medical profession.
Appointments not processed, and waiting lists that move eternally like
    an ever moving tide flowing relentlessly outwards away from the
    shore.
The shore on which myself, my sons, my mother and friends
Wait patiently,
Wait silently,
Wait simultaneously,
For the tide to flow inwards, and for long awaited help to be given.
Meanwhile, concerns deepen, my physical condition falters,
And yet ~
Like a pebble in a pond I am thrown,
Whilst ripples of fear of the unknown are recurring.
How I wish I could prevent the ripples from touching those whom I
    love so much.
Phoning friends to prepare them, that I no longer am physically present
    as I once was.
And yet ~
Still their eyes betray them when we meet.
And yet ~
I tell them not to worry as,
I clean my teeth so carefully each night.
I swallow 12 grams, of Warfarin each night.
I equally carefully, take an artist's fine sable brush, and with a satin finish
    polyurethane, paint the precious, oh so precious marbles, inside my
    head each night.
(To secure them hopefully to morning and beyond!)
I lay my head down as I go to bed, and smile,
At the two moons I now see each evening, thanks to my recently
    acquired double vision.

Life seems so unpredictable and strange for all of us now.
And yet ~
The sun shines as brightly,
The daffodils raise their heads in partnership of a new day,
The boys all joke, laugh and enjoy life,
Bertie the puppy nuzzles the rabbit coaxing him to play,
Then proceeds to demolish yet another plastic flower pot,
The cats take up their positions on the boys' beds, basking in the sun
    streaming through the windows,
Mum folds yet another heaving pile of shirts and trousers,
Defying arthritis,
as I, her daughter defy,
The new challenges that almost daily present themselves,
And yet ~
We remain a truly lucky family blessed with each other, and the support
    of so many wonderful friends.

and yet ~
Life could be so much worse!
Sainsbury's, Homebase could run out of polyurethane,
Then, where would the marbles be?!

29 March 2000

Update: As the book goes to press Wendy reports that she has experienced a
further minor stroke that has affected her walking and well-being. The main
change, though, concerns a full return of her foreign sounding accent, and feeling she has to start all over again explaining to people what has happened and
that she is still the same person as previously.

Kath's experience is common to so many people who develop an unwanted
new accent – the sense of loss, bereavement, searching. Her painting depicts
a lifetime of development of one's identity, experiences enriching in their colour
and progression. The arrow of speech disorder and FAS intervenes, severing
all that, thrusting one into a monochrome world, lost for words, the tantalising
coloured door back to a life beyond FAS. But how to unlock it?

'Robbed of a precious gift, my identity'

KATH LOCKETT

Lost in translation

Illness always changes you. I have had health issues for a few years now. My health problems have been different to say the least, very challenging at times. But nothing could of prepared me for what was about to crumble.

Talking to my sister-in-law on the telephone late Sunday evening, I noticed a lisp sound in my speech, as if you had been to the dentist. My head was hurting more than usual. I thought I had over strained myself, I do get fatigued a lot. I had early night's sleep. The next morning nothing changed, the lisp, the numbness on one side of my mouth. I thought "shout up and rest". The following morning my speech sounded odd. My family were getting very concerned. I telephoned the neurology department I was under and left a silly message. Heaven knows what it sounded like. Nobody got back to me, don't panic I thought, "It will pass".

Three days passed and the problem was now getting worse. I could not talk properly, my swallow was becoming difficult. By the fourth day I had lost all normal speech and I sounded like a alien. My husband telephoned my neurologist. He got an answer machine too, he hates telephones, so I grabbed the phone in frustration and spoke alien down the phone. Within moments the secretary rang back. She had put the two messages together, the better one from earlier and the recent rubbish alien message.

I had to go to hospital straight away. It took time to get to the hospital. I had to be admitted but it was late, I had brought no clothes. I was allowed to return home and return the next morning prompt.

The word tumour was mentioned, alongside my own health issues. It was a weekend and I had to have various tests done. My swallow was difficult. I had horrible mixture to take for that. I was told to say my alphabet, name, address out aloud, read anything from a book, even if it sounded alien to me. It was embarrassing. I was in hospital for thirteen days and in that space of time I lost half a stone of weight. I was using pen and paper to communicate with doctors, nurses and other patients. It was difficult, I felt so sad, scared and alone.

My head still hurts, but it was not a tumour. I thank God for that. It was put down to my own health issues, Cerebral Vasculitis. I was referred to a speech therapist. I was allowed home, my head pain was still terrible and I still felt sick, but my own bed was comforting. I felt ripped into two halves "where had I gone". I was falling apart, I looked in the mirror, I tried to speak, and the person looking back at me was an alien. I slept and rested for over a week. I was so exhausted.

When I started to try to speak it was like a bad stammer, slow and hard. Every word I could hear in my head sounded correct but I could not get it out correctly. I kept doing my exercises, my A to Z's, numbers, it was so frustrating. I cried a lot of the time. Then I did start to get some words. They did sound different but I just put it down to my problem of expressing myself. I had not been out for along time, so my daughter decided to take me to our local art gallery in town. I was talking to my daughter about a piece of art and one of the staff asked me to fill in a questionnaire. I instinctively turned around and said "no thank you" She looked puzzled, and then responded with "what part of Poland are you from?" I looked at her in surprise. She said "we have leaflets for all nationalities". Both my daughter and I looked at her and said "No thank you". My daughter said "my mum is English". I felt sick and scared again. I felt I had done something wrong, in my head I was saying I am learning to speak again. Why can they not see that?

Then on the bus on the way home I spoke quietly to my daughter about the gallery. Then a man two seats back asked me "What part of Russia are you from?" Again my daughter said "My mum is English" I started to have confidence issues, thinking I was doing something wrong, I am an English lady. When I went out I could see people looking at me when I spoke. One man asked me if I had a sister, I did but she died 29 years ago, have you got a twin. I could not understand why I sounded different to everyone else. In my head I sounded like me. I felt like I had died alive, I feel so lonely, isolated, scared. I feel like I have bereaved a good friend. I was having a identity crisis. Then one day my daughter noticed an article in a newspaper, a lady in Newcastle-on-Tyne with this problem. "Look mum, this lady is you", "What do you mean me?" I replied.

I felt a whole rush of emotion, I cried. The lady had a condition called Foreign Accent Syndrome, finally it had a name. I did not understand all the details. In the article there was a study at Newcastle-on-Tyne University. I had to try and contact them. With a little bit of phoning around and leaving messages, I hoped someone would get back to me. I didn't want them thinking I was a crazy person.

Finally I got the telephone call, I spoke to a Professor X, and he is my saviour in my eyes. He understood what I was going through. We spoke about what had happen to me and felt so overwhelmed in emotion. I had lost my native speech in only four days at 47 years old. Now I sound foreign to other people. But now I was being told it is a speech impediment, which made more sense. The University were going to send a team down to record my speech for a study and research. This became a lifeline to me, listening to them, explaining there were other sufferers like me, with not many in the world, it is a rare condition. I had better understanding of FAS, it helped me but I had a long road to go.

I was going to the speech therapy doing exercises for the five year old children. But now I told the therapist about FAS, she contacted the University, providing extra knowledge helping both me and the therapist to understand a better plan to help me. FAS is a very rare condition and not many speech therapists ever come in contact with sufferer. My husband and grown up children were great support, it was very difficult for them. I could not say my name and their names correctly. This broke my heart.

My husband thought there was a foreign person in the house, he never showed it to me, but he missed the old me, the woman he married. I helped choose my children's names, saying them was impossible. In my head I could hear it correct but when I would say it aloud, it sounded wrong. They said it did not matter but it does. I used to be able to sing; I sang in the school choir, knew hymns, carols, sang-a-long with the radio. Now it was gone. It is now rubbish, I cannot say the Lord's Prayer, and everything was different. The sound I could hear was British, my speech had changed but I just thought it was because I was learning to speak again.

The only time it totally dawned on me completely was when my regional television station found out about me. I had to find something with my natural voice on it. I managed with difficulty, to find a very old tape; just as the interviewer came to interview me. I just cried with joy and sadness because I had found myself again not because the television was about to interview me. After the interview was finish I saw the complete interview on television. Seeing it like everybody else made me cry again, this time because I looked at myself speaking. I felt lost again, more than ever. "Where had I gone"? My Mum, Dad and brother could not understand, their love for me was the same, but I felt like I was adopted, the dynamic had changed. Your speech is made up of factors, your culture, upbringing, education, relationships, and your characteristic of a person group. I am a very patriotic person, I am very proud of this country where I was born, now I cannot be British freely in my own way. Now I get asked all the time "where are you from" or "I know you live here but where you from". I have been told now I am from all over the world. Polish, Russian, French, Italian, German, Hungarian are many to name to date. I keep telling people, "No I was born in England". It is very upsetting; I know I am English right to the centre of my core. I think you cannot be totally British now, because when you make spoken comments about issues to do with this country, it doesn't feel right anymore. For e.g. when I buy British strawberries I will say "British strawberries are the best in the world". I support British products but feel embarrassed because my speech sounds foreign to others. It is like I am doing disserve to other countries.

I have had racial comments said to me; I had a taxi driver try to charge me double fare for a journey I have taken before. Two bus drivers treated me like I was deaf, stupid and belittled me. I tried to explain to the drivers, they just carried on. I had to use my trusted 'idiot card' I had made with my speech therapist explaining my speech impediment and that I could understand everything that the public where saying to me. I did not think this country was like that, how wrong I was. I always treat people like how I would like to be treated. I know I have a speech impediment but the sound seems foreign to others. Now I can see the obstacles people of other countries face, I hear people murmuring behind my back about foreigners coming over to our country.

I was told people from other countries would know I am not from their country. On one occasion there was a Christmas German market being held in Stafford town centre. When I was speaking to a stallholder he grinned happily at me and changed is English to German. My husband said "He thinks your German", I felt my face redden.

A simple thing like saying my own name is a nightmare. One Christmas Eve I went to a midnight mass. I told the vicar my name three times but he still blessed me with the wrong name. I went back to my pew and cried. I cannot sing, say a pray correctly anymore. My speech gets mixed up so much I cannot join with these sorts of celebrations. My debit card was cloned, trying to explain I had not been aboard and that I was the person on the card. When I went into my own bank, the cashier knew who I was. My identity was not questioned. I got my passport updated because my birth certificate does not have a photograph on it. My name does not fit my accent.

I have a special card made for me; it shows my personal details explaining about FAS. When you have FAS you do a lot of explaining, sometimes I will say nothing at all, just use the card for people to read. I go to the same shops because they know me and what has happened to me. I am trying to use my condition to help other sufferers and the general public to understand the true problems with having FAS. This could be some television programmes, helping students, radio or newspaper articles. One programme I did brought me in contact with a lovely gentlemen who had FAS, listening to him was easy because he knew the problems you face with having FAS. There are no clubs you can go to. So it is a isolating condition. I do miss the old me, I feel like I bereaved a good friend. I now feel a foreigner in my own country. I lost my native accent in March 2006, which as I write is now 6 1/2 years ago. I still have not got my old accent back or the ability to sing, say prays, and read out aloud. One day when I get Grandchildren I will not be able to sing or say nursery rhymes to them, all the things I learnt as a child. I will have to find a new way, a fun way to explain tales to them. I feel like i have been robbed of a precious gift, your identity. Something we all take for granted.

'Where Have I Gone'

'Where have I gone',
I knew I met you,
My direction was clear,
Now you have gone,
This place I call England,
Now I am invisible,
You are now a shadow beside me.

'Where have I gone',
My years of learning,
Why can you not see me,
I am still here,
But you do not hear me anymore,
You ask me questions.

'Where have I gone',
My native tongue,
I am not from faraway,
Of exotic lands beyond,

A flicker of light beckons,
New steps I must follow.

'Where have I gone',
My changing shadow,
She sits side-by-side,
We will learn our new journey,
Together we will walk,
Our own path once more.

By Kath Lockett
Foreign Accent Syndrome Sufferer.

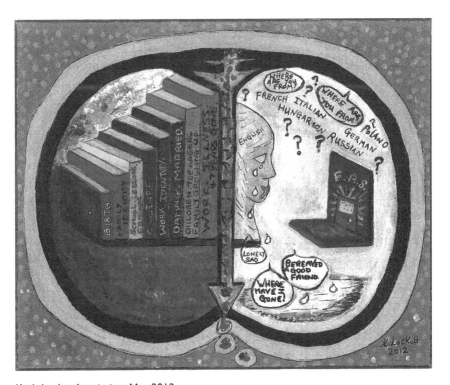

Kath Lockett's painting, May 2012

Craig Lockett, son of Kath Lockett

From the early stages of FAS developing I was unsure what was happening, just like my mum was feeling. To me nothing changed, she was still my mum. She found it very hard and upsetting not pronouncing our names correctly. It didn't bother me nor anybody else in the family. I know she still felt upset by this though.

The presence of bad speech, bad balance when walking and blurred vision was too much at the beginning. She was wearing an eye patch for the blurred vision and a walking stick for the poor balance in her walking that had developed.

I personally felt angry at members of the public and their hurtful comments. I used to make sure how I felt towards them and to ask them to think before opening their mouths. Once I knew what was happening, I was able to tell people what was wrong and provide a better answer to people!

The introduction of the blank eye contact lens provided a bit more confidence than the eye patch. That stopped the comments from people about the eye patch and the jokes, but there was still the speech.

The speech that was coming out was difficult for other people to grasp. I found it a bit hard at the beginning but got used to it quickly. But the general manner of the public was shocking because she spoke with a foreign accent. Taxi drivers charging more for a trip which she knows isn't that amount or even taking her on a longer journey to charge more. The older generation were just as bad. Bus passengers muttering under their breath whilst she is sitting near them. She can hear every word people say!

Because sometimes words take longer to come out, I can get frustrated waiting for a reply. I know I shouldn't but it is hard. It is hard for her to keep up with the rest of us and just as hard for the family to slow to her pace. That includes pace of walking and speaking. The speaking was very hard for her and us at the beginning, but we have got used to it quickly. You still get comments from some members of the public. I find it a bit funny when people of other nationalities speak to her in their own language. Or ask her what part of the world she is from!

I can't imagine what it must feel like, but I would feel lost and sad if I lost my native speech and it had still not returned after several years. I would hate for people to be rude or spiteful to me because I spoke with a foreign accent. She will have her bad days, and that is when we do our best to give support. People she knows have also become used to it.

Kath Lockett's daughter Amanda

Having to get to grips with the reality of your own mum not being able to speak and articulate her words properly is hard. Hearing her talk with a completely different accent took a long time to understand.

I had mixed emotions. I was frustrated at the start because she couldn't say my name correctly and I had to learn to remember certain sounds and recognise words that she was saying that obviously were now phonetically different. In some respects it was embarrassing because some words were just coming out all 'mumbo jumbo' and in front of the general public you would just see them sniggering or even looking down at my mum for the way she was speaking. It knocked my mum's confidence to rock bottom. Amongst other variables to her illness, the speech I think was the pinnacle of her self-esteem just being non-existent.

She became a recluse in her own home for a long period of time, which I felt very upset about. I couldn't always be with her due to my own life, so when I heard that a lot of the time she would just be indoors and scared to go outside, even to the local shop, it was terrible. The general public wouldn't understand her speech and instead of just being courteous and just giving her that extra time she needed to get her words out, they would just ignore her and some would even laugh and comment 'what part of the world are you from 'cause it's not England!'. A taxi ride home once cost double because the driver thought my mum was a foreigner so tried to rip her off!

Another example I remember quite clearly was when we visited the local gallery and were stopped by a worker who wanted us to fill out a questionnaire about the art and our opinions etc. As soon as my mum opened her mouth to speak, the worker abruptly cut in with 'Oh I see you're not from round here so you don't have to fill out the form if it's too much to understand the questions.' My response was one of anger as you can imagine: 'My mum IS British' I snapped back.

Obviously the foreign accent syndrome has completely altered her speech and it baffles me why it happened to my mum. I don't know much about the syndrome and as my family gets to grips with it, we do hope for more people to become aware of it so that it's not something hidden and forgotten about. Even though her accent is different, my mum is the same and I salute her for all the courage she has shown over the years, and her determination to not let it ruin her life.

Neurogenic FAS. The family theme again, but emphasising how little this is appreciated by others, especially the media. Support from work, but the feeling here that it's harder to get support from the health service.

'It does affect the family . . . a little part of you goes with your voice change'

JUNE MALDONADO

June Maldonado 2010–13. Small strokes in August and October 2009.

Looks like the beginning of 2010 is looking better (except weather wise) for me than the last few months of 2009..thank goodness! It is not good to feel your are living in some sort of mystery sphere..asking all the questions but being fenced off with no real answers..I was beginning to think this Neurologist was playing some sort of "mind game" with me just to see if I was aware of him not committing himself to any form of diagnosis .... but you can't make someone answer who has no intention of doing so!! My husband said I should have said "I'm not moving until I get an answer from you" . . . .can you imagine the response would have been probably he would have got hospital security to escort me off as being an unco-operative patient when in fact he was the person who was being "unco-operative!" Well that is in the past now and cannot be undone so better put it aside I suppose.

The Occupational Health Doctor at work has been doing monitoring of my condition since October last (being that I work as a Receptionist) the department know I am very keen to get back to work . . . .it is three months nearly since that fateful day in October with that strange headache and neck ache and I have not worked since..being a receptionist I do need to speak clearly to visitors etc., and on the phone. I think the Occupational Nurse said she was going to speak to the doctor about formulating some sort of plan for me to return back to work . . . can't include the greeting of "Good Afternoon" I just can't seem to say this properly . . . .if "Hello, can I help you" was allowed it would be more feasible . . . .but it sounds rather static even saying that!

My Manager wants me back as soon as and says even the friends of visitors have been asking after me and how I am . . . it is comforting to know you are missed not just by visitors but by their families as well you find out how much you appreciated. I really enjoy my work . . . have been working nearly 7 years there. My next appointment with Speech Therapy is beginning of February . . . may be I may have seen the Physician for Stroke by then . . .

. . . .

I saw my Doctor at the surgery to-day (she had already got the report from the Speech Therapist at the hospital and I mentioned to her about the Foreign Accent Syndrome . . . she was surprised at that, I printed out your reply and gave her a copy of it for her information and also mentioned about the video clips that can be opened up when on Google when putting in FAS (it is easier when you use the abbreviation) saves typing it in each time . . . .anyway . . . my Doctor said to-day after she read the therapist's report she was going to contact a Prof X

. . . .

Well last night I was travelling back from F where my daughter and family live after seeing my grandchildren . . . it takes about an hour to get back to P . . . When I got off the bus . . . I then needed to get another bus to get home . . . I asked the driver for a timetable of another service that runs from F to P a No.57 bus. Well the Driver who I gather was not English said to me when I asked for a Timetable "You are not English . . . Which Country do you come from?" . . . I thought here we go again!!..I said I am English but because of a stroke related problem I speak like this now with a bit of an accent" I could tell he did not really believe me though he said was I going to be alright waiting for another bus outside a deserted Shopping Centre and well I was on my own and it was 20.00hrs. I said I was fine and thanked him for asking. I think he was a bit concerned for me . . . quite sweet really in this day and age . . . he even took the trouble to show me the page in the timetable where the No. 57 bus timings were!!! He still had a few more stops before finishing the route although I was the last passenger the service stops last at SP . . . if I started to explain about FAS his bus would be delayed getting to its final destination . . . I did not want to be responsible for a delay in the operation of the Buses..I know they try to run on time..sometimes!! .....That hour on the bus the getting there and the hour getting back seems to give me the time to reflect on things ....a "switching off" time so to speak. I have certainly done some reflecting since I have known about FAS I can tell you. I wonder if I will just simply wake up one morning and talk just as I did before . . . just something that one never gives a second thought to!! You just take speaking for granted don't you . . . like breathing I suppose!

Well Y (another person with FAS) phoned me this evening and she was one the phone for about an hour telling me about her experiences . . . . it was sad she did not get any support from her work place or work associates even though she had worked there many years . . . .I have been fortunate with my work place and colleagues ..I get regular calls and visits from my workplace which is much appreciated doing a time of not knowing what was wrong with me even though my boss made regular reference to me sounding like "Mr Shut Uppa your Face" (popular song in GB from a while back) .....Thank heavens it seems as though we have partners that support us ..though I am not sure my husband really takes all this in . . . he does ask me how long will I be like this . . . I feel I want to answer "How long is a piece of string!!!"..Can't answer that one I am afraid!

The Physician I saw back last mid October in Medical Assessment Unit at the Hospital well I phoned him to encourage him to watch the programme (on TV about FAS) and ended up with having quite a long phone conversation with him. . . .he had not heard of FAS and was keen to learn more about it . . . I explained some of the problems I had come across with Neuro people mainly because of their lack of knowledge (e.g. saying it was all in my mind . . . me needing counselling, no tests etc), but that I had a marvellous Speech Therapist who was helping and very supportive of me.

I started back at work this week doing just two and a half hours on Reception but felt quite exhausted when I got home the first day and my speech that evening was not good at all. My Speech Therapist told me I was not speaking very well this morning and although she knows I am keen to get back to work she said she would not like to see me taking a "step backwards" so to speak because of wanting to do the three and half months to complete my contract and put at risk the months of improvement I have made and putting myself back and risking any further health complications. She likened me working to someone doing mental arithmetic non stop for two hours with no brain or speech problems . . . she said that was the best way to illustrate how it was for me in my position in my workplace! She said people in my workplace probably do not understand how much harder it is for brain things to work after damage. My daughter said since being back at work I am not speaking as well as I was and said no job is worth my speech getting bad again and everyone struggling to understand me like they did for several months. One of the people at work did me like an "In an Emergency" a little card just explaining about I have some speech disorder and in event of an emergency
. . . . . .

My visit to see a Stroke Specialist did not offer anything more than the consultant saying he knew nothing of this condition he had to spend time looking at the computer ... he had never heard of the condition before ... and tended to side with the Neurologist I saw perhaps I needed counselling, too pre-occupied with my health etc. Well my Speech Therapist saw him having coffee in the Hospital and was quick to have a chat with him and give him her professional opinion as she is Chief Speech Therapist and is well qualified in her profession and works between two hospitals.. She said afterwards he seemed to change his opinion and accept that this a very real condition and that it does exist!

.....The long and short of it (from all the tooings and froing about referral on to specialists) was that an appointment was arranged for me to see a specialist neurologist at the university hospital ....Well after nearly six months it is a start in the right direction ....I have cut down my hours at work I was feeling so tired and drained .....I am working only two and a half hours 3 days a week instead of 5 days a week ... to see if it helps.

..... (entry following case of another person with FAS being all over the media)..I expect when I get back to work next week everyone will be asking me if I saw Z in the Newspapers .....I expect they will say ... how come you were never mentioned in any article. ... Z contacted the Newspapers herself and sometimes the Press inundate you and you family but there was no comments made by her husband or photos of her husband or children as to how it affects the family. ... it does affect the family ... it did with the other person with FAS I contact ... a little part of you goes with your voice change.

I am still being asked where do I come from .....well I have been told I could pass for a Continental ... must be the brown hair and brown eyes and I always tend to use my hands when talking ... seem to use them more now as I try to say some words I do not find easy to say and it takes sometimes three parts to say one word ... but I do not give up ... get there in the end ... after three tries if I can't say it I give up ... it gets tiring sometimes.

.....an update (Dec 2010) ....finally got to see the university specialist ... his report stating the following (amongst other things): brain scan did not show any new areas of ischaemia and as before showed on a few small scattered vascular lesions ....suggest that she has had a small ischaemic stroke and that some of her residual symptoms are due to this ....but if they were able to pick this up at the university hospital, why didn't they see this over a year ago and they took no notice of me reporting double vision!!! I feel really confused by the whole thing ... or is it my brain is "so out of order" I am simply "missing the point ...". Since FAS arrived, I have found out that there are lot worse things in life. FAS may change one's life but does not shorten one's life. Cancer and the like may, but not FAS. It is important to place it in perspective. Life is for living.

A successful businesswoman. The advent of FAS. Am I mad, or is it the others? Finding the answer, as many others attest, is not easy.

'My glass is always half full, but I do shed the odd tear'

JULIE MATTHIAS

In the beginning

I own a Hair Salon and Training Academy in Kent and was diagnosed with hemiplegic migraines (H.M.) 9 months ago in September 2011 after a very long and worrying summer of being treated for a stroke, then told I had M.S. then Drs were unsure and thought I had a very rare condition where there was only one other case in the country.

My symptoms started after a major headache in July where I thought I was going to die, after suffering from migraines for the past 10 years this was totally different as the pain was in the back of my head. I recovered being left with symptoms of confusion and forgetfulness. 2 weeks later I was rushed to hospital with suspected stroke I lost the ability to walk and talk. I spent a week in Hospital where I had a CT scan, numerous blood tests and approx 8 unsuccessful attempts at a lumber punch. I was discharged from hospital the same as I went in with the information that I had not had a stroke. WHAT WAS IT I HAD WAS THE QUESTION !!!!!!!!!!!

I made an 80% recovery and thought it may be a viral thing but was rushed back into hospital 10 days later as I had collapsed like a rag doll at home.

After 8 more days in hospital and more tests and a successful lumber punch I was diagnosed after seeing a Neurologist 6 weeks ago as an outpatient as having H.M. my symptoms are full body paralysis and my auras are right sided weakness with slow slurred speech. My internal functions (bladder and bowels) are also affected in addition to the hot and cold moments.

I deal with the general public, heads of school and local authorities on a daily basis who either think I am drunk or stupid by the way I talk and I constantly have to explain that I am struggling with my speech at the moment. I also need the aid of a walking stick on occasions. The medication so far that I have tried had poisoned my body so am due to see my neurologist for the next batch

I rule my life not H.M. rule me I make the most of my good days and still guide to very successful business' which we have just won The Best Training Provider Award in Medway and my company has only been going for 3 years. This is a dreadful illness we need to make people aware

On a daily basis I struggle with speech and walking along with many other symptoms, I am losing faith with the medical world and beg for someone to help me.

I feel that there is not enough know about this dreadful condition and feel I need to let everyone know so we can help others, and reduce the number of suicides because of Hemiplegic Migraines.

Update on my condition

To add to my symptoms about 4months ago the end of February 2012 I started to speak with a foreign accent to every body's amusement. This was better than the speech before which was slow as at least now people would not speak to me as though I was stupid. Or so I thought!

I have now been diagnosed with FAS which has affected my life in more ways than one could ever imagine. I was a strong independent business owner who was achieving her dream, endless awards for the business, and frequently requested to participate in public speaking.

Now I feel that I hardly know myself, I cannot look in the mirror as I have lost my identity who is that strange speaking person looking back at me? I put on my make-up by looking at small parts of my face.

I try to stay positive but this condition has taken away my independence, I cannot go out alone in case I have a 'melt down' (this is what my children have nicknamed my paralysis and major fatigue moments)

I constantly get asked where do you come from.

I have experienced racism!!!!

My confidence drains away in different situations,

I cannot answer the phone at work unless there is an explanation as no one recognises my voice.

My working life as it was is nearly non-existent as I cannot commit to anything; this has put major pressures onto my two wonderful daughters and increased their work load and responsibilities. Financially it has started to become a struggle as I have not received any sort of financial help from the government.

The doctors that I have seen so far have told me they have no answers and my neurologist has said he is not a magician although he has referred me to a cognitive behaviour therapist, I asked him does he think I am mad???????

I live from day to day to see how I am physically, although my voice now is predominately in FAS mode and I find that when typing e-mails or writing I write how I speak (missing words and saying things around a different way just like a foreign person trying to speak English) So it is a strain to keep checking my written work.

On the positive side my husband has said that I have developed a sense of humour, making little quick jokes.

Thanks to the wonderful support of my fantastic family I am able to carry on fighting to get some answers regarding Foreign Accent Syndrome.

MY GLASS IS ALWAYS HALF FULL but I do shed the odd tear.

I look forward to a response

Kind regards Julie Matthias

Many accounts speak of the importance of family, the fact that the family can be as much impacted as the person with the new accent. Here and in the accounts from Julie and family we gain glimpses into this wider web that FAS and chronic conditions cast.

Julie Matthias' young daughter

When my mum first started to get ill it was a bit of a shock to me, as she was fine one moment going to work each day and doing clients' hair, plus teaching the National Vocational Qualification (kind of apprenticeship exams in Britain) Level 2 and Level 3 classes. The next moment while doing clients she got worse and was put into an ambulance.

On that particular Saturday it all happened in a blur. One minute Mum was fine, and then she went out the back, excusing herself from the clients. I had no idea what was happening, my sister C told me to transfer all of her clients over to other stylists so she could go home. C then left as she was going out for the day. I then went in to check on my mum and got told to go outside and get the ambulance.

I was scared and confused when mum got taken into the ambulance as no one told me what was going on or what was happening. My auntie was in the salon so she went up to the hospital with Mum. I felt as if I should have been informed more. While trying to keep reception going I was also trying to get hold of my dad who was at work, and C to let them know that Mum was at the hospital. After finally getting hold of Dad, he went up to the hospital and I then felt relieved, I knew he would look after her.

Dad kept me informed all day with what was happening. Finally it felt like someone understood how I was feeling and what I needed. I finished work and went home, waiting for another update and getting ready to go out with my sister. While we were out we heard that Mum was staying in for the night for tests and to be kept under observation.

We went to visit her the next day; it shocked me as her voice went from being so strong to very weak and slow. We stayed there for a couple of hours and then we had to leave. It was heartbreaking. Mum was in hospital for a week, which seemed unreal. Work was quiet, even home was quiet, I hated it. When she came out it was so good to see her. Over the next couple of weeks she got stronger. We were hoping that she was back on the mend, but then all of a sudden she got worse again and was taken back into hospital.

I felt guilty, as I had been away for a week with the Girl Guides camping, then on my first night back she was taken away in an ambulance again. She was in there again for another week, which is when we finally found out that she has Hemiplegic Migraine.

Mum is home now and has only been back in hospital once over the last year. Now her voice is different, stronger, but she sounds like she is from France or Spain. It now has turned from not only her having Hemiplegic Migraine but she also now has Foreign Accent Syndrome.

When Mum first started to speak differently I was in denial at first, as before her voice was strong then got really slow, and then her voice would come back to normal for about three weeks. It became a shock to find out that she would never return to normal. It was quite upsetting at first, as I realised I would never hear her voice the same as when I was growing up.

But although she spoke differently she was 90% better, which was better than what she was like when it first happened, and I found I could cope with her foreign accent if it meant she felt OK.

It has been really hard to watch someone who has always been the strongest person in my life to now seem so weak. Instead of being the independent woman I have always known her to be, she now has to depend on someone all the time, whether it is my dad or one of us, her daughters. We have to take her to places and sometimes even translate what she is saying.

I can see that she hates it, having to be so dependent on people. I'm just pleased we are here to help her, and for her to have us to depend on. Now it is our turn.

Although I hate seeing her the way she has become and it upsets me most of the time, I could not be more proud of her. She has said since the beginning that it would not beat her, and though the doctors keep on saying that she will get depressed, she has proven that she is not weak, it will not beat her. She is the same strong willed person she was before she became ill, that has not changed.

By Mum being diagnosed with Foreign Accent Syndrome it has actually come to light that she will not return to her old self. It makes me want to cry all the time, seeing her at her lowest. I never thought as a daughter that my mum would be dependent on me, as I have always been dependent on her. I am grateful that she is still OK; it is just sometimes I feel like I have lost my mum. I do miss the old her, but now she has changed she has more of a sense of humour and can actually let people help her.

Julie Matthias' husband

After many months of J battling her Hemiplegic Migraine condition with the utmost determination, we were aware of an intriguing change to J's voice with the slight overtone of maybe a Spanish or French accent.

Initially my thoughts were of disappointment as 6 months down the line J's condition was showing no signs of improvement and had in fact gained another ailment. When the condition was diagnosed as foreign accent syndrome I felt some kind of relief in that it was a known condition, as up until then we had very little idea as to what was happening to J, but upon further investigation 'deflation' probably sums up my feelings, as we learnt that less than 100 cases have been reported worldwide.

Julie's condition has meant subtle little changes for me in regards being less playful or hands-on and trying to be more supportive and understanding and to absorb the condition and treat J as normally as possible.

Not knowing whether there is a cure out there is a worry, and the sporadic attacks are a concern, and although some concerns are put at ease with scans giving the all clear, it would be a boon to ascertain what is triggering the leg and arm paralysis and slowness of speech, but as yet we have not had proper confirmation of the cause.

Unfortunately, with the rareness of the condition most doctors seem to have a limited knowledge of it, and unless J was to be under observation 24 hours a day and was electronically wired up, educated guesswork would seem to be the order of the day. It would be great if someone could be determined enough to put something like that into practice, as the condition does appear to have a less than serious approach. If all sufferers have the same debilitating conditions as my wife, my heart goes out to them, as it does to J, whose determination and fight to deal with and beat FAS is an inspiration to us all who have to live it with her. J, I Love You.

Debie's image of the girl adrift in a rowing boat on the storm-swept waves, the oar broken, is a powerful image that many people experiencing FAS (and life's other tribulations) will relate to. The theme of the journey runs through many of the accounts in this book. Formerly Debie was a classroom assistant guiding children who needed extra support. Suddenly the tables turned. The poem encapsulates her call for help. Her story, despite the trials, sets a compass for her way out of the storm.

'Life isn't about waiting for the storm it's about learning to dance in the rain'

DEBIE ROYSTON

The journey

Id like to thank my family for support me
And always be here for me through my struggle

The flu become so bad that the day never come when I feel a turning point to recovery and what I don't know is that things are go to get even worse . . . . . .

My doctor look at me and say you have a flu virus take time off work and get better . . . . .

I went back three weeks later and said I feel worse she said you should be starting to build yourself up go out do some light exercise . . . I looked at her in disbelief but thought if that's what will do it I'll give it a try.

My right side became week I couldn't use my leg and arm properly the signals seemed to not get there when I needed to use them.

My husband wasn't happy with what the doctor was saying and came with me a week later to see her again, she said it's a virus or are you stressed, wow! why is it when you go to the doctors the word stress is always top in their dictionary .. ..The only other thing it might be is fibromyalgia I will send you to see a rheumatologist and I will give you a low dose antidepressant to take daily ...... no thanks ...... I'm not depressed and if I am it's because I want to be better. ...We left there and I decided that I would need to get harder on myself and make things happen .. ...My husband was still amazed that the doctor wasn't taking anything seriously ....

I decided to go back to work, I woke up Monday early, my body hurt all over it wouldn't function. legs so painful my feet hurt to touch the carpet; I thought they would break at some point from the pain ....I tried to dress myself, my arms had no strength, my fingers wouldn't coordinate to grip the buttons the more I told them to do it the more they wouldn't work. I tried to lift my leg to put my trousers on and my other leg buckled underneath me ....okay sit on the floor its easier ... now stand, no strength don't give up Deb you can beat this be strong I told myself ...... My head pounding, the strength I had recharged was gone .. ..I was fit for nothing ... I lay back on the carpet and closed my eyes I fell asleep exhausted ...... i woke up and tried to function again, I needed to remember everything I needed to take downstairs, I wasn't going to be able to come back up If I had forgot something .... I sat on my bottom and step by step went down the stairs ....the pain in my head felt like a hammer banging against the sides ....The migraines I described as thunder storms I would get a dull aching in the left side of my head and a pain would come through to my eyebrow, a flickering around my left eye would start and then when I closed my eyes it was like lightening flashing in the sky on a stormy night ....

The working day at an end, I came home exhausted head pounding I fell asleep. Crying about everything made the pressure worse in my head so I avoided it.

After trying to go to work I came to a decision I needed to reduce my days down so after speaking to my Boss she was very helpful and agreed it would be okay ...... The next week passed, same scenario painful headaches no coordination ... I was chatting to my daughter in the kitchen and I felt my cheek and my tongue tighten, that was it for me enough was enough time to go to hospital! ....

I was examined by a nurse who said something isn't right and sent me up to wait for a doctor to assess my condition .... the wait was very long and the tests consisted of can you lift your leg can you touch your nose ...... One doctor questioned how pale the back of my eye was, the lights were so bright my eyes hurt ..... I was so tired I just wanted an answer and please get me better .....

I was admitted into hospital for the start of my nightmare .....

I was on the ward a few days when the neurologist appeared he began examining me he moved my arm and my arm began to tighten to the point he couldn't move it. He began moving my leg that did the same then bit by bit the more the doctor moved me the tighter my muscles became I was locked in a spasm I couldn't move . . . . it lasted for about 20 minutes and then bit by bit my muscles began to relax. He examined me, never said anything and walked away in a trance at what he had just observed . . . . . . .He didn't come back and I was left waiting . . . . the rheumatologist came to see me just after and the same thing happened he began to examine me and my muscles one by one began to lock the more he examined me the worse the locking became

I noticed a sensation in my right leg that felt heightened when this locking began . . . .

The next few days the locking of my muscles would happen without being touched. I would feel very vague and then feel the sensation in my leg and then my body would go into a seizure when it stopped I would be very tired and vague again . . . .

When the seizure had stopped the doctor said I can help you and he said he would put me on Epilim . . . . .That night the Epilim was introduced and I went to sleep. I woke up from my sleep having a seizure my body was jerking. I was so frightened my whole body thrashing about nurses all around me I couldn't speak. I thought it would never stop and slowly I felt it begin to subside and I was relieved but very afraid . . . .The quiet spasms that I had began with had now changed the sensation would begin in my leg and a feeling of not hearing what was going on around me when the seizures happened I couldn't speak and after the seizure it was exhausting . . . I would fall asleep unable to communicate . . . ..

My family visited me everyday and afraid of upsetting them my husband would draw the curtains around me whilst having these seizures . . . ..There came a time though that I realised they were going to have to see it happen because I would need looking after when I got home . . . .They were upset that something so awful was going on but credit to them they were very supportive.. I saw my mum cry at what had happened and I didn't want to be like this . . .

Everyday at home I would have these seizures where my body would slide off the chair locked in spasm and began rolling around on the floor. I hit the furniture so hard sometimes I felt I needed to wear a crash helmet . . .

I had developed a shaking, my head would bang over and over it was so painful until I couldn't bare it and when I held onto my head it would throw the shake into my arms . . . . all day every day these random things would happen . . . I remember my daughter wanting to show me something on her computer and i couldn't see it because i was shake so bad.. she held my arm without question whilst i watch the computer screen . . . . nothing was say i was grateful . . . ..The shaking got so bad and my body spasms were now of the case that if I had one someone needed to be with me because I would crash into furniture and end up rolling around on the floor . . . ..

I would walk round in circles and to stop it would drop to the floor and hold onto something to stop the sensation of needing to do it . . . then to get from the kitchen to the living room one day my body just decided to turn around and walk backwards . . . . My movements were clumsy and when I made steps my legs would need to lift very high of the ground to move . . . . . . .like I was stepping over something . . . . . .

In the mean time I hadn't been able to go back to my job and couldn't give a reason for the illness . . . . I wanted it all to go away I was fearful of what the future would bring and scared that my family were watching this happen to me . . . . . .

I didn't like people coming to the house, I didn't want them to see me in this condition . . . I feared someone knocking the door. My husband would calm me before opening it and say it's okay and the reassurance came when the living room door was closed and I would feel safe . . .

The days passed living like this when an appointment came to go and see the rheumatologist the GP (family doctor) had previously sent me to see. We went to the hospital he was very concerned as he had visited me previously when I was in hospital but now my condition was much worse . . . . . He looked at me distressed that I had been left to cope like this and he paged neurology and said I can't examine you like this can you go to mau and wait there they shouldn't be long . . . ..He thought I had uncontrolled epilepsy . . . .

I waited in mau and no neurologist came . . . they gave me a bed for the night and the next day still no neurologist people stared at me wondering what was wrong . . . . . . I hated it, I wanted to go home . . . ..the doctors from my first visit to hospital appeared and were slightly shocked at the now worsened condition and were concerned . . . . . .

That evening my husband and daughter came to visit and I had a shaking seizure . . . . it gained strength and I felt it would never stop . . . . suddenly I felt release as it lost power and slowed down and I lay there exhausted . . . my husband looked at me and said are you ok . . . .. I looked at him and my mouth wouldn't move I was talking in my head but no words would come out . . . . . . .he could see there was something wrong, my eyes must have give away the panic I felt at not under-standing what had happened . . . .

I sat up and looked for something to read . . . I got out of bed to read a notice, nothing would come out . . . .. I thought this is silly just talk you can do it but nothing. I began panic to panic ..

The nurse was called and she said she would send for the doctor hours went by and it was also late she said we are moving you to a ward . . . .

I was wheeled to the ward it was dark my husband leaned over to kiss me and left. I had the curtain drawn around me, what was happening to me! I was afraid, scared and I couldn't answer the nurse when she spoke to me . . . ..

The next morning I woke up and thought the day before had been a bad dream . . . Could I really not speak. I wanted someone to ask me something . . . .. I eventually was asked if I would like a cup of tea.. I looked at her and tried to talk but all that came was breathy sounds..She nodded with a look of sympathy and went . . .

Nobody come to ask me how i feel or tell me why this have happen nobody seem to care i couldn't speak . . . .i did wonder when they would ask but nobody did . . . .why didn't they?

Breakfast was hard to eat, my mouth wouldn't move; chewing was tiring so I gave up .... I opted to eat softer foods ..i dribbled tissues were at hand to save embarrassment and when i swallow food would go up my nose or i would choke . . ..

Days passed shaking no speech . . . it was suggested I might want to see a speech therapist and one of the doctors walked passed my bed and uncaringly said shake rattle and roll only to realise what he said he shouldn't have . . . .

I was sent home . . . . . .

My speech in the beginning was very breathy and trying to speak was tiring my mouth wouldn't move my tongue tied not able to move it to make the sounds that i did before . . . . My shaking eventually became less and less but the seizures were still there and to add to this cold temperature brought it on too . . . so now I had to wear more layers to stop seizures happening in the cold . . . ..

Eventually my speech was understandable to a point but wasn't me I could hear .. I have a Brummie (Birmingham, GB) accent but this accent sounded alien to me . . . . not much was said, family were happy that I could communicate as it was tiring for both sides trying to understand me and me trying to make them understand what I wanted . . . . (A lot of note writing and charades.)

I didn't like the change, everytime I opened my mouth I could hear someone else speak. I tried shouting in frustration but I couldn't make my sound come out ..

I walked around the house not understanding my surroundings i know this is where i live but it felt unsure . . . i looked in my wardrobe of clothes and didn't know why they were all there, come on Deb what did you buy them for what did you do with them . . . .tired at looking at them i close the doors and sit down . . . . im staring at a wardrobe life is passing by but i just stare . . . what is happening to me . . . .

The handbags that i used to love sit gathering dust . . . .i pick them up and look at them like they belong to someone close to me . . . .. i feel i mourning a death and all of these clothes and bags belong to someone else . . . .. i admire what i am look at but i don't want them . . . i try an old coat on but it feels wrong like it's not mine . . . ..

I opened the front door to get the post one day and my neighbour was there with her grandson and daughter, she said I haven't seen you for a long time. and I began to explain. She looked at me and I knew what was wrong instantly .. I didn't sound like me and she was listening to my accent . . . . . . her grandson said hey Deb why do you sound French . . . ..apparent he have a French doctor and that why he likened my voice to it . . . ..the realisation of who I sounded like become clear to me . . . and then when my family came home I questioned them, do I sound Foreign .?. . . . .

I went to see the speech therapist and had a few tests done and then she said you know what you have is very rare don't you .. I said I don't know what I have, she said it's called foreign accent syndrome. I looked at my husband, I was glad that there was a name for what it was but not that they can't cure it . . .

People who I know would stop and ask how I am and look at me as if to say why are you talking like that. If we went shopping I would get hand signs and mouthing the words much bigger so I could understand or the other thing is people would speak to my husband instead of me.

Dealing with the loss

I had lost myself this person I could hear I didn't know ... my family would say yes we no it's you but I couldn't feel that they could see me as their mum and wife..

I felt very lost ..I was grieving for the death of myself .. I looked in the mirror everyday and felt like I was very far away from the image looking back at me ... tears would roll at the feeling of being so sad so frustrated ......

In our house I would always be the first person up. I would get out of bed I would say to myself in my head don't speak and on my bottom attempt to go down the stairs .... my two cocker spaniels Alfie and Molly at the bottom of the stairs to greet me and without thinking forget what I had asked myself and the silence broken I would hear the sound of a stranger ......

When everyone began returning to work and school I found this very hard I wanted to go back to my life .... I would have tantrums like a child .... no understanding at why this had happened to me ... My husband would get distressed because didn't feel he could leave me like this but it was always when he was walking out the door for work that the confrontation of why me would happen ....

Not talking helped me to not have to listen to this new sound but it also didn't help me because I needed to speak to help my speech become more fluent but the silence in the day was the only escape from this person, locking it in so it couldn't get out but school and work would end and the stranger would be back in the house ....

My memory is very poor and I forget from one room to the next ... sometimes the second something was said I would forget it ....multi tasking is very difficult. If somebody ask me a question my head would decide to talk about something else and sometimes answer a question with a question ... My family had to learn that if I didn't answer them it wasn't because I didn't care ... I am not able to have a conversation if it is too noisy and I have difficulty reading writing and sorting out important text. I find it difficult to multi task.

My husband looked after me for a very long time as my seizures were unexpected and just come and go as they pleased. He is my rock that I cling to when the waters are very rough and uncertain. I have been to the depths of despair and he has been with me and whilst holding my hand he has lead me down through the dark pathway to a clearing where I can breathe again .....

My children have grown up so much during my illness and have shown me how mature and responsible they have become and if anything good can come out of this I am proud of them for showing strength and courage at such a young age ....

The hospital refer me to a neuropsychiatrist who was the first doctor that actual sit and listen. He send me to see a speech and language and my neuropsychiatrist also arrange for me to have Wechsler testing done . . . . . . because of how nobody actual know what have happen to me when I was introduce to a psychologist I was very dishearten and say to her if you can't do anything don't worry . . . she say did I read my test or understand them . . . . No I didn't see anything in there that was hopeful . . .

She tell me that my brain have suffer a trauma and that this is why I am struggle with everyday life . . . she give me lots of ideas to use at home which I was about to find very helpful . . . .

When I couldn't deal with noise she tell me to use my ear phones . . . . Not only does it alert people not to bother you but it also helps you listen to something that helps you regain composure to carry on . . . she also advise me to use alarms around the house to help me remember what I am doing and to have the tv on in the kitchen to stop me get distracted and walking out the room when I am cooking . . . . . . And also when life gets to overwhelm for me as a family we choose a word to use to let them know I am not coping with a situation without have to explain . . . . I say the word and everything stops without question . . . ..

A while ago I want to try and paint what it feel like to have fas . . . . I thought of a me sitting in little row boat in middle of rough sea lost its dark and i don't have the strength to save myself the waves throw me about and i am holding on with every last breath . . . . Eventual the storm calms and the boat reaches land and there i am waiting for myself on the shore . . . . . .

Have you ever watch the series life on Mars?

The synopsis go, sam tyler is an ambitious young detective determined to keep the streets of 21st century Manchester safe However, the hunt for a serial killer becomes a personal vendetta when sam suspects his girlfriend has be kidnap by a man he is track down

But after a near fatal car accident, sam wakes up dazed and confuse in 1973 struggling to understand whats real . . . . has he gone back in time ? is he in a coma? or has he simply go insane ?

Thrown head first into his new world sam faces some of the hardest cases he have ever know he have no idea why he is in 1973 but maybe if he can work out the reason he can get home . . . .

that series is how i see my life . . . .. im not a policeman hahahah. i connect with how he is

stuck in a world he cant get out of he doesn't know what have happen to him and is look

for ways constant to get back to his old life . . . i feel my old self is getting further away as my new self grows stronger . . . . . .

memories are random flash at me .. for instance one day i was walk to the toilet and a memory of the school custard jug flash into my mind . . . i can see it a metal jug gold

colour filled with hot thick custard . . . . and feel so real to me they could be right infront of my face .. the memories my brain show me are my most connected ones . . .

this is how my brain work it shows me things and i am sad that what if i never remember something that is very important to me and will only know it again when my brain decides to show me .

i can talk about some things in my life but i don't have a real strong i was there connection . . . .

in one part of the series a girl is sit on a three wheel trike and i remember a picture of me and my brother . . . he have a car and a cowboy outfit i have a trike and a nurse outfit . . . i get strong feeling of how our christmass used to be . . . . the wall paper .. making things to hang on tree . . . . . a tin of toffees that all were gold colour and look like treasure,,,,

i was born in the 70's and watching this series i can connect strongly with the cars the music the life styles . . . . it feels real to me . . . . . .

i understand my life isn't two people but i feel like i am be show my past in a book that i have read somewhere . . . . it is familiar but i have no emotional connection . . .

i was ask if i can have my old self back would you do it . . . . in the beginning i would exchange without question . . . .i was afraid and lost . . . .

but now i think no . . . . . . .this is my life now . . . .

These are my poems that i have make to help me understand what i am go through

In the darkness

In the darkness i close my eyes
I lay next to my husband
There is no illness between us
There is laughter of past times
Great memories we share . . .
Talking is not difficult
i see pictures in my head of the happy times like watch silent movies
    that i feel we can both see
of how we laugh and cry at memories go by
connection back to who we were is easy in the dark . . . i chat to him in
    my head
it is not awkward it is easy he knows me i am safe . . .
it is peace

Lost

Home sick
I want to go home
I want to be where i am understood
I want to feal peace
No struggle
I am trapped in a mouth that wont let me out
Someone switched the channel when i wasn't looking
I m lost

FAS

Locked in a world where nobody understands
I cry out . . . . I am lost
I search inside myself looking for me . . . desperate
Please help me open the door and let me out
Will this nightmare end?
Wake me up someone shake me please make it stop.
Curled up afraid and I try to speak
I don't know who this person is
Silence is my only respite from the stranger I can now hear when I
     speak..
I look at my loved ones, please see me, please hear me . . . I am your
     wife you mother!
We see you we understand! . . . . I can't reach them . . . .
Silence is my only respite to connection
But it is broken and I am lost once again

By Debie Royston
July 2012

Time have move forward i am happier me i write how i speak i cant help it before
i would try hard to change it but Cant do anymore i can be free when i am me
. . .

My family life is happy and although i cant change the way i am i am adapting
to doing things and i am learning to accept life how it is . . . . . .

I can draw now i can't draw before i get ill but i can now . . . i like draw my
loved ones it keeps me connect in a deep way ..i am more creative . . . ..i bake
better too hahahhhhhahah

The sad thing is I know i am impaired and it make me embarrass i don't want
to come across as stupid . . . ..it hurts me to not be able to just fit . . . ..

If i could want for anything it would be that the medical profession understand when they are present with this condition ... and give the person who is suffer a bigger understanding of what they are go through ....

We can all live in hope that we will get peace one day and to remember ... Life isn't about waiting for the storm it's about learning to dance in the rain ....

Thanks for taking the time to read

Debie Royston

About the impact of FAS, but about the need to educate too. About self but about importance of others too. About appearance, but what is the reality?

'Not everything is as it seem, not everything Is black/white'

KAY RUSSELL-ILIFFE

Journey into the unknown

Its just past my third anniversary, strange to call something as unusual as what happened to me 3 year ago when I was launched into a journey of total unchartered territory, complete life changing, isolating, bewildering, an anniversary but how else do you describe it. In fact, calling this an anniversary is as strange as the journey of Foreign Accent Syndrome is in itself. The sheer name of the condition isn't necessarily right, the only part of that is correct is the definition, which does pretty much sum it up.

In January 2010 I suffered a Hemiplegic Migraine attack; I have suffered from these for over 30 years. This type of migraine is also on the rare side, its impact and effects mimic stroke, so create speech problems – from none to slurred, paralysis of limb or limbs, etc. Affectionately by my family known as "wobbles" which can last hours, days or since January 2010, weeks.

On 5th January 2010 I woke up with the usual numbness of mouth, limbs heavy. 'Oh no,' I say to myself, 'here we go again, wobble time, the boss is going to love me after 10 days of holiday for Christmas and now am out of action again.' The following few days continue as they normal do for an HM attack, no speech or slurred speech, but unusually after a few days, the speech didn't return to normal. The following weekend, it deteriorated, so I had a bath to help soothe the back of my neck/head which the pain is always worse. During this bath I lost all use of limbs, couldn't feel a thing from head to toe. The water was gently soothing but I felt nothing and couldn't move. This was so unusual for me whilst having attack, had been partial paralysed before but never total, was I dying? If I did how would anyone know until it was too late? I live alone. The front door was locked, couldn't reach my phone to ring or text anyone. Didn't really feel scared just had strange thoughts that I think at times like these, the body gives you as a safety mechanism to stop you from panic and despair. Weird thoughts such as how would I feel or what would I do if a tarantula was to come over into the bath and crawl over me or a snake (I am petrified of both), this was very unlikely to happen living in England and in a bathroom that was upstairs in a mid-terrace house. However, the thought of that scared me more than the though of potential dying. Many peoples have said to me since, I could have drowned, that never crossed my mind. After about 30 minutes I regained some use in upper half of my body and manage to launch myself by hanging onto the bathroom sink and hoping it would take my weight as legs were not functioning. I survived my launch and text my friend, my parents came and eventual the use came back.

Over the next three to four weeks, this cycle continued, poor speech, paralysis of limbs, stuck in the bath for a further two occasions, launching across bathroom with no legs became a bit of a regular exercise, not recommended though. Eventually I was sent by my GP to see a neurologist, who booked me in for an MRI. In the meantime was put on Topiramate. The MRI took place about 7–10 days later and I saw my neurologist for the results 7 days post MRI. What happened during those 14 days or so between seeing neurologist to book for MRI, having it and then the results meeting, was what changed my life. Up until this point, my speech, albeit slurred, difficult to find words (aphasia) undertones still sounded like me. However, my undertones of speech were sudden total different, nothing like me. They sounded to me and to anyone who heard me that I was either French or Eastern European. I couldn't work out what was happening to me. I looked in the mirror (not the greatest sight to see), I looked the same physically but somehow, something had gone, my speech and how I sounded wasn't me and I felt that all I knew about me was the outer casing. Where had the rest of me gone and why? That's a question that I asked then and so many times since and even since having a diagnosis of Foreign Accent Syndrome subsequent and now knowing more, no one can truly explain what happens nor why and where the person that you were and what your capabilities you had appear to have completed deleted or gone into a re-cycle bin.

The following few weeks were probably the worst of my life, total bewilderment, suspicion, disbelief from the medical world and friends. Even one of my grandchildren accused his Mama of lying to him because he said I wasn't his Nanny any more when I spoke to him on the phone; going out into the big wide world and realising that I couldn't cope with noise and speak at same time. The only description of this I could then and can still now only say that for me it was like a stunned, scared little rabbit in car headlights. My concentration was affected, I can't read out loud and comprehend at same time. I couldn't read very much. When I read, I read in FAS (Foreign Accent Syndrome). When I wrote, I wrote in FAS (handwriting and even on computer). If I tried to write in grammatically correct English as I always could, my hand writing when from adult joined up writing to child like print that took me ages to do. All of my communication skills whether written or verbal seem to be affected. For me, some of my communication skills that had always been my forte had been reduced to those of my 5 year grandchildren, 45 years of my life just gone! I told my speech therapist that this condition was "The incontinence of mind" as its impact rendered me so useless; it was taking the P out of all my mental ability and agility.

I can't still say certain words; I never used to call my parents 'Mama' & 'Papa' but can't say those words any more. Sometimes when I get tired and this still happens, the "thingy's" appear a lot in my vocabulary and on one particular occasion in the early days, whilst potting some bedding plants with my dear friend, the 'compost' that we were putting them into sudden as I tired turned into "cinnamon." Bless her, she eventually worked out what I was trying to say but the words escaped me complete when tired or stressed never mind whether or not I can actual say them or not. I even dream in FAS, I cannot now remember what it was like pre FAS, though I have copies of my pre FAS voice, to do all the communication, thinking process etc is so vastly different. I have a "handybag", I do things in little minutes, rather than a handbag or in a minute, I say "Yedda" for 'Yes' and "Yeddaday" for 'Yesterday' . . . .how strange is that, these are just a couple of examples, but there are many, many more.

My memory was also affected and my ability to multi task went out of the window (rich coming from someone that lead a very busy working life as a sales executive, driving and undertaking several tasks in one day and several times during the day). Everything just went in my words – total upsy down.

Because no one has answers, because no one has heard of this, because of the looks you get, the questions where are you from? People who live in the same village/town as you, and the town where you were born, because when you look at yourself and you can't work out where you've gone. One of the hardest parts to come to terms is, where have I gone, will I ever find me again? I have used on my first and second anniversaries of this to use the words of the song "Still Haven't Found What I'm Looking For" by U2. I have also suggested putting an advert into a 'Lost and Found' section of newspaper in case someone might find me.

At first, its total desperation, depression, so much isolation and confusion, locked away in this world that no-one knows, understands or at the time you think anyone else is going through due to its extreme rarity. Then anger kicks in, why has this happened to me, why don't people believe me, why is it all people can say is . . . well never mind you sound really sexy . . . ..like that's supposed to make up for everything is it? Wow, think not. Don't they understand that this feels like an amputation, that part of you has been amputated but it's just not as visual to them and they can't cope with it any more than you? The amount of times that it was suggested that I could use my voice to make myself a lot of money . . . ..I guess for some they thought it they made light of it, it would make it better. But bless them, better for whom, them or me? Part of what happens; I believe happens in many situations. The person suffering from the loss or the condition seems to have to kind of compensate for everyone else and make them feel better. Its one of those, and I believe it is not done with mal-intent, just they don't know how to handle it so instead of them making you strong, you have to be strong for them, so you learn to cover, because it makes the rest of the world feel better. It never though takes away how you feel and what goes on with this condition however I am sure this can be also said at times of bereavement and/or with other conditions too.

The impacts and effects of this condition, even after 3 years have not gone away, the best advice I was ever given was by my speech therapist who told me to take everything in "baby steps". The speech therapy itself didn't help masses and of course every time I have an HM, it puts me back. But I'm learning how to manage it, rather than let it manage you is the key.

Over the last 3 years I have gone through some extreme highs and lows. I managed to contact a couple of other of FAS Sufferers in the UK over a few months and in turn that lead to being in contact with others not just here in the UK, but across into the USA and Canada initially through social networking. During the last 3 years, whilst this condition is still extreme rare, a social network page has developed and I am fortunate to have been appointed one of the administrators. Our site and as we now call it, "our FAS family" has grown not only in number of members, but in reaching far more corners of the world, which is amazing. I am privileged to be a part of this group of amazing, inspiration, supportive people.

After about 6 months into my journey, I ventured into the media, undertaking TV both National and International interviews. There were Radio interviews and (without my permission) it was covered by the press all over the world. My reason for doing this was to educate about what this condition is truly about, that its not just an accent, it has far more reaching impact. We are not 'nutters' or psychological cases or freaks, and there's no way you can fake this, as many (even in the medical world) think or deem us to be. My most burning desire was though to reach out to other FAS sufferers anywhere in the world, because as this the case in many conditions. Only another sufferer knows how this truly feels and the isolation and despair you go through.

Having gone through what I did, I can't stop others who may have FAS stampede into their life. But what I and others can do is to ensure that they don't do it alone. Family and friends can be amazingly supportive, it is immensely difficult time for them too, in some aspects we can't know how they feel watching us, as indeed try as they may, they can't totally understand what it's like for us, but what I do know is that without them, life would have been hardly worth living and there were times when in the middle of the night, alone and crying I felt it wasn't. Some of the general public and press response wasn't easy to deal with, but I just decided to put on an imaginary wax jacket and not allow their comment to get through. My motivation for doing what I did far outweighed small mindedness, ignorance, tunnel vision, judgemental attitudes and so I didn't let it effect me. Going into further uncharted territory of the TV and media world, was new to me and I had no experience in how to deal with it. However, despite its challenges, it helped me as a person to become even more determined to educate the world about it and reach out to other sufferers and be damned to the critics or sceptics, to turn something negative into something, hopeful hugely positive.

During my journey of desperation, depression, anger, confusion, unable to see anything good coming out of this, I have, partially through the inspiration of one of my co-sufferers, the advice of my speech therapist, the love and support of my dear friends and family, now taken a different approach. I still have FAS and may always have it. Has it changed my life? In many ways, 'yedda it has!' However, now I challenge myself to try and do some of the things I used to be able to do in my life pre FAS. I acknowledge I have FAS but don't accept that I have, and to me there's a world of difference! If I accept I have it, and then I give up, I acknowledge I have it. It means that I can still do things to improve and enhance my life. In the last twelve months, I have now returned to full time employment, started out 12 months ago doing 15 hours a week and getting back to full time 8 months later; working in direct contact with people, talking on phone or face to face with customers at same time as having to use computer. No, I don't have as much multi-tasking skills as I had pre FAS, however never in my wildest dreams two years ago would I have thought that I could return to work, never mind talking with people in a busy environment, despite having a speech impediment and a condition that makes speech in noise environment incredible difficult if not impossible, using computer, writing emails, etc. etc. could have been possible.

I have also recently become engaged to a man who I have met in the last 12 months, since having FAS. Our first date was a bit like a TV interview as he was so interested in FAS, how it affected me etc. He had loads of questions, however amazingly, we then went onto a second date, and the rest, as they say, is history. I think he would as indeed some friends I have made since FAS find it equally as strange and weird as my family and friends did when I developed FAS, if the impacts, effects and everything associate with it, did go. One of my friends who I have made since FAS, calls it the "Kaylish" language.

I have undertaken many challenges during the last 12 months, some of those steps and challenges have been small and others big ones but as I accomplish each one, my confidence grows (lost that big time when FAS first happen).

I guess what I would say to anyone with FAS or someone who becomes a sufferer of it . . . its hell initially. You feel you lose so much of you that no one else except one of us, no matter how kind others can be, truly understands what you go through. However through the help of other sufferers, your family, your friends and now that the medical world is slowly, slowly, together with the advancement of understanding, that is now starting to take place with the general public, you can re-build some of your life. It may not be exact the same and it may never return, but you can learn to laugh again and most importantly within your own individual capabilities, live your life albeit with it, despite it. It is an amazing twist to a journey in life, puts you down an incredible path and on one that you never know what is going to happen. But you learn so much, some good, some not so good; knowing however one lesson you have learned– never underestimate the unexpected, because you have and do live it.

To the outside world – FAS is a classic case of 'Never Judge Book by its Cover' as what you see and interpret you hear, truly often isn't what you see or hear.

Maybe open your eyes to a different panorama rather than one that society generally only looks at – tower blocks. The vista, your understanding and interpretation of not just FAS, but many other situations in life too may change and for some positively as a result. Not everything is as it seems, not everything is black or white and the unexpected can happen to anyone at any time or stage in life!

Maybe that's what a book about FAS should be entitled . . . . . . Never Judge a Book by its Cover!

Kay Russell
January 2013

USA

Teshera Bowser offers us a glimpse of FAS through the unique lens of a very young lady. Her perspective is rather unique since it more typically strikes individuals at later points in their lives. We come to understand just how much solace a good friend can offer, and how much pain a bad friend can inflict. We come to understand how critical our social networks are in our youth and how they affect and colour our entire life view.

Dream turns into a nightmare

TESHERA BOWSER

My name is Teshera Bowser and I have Foreign Accent Syndrome. I am 21 years old and was born and raised in Washington State. I have what most people describe as a Cockney accent. It's somewhere between an Australian accent and a British accent. I wasn't always this way though. In 2012 I got three concussions within five months.

My first concussion happened in June. I was in Idaho cleaning my Aunt's garage when something spooked me and I jumped up and back and hit a shelf. I woke up on the ground. I was alone so I don't know how long I was out for. It could have been anywhere between seconds and hours. I had an awful headache, but I finished cleaning the garage and then went to lie down. I had pretty terrible headaches for a week, but I didn't complain. I was raised with four brothers and showing pain is a weakness so I have always been used to showing as little pain as possible. After a week I had headaches come and go. I started getting used to having headaches.

My second concussion (which might not have been a concussion) was in early September right when I started a semester at college. I was going to Brigham Young University-Idaho. One night I fell off my bed and hit my head on a desk. All I remember is seeing this white flash, and then blackness. It was around midnight, so I just got back into bed and went to sleep. The next morning I was stuck with this accent. I couldn't believe it! At first I was excited. I mean, who doesn't want a cool accent, right? Well the problem was I had this terrible headache. This time it lasted about two weeks before it subsided to smaller headaches. Now once again I just ignored the fact that this happened.

Well sometime later in the semester I met this guy and he asked me about my accent and I said that I really had no idea. One night I had an American accent and the next morning I didn't. He asked me if I had hit my head and I said yeah I did. He then proceeded to tell me about Foreign Accent Syndrome. My friend and I laughed. It doesn't sound very realistic. We thought he had made it up, but when we got back to our apartment we looked it up and sure enough it was real. It was really rare, so at first I was hesitant to think I had this syndrome. But I seemed to match so I finally accepted that I might have it.

For the rest of the semester I was constantly asked where I was from. I always replied that I got the accent from a hit to the head. And I have to say that most people believed me and were very nice and supportive. So it didn't bother me all that much. I was a little annoyed about being asked where I was from all the time, but otherwise I wasn't all that frustrated.

Then in November my friend invited me to go to Utah for Thanksgiving at her grandmother's house. Well the night before we left my friend was messing around and she accidentally kicked me in the face. My head was slammed against a wall behind me too. All I remember is being stunned and just coming back into focus. She kept apologizing and I said no big deal and we went to sleep. The next morning I woke up with this awful headache. I was given Motrin and then we drove back to Idaho. Well the next day my headache was even worse and I started feeling nauseous. So I took some ibuprofen. I did ok until the next day when the ibuprofen didn't work anymore and the headache was worse. I kept feeling light headed and blacking out all the time. My balance was off too. I took Excedrin, which also worked for a day. But again the next day the headache was worse.

I finally went to the doctor. I ended up getting a CAT scan and an MRI, but they didn't find anything, so the doctor gave me medicine for my headaches and nausea. The nausea pills didn't work and I finally ended up throwing up. The headache pills worked for a day and stopped, so I went back to the doctor and he gave me another prescription and this went on for a couple more days until he gave me narcotics. But it was same with the narcotics. They only worked for one day.

During all this time I had these weird mood swings where I would just get very emotional. It happened two to four times, but they stopped. The headaches were so intense that I passed out several times. Light and noises just spiked the pain. I finally had to leave school. My mum and younger brother drove all the way to Idaho to get me around December tenth. I went home to Washington and stopped seeing doctors, they didn't seem very helpful. I do remember this doctor asking about my accent and I told him about hitting my head and waking up with it and he just said that was interesting, so I assumed it wasn't a big deal.

After I got home, I stayed in bed until New Year's Eve. I decided to go to a party with one of my best friends Ariana. She was very supportive and believing of my accent. So we went to this party, but the flashing lights and the noise caused my headache to get really bad. Ariana kept getting really worried about me because my eyes kept glazing over and I wouldn't respond for several seconds. I went home and didn't go out for a couple weeks after that. I stopped throwing up by January. I still felt extremely nauseous at times, but I never threw up again.

I always had a constant headache. I just got used to it. At first the headache would turn intense at least once a day for an hour or so, but the intense headaches diminished to only once a week by April. And that is how it has been ever since. Ariana and Nicolle were two of my best friends that helped me get back into social outings. I grew up in Washington, so there were many people who knew me from school or church. A lot of people thought I was faking the accent or lying about it and it was really hard to deal with especially since I am a very honest person. Ariana, Nicolle, my mum and my brothers always backed me up.

Only a few people would call me a fake or liar to my face. The thing that was really hard was that I could tell that people didn't believe me. Another struggle was that even though people believed me they made fun of me constantly. They teased me about my accent and mocked it and they teased me about getting hit in the head so many times saying I was going to get hit again if I wasn't careful.

In mid-February, Ariana moved to Utah. I did ok at first, but slowly got more and more frustrated. Ariana always spoke up for me and told people they didn't deserve to talk to me if they treated me in mean ways. Nicolle always liked a good joke and joined the teasing. Coming from her, of course, made the teasing easier to bear, but it was still frustrating and annoying. Nicolle really has no idea how much she has helped me. With Ariana gone I really needed someone to be there for me and Nicolle has been. She is kind of the only thing keeping me sane at the moment.

I am asked all the time where I'm from and it starts to get really annoying and frustrating, especially since I don't have a genuine accent. It happened from a blow to the head. It doesn't make much sense to me. I was away at school when it happened, so when I came back from school everybody bombarded me with questions. I explained best I could.

My mom and brothers have been supportive from the beginning and that has made it a bit easier on me. Some of my friends didn't believe me in the beginning, but most have accepted it. Everybody says the accent is so cool and how I got is cool, but at the same time they seem to think I'm a fake and a liar. It's really hard for me to take because I am a very honest person.

A lot of times people ask me to hang out and it just seems like they do it because they want to show me off since I have an accent. I also now have headaches that won't go away and it makes it even harder to deal with everything. I have honestly never felt so alone in my entire life. Sometimes I feel like just shutting myself away in my room and never coming out again. I seriously have no idea how to describe to you how frustrating dealing with this really is. If I could have my American accent back I would take it in a flash! Nicolle won't let me lock myself away though, and I am grateful to her.

In May I started researching FAS. I knew there were others like me, but I wanted to know if I could communicate with them because they would understand what I was going through. And that is how I found a FAS support group on Facebook. I found out that there were several more people like me all with different sort of accents. They have all been very supportive and understanding and they give great advice. They check up on me constantly asking how my days are going and if I need anything. They all understand my frustration and tell me it is very normal in the beginning.

One of the first things I remember asking was if my accent would go away. The answer was that there is a chance it could fade away in one or two years, but that I shouldn't get my hopes up because most likely I will be stuck with it. Shortly after joining this group I also emailed Dr. Jack Ryalls, who has also been very helpful. Even though I am still dealing with a lot of frustration I know I will be ok. I will always have my family, best friends, FAS family and Dr. Ryalls to help me. The advice I have been given the most is to just have fun with it and that is just what I plan on doing.

Kenley Byrd is a teacher and scholar. It is interesting to observe how many of those willing to contribute are teachers. Perhaps teachers implicitly understand their important role in sharing their stories. Kenley is unique in that he was the only male willing to share his story. He shares with us his own observations from this perspective. As editors we feel compelled to share with our readers that, since sharing his story, Kenley has lost his beloved wife to a tragic automobile accident.

'I'm still me'

KENLEY BYRD

I

Some people can tell you where they were the day President Kennedy was assassinated, while others wax bittersweet about where they were the moment they heard of the attacks of September 11, 2011. I have the same type of memory regarding several moments in my life, but none of them compare to what happened to me on April 23, 2010 at 2:15 in the afternoon—the day I developed Foreign Accent Syndrome.

The day started like any other day since having a mini-stroke two months prior. I went to work and taught my classes as usual but that day I was fighting through a major headache all day long. I called my wife during my planning period to ask her to pray for me and to check in with her. We developed the check in after the stroke so she would know how I was making it during the school day after returning to work. I thought the call went fine, little did I know she later revealed to me that she could barely understand what I was saying.

The headache passed somewhere around 1:45, and I was able to continue to my last class. The class was nothing out of the ordinary; in fact, it was business as usual. We were in the middle of a class discussion. I was answering one student's question when I noticed a child talking to another student while I was trying to explain a concept. I made my way over to her desk and opened my mouth . . . what happened next changed my life forever. Instead of my deep South Mississippi drawl came out the following in what can best be described as British English:

"Yagonna keep talking that? I'll get out me phone and we'll call ya mum yeah?" My student's eyes grew large," Coach Byrd, why are you talking like that?"

"Like what?"

"Like that," she said confused.

"I don't know ....." I had no idea what happened to me. My thoughts began to race. Did I have another stroke? Did I have a mental break down? Was I going crazy? All of these things began to flood my mind. I wrote a note to the teacher next door and asked her to cover my room while I went to our Assistant Principal's office. I checked my blood pressure, and it was fine, I called my neurologist and left a message. I prayed they would call me soon as I was lost and confused as to what was going on.

My Assistant Principal and I talked for a few moments; she asked if I thought it was stroke-related and if I needed to take off the next day. I decided to try to come back the next day, because I may have to take off multiple days depending on when the doctor told me to come in and what he wanted to do.

Football practice that afternoon was unusual to say the least. Here I was trying to instruct boys with a voice that wasn't mine, while trying to fight through the confusion and fear that gripped my heart. At the end of practice my head coach called off practice the next day. He told me what I already knew, I had to get up with a doctor because whatever was happening was not normal.

After I got home that evening my wife and I did not talk much. We knew something was not right, but we could not explain it. I searched the internet in silence trying to find something that even sounded similar. Somehow my mind returned to a video of a news story I had watched online some seven months before. In the video, a woman was interviewed who had developed an odd speech condition after a car accident; Foreign Accent Syndrome they called it. I looked up the story again and watched the story again. I was certain this may be what was going on, but I needed to make contact with my neurologist to make sure everything was fine and I faced no other possible problems physically. Later my wife would tell me, she initially thought I may have been faking until she prodded me in the night to put my Cpap mask, she said I replied " ok, ok if you will give me a moment I will put it back on . . . " in a perfect British accent.

The next day was a whirlwind of confusion as I tried to explain to my students what had happened to me and what we think happened while all the time trying to contact my neurologist, who I prayed would call me soon. Some students looked at me as though I was crazy, some looked shocked. One boy even refused to be in my class because he believed I was lying. I received the same looks from my coworkers as well. The most encouragement and support came from my Assistant Principal, who had emailed me a link to the same story that I had watched the night before. That was her way of saying, "It's going to be alright. We are here for you." The team of teachers I work with stood strong with me, even correcting students who thought it fun to laugh and snicker about the trial I now faced.

Finally I contacted my doctor's nurse. The response I received from her angered me and hurt at the same time.

"The doctor said to tell you that's odd. He has never heard of that before, he will put a note in your chart." Click . . . the phone call ended like that . . . a note in my chart?! Here I was sounding like a stranger in my own land, and my doctor does not want to see me. He does not wonder what may be causing it, he simply wanted to document it. At that moment I realized that my greatest advocate would not be a doctor, I would have to be my greatest educator, my greatest defender, and my own advocate.

I called a few neurologists in our local area and finding one which proved to be a chore. Waiting lists, referrals, and pre-authorization all made finding a doctor difficult. I would not go to an emergency room. I was certain that I would have a psych evaluation done instead of a neurological consult and my mind was fine, but my vocal cords, lips, and tongue was not. Something was amiss, and though I had my suspicions I could not say for certain that I had Foreign Accent Syndrome or not, nor could I say what I would do or could do even if I had an official diagnosis. A coworker gave me the name of a neurologist in Hattiesburg, Mississippi. I called and received an appointment for Monday. Finally I would be able to make sure that I was ok and see what my options would be.

2

I took a disc with me speaking on it to the neurologist's office. I was scared at not knowing exactly what was happening. I spoke with the doctor and he listened to the disc in his personal office. When he walked in he said,

"Foreign Accent Syndrome huh? Yep, you've got it. To be honest, you have a 1% chance of your old voice returning from what little we know about the condition. Foreign Accent Syndrome itself isn't life threatening so doctors really haven't done much research with because of the low number of people with it. I want to run tests to see if there are other issues physically, we need to address then we can go from there in regards to your speech."

Finally, a plan of action that made sense was put out there. I went through the tests only to find my health, aside from a small blood vessel malformation at the base of my brain, was very good. The MRI showed no visible tissue damage to my brain. My doctor explained that even though there was no tissue damage, obvious damage did occur, "Well something had to happen, you used to sound one way and now you sound like this. Something happened to the nerves in the speech area but we can't see that on scans. If you want to proceed with speech therapy we can help you find someone; if you choose to go without speech therapy you will be fine."

In other words I would be ok . . . I might sound like this for a few weeks or for the rest of my life, but otherwise I was healthy. I could live with that diagnosis. It beat being told I only had 3 weeks to live. I really didn't want to have speech therapy. I searched because I thought I had to do it. I felt like if I didn't people may say I was faking and wasn't trying to shake it. I talked with my family about it and everyone said the same thing. If I wanted to try the therapy they would support me, but if I did not they would support me as well.

My grandmother gave the advice that cemented my decision not to pursue speech therapy. "You can talk can't ya? We can understand you can't we? You can still work. You can move about ok. Don't be a fool and waste your time with it. Live life and enjoy yourself completely." With that said I purposed in myself to go forward and be as positive about my life as I can be.

It was then and there that I had an epiphany. Those who mattered did not care, and those who did care did not matter. It sounds harsh but this new mantra helped me remember that no matter what happens in life, those who care for me wouldn't care about the circumstance. They would be there for me, period.

3

Six months after learning to adjust to being the "odd man out" wherever I went I searched through Facebook on a whim to see if there may be anyone else who lives with FAS. I found a group of people who communicated through an open group. I asked to join, and was accepted into the group with open arms. Now I had community where I once walked alone. I could ask questions and see if others faced similar situations or ask advice regarding things I was going through as a result of feeling like a stranger in my native land.

For the most part, people I knew pre FAS have been awesome. There are a few people who did not believe me at first, and even were adamant that I couldn't be going through this; however, the majority of people have been great. My church family, coworkers, friends, and my family have been so supportive of me. My wife, son and parents have been the greatest source of strength for me in all of this. They have stood up for me, explained my condition to others, and defended me to people that really didn't understand what was going on.

Day to day life and interactions with people provide humor for me and frustrations for my family, especially my wife. I really do not mind answering questions to people that ask. I admit, it is odd and people are curious, especially in the Deep South where foreigners are an oddity. My wife does not find the same humor in the issue. She is very protective of me and sometimes I just tell her, "Its ok, I can do it." She doesn't want people to view me as a freak or someone in need of pity.

My son handles things the same way, and both of them know that if I am having a bad day, speech-wise or if I am really frustrated that day then if "the question" is asked then its up to them to handle the inquiries.

4

The greatest challenge for me, living with FAS has not been acclimating to my new voice. I admit, there are times I do miss my "southern twang;" after all, it was the voice I proposed to my wife with, said I do with, welcomed two children into this world and said goodbye to one with. It was part of who I was . . . a deep southern drawl associated with a good old boy football coach who lived in Buzzard Roost, Mississippi. The greatest challenge for me has been learning to live with the questions, the stares, and the disbelief that comes from such an odd life changing experience.

If it didn't happen to me I probably wouldn't know how to react to other people with FAS to be honest. It was one of those "out there" video pieces for the end of a program like Inside Edition, you know the ones. They tease you with the story all through the program to keep you watching then at the end they show you the piece and you are left going "Wow! That is some crazy stuff!" Now I tend to be more considerate when I hear the outrageous. After all, I am one of those stories.

I have not felt the need to put myself out there on television interviews. There is nothing wrong with those of us who have. I am grateful for them and encourage all that have done the pieces and will do them in the future. For me, my balance in this was being who I am, no matter how I sound and reach out to those who may feel as lost as I did at the beginning of this long and strange journey.

5

What constantly amazes me is the number of men who live with FAS. I know two personally and know of three more. For some reason, the majority of people I have been in contact with, and that I have heard about in other mediums, have mostly been female. I do not know why this is. Now not only am I an oddity in the realm of "normalcy," whatever that is, I am also an enigma in the scientific community as I am one of the few men who live with a condition that for some reason usually manifests itself in the female population.

I have never really given thought as to why this is. Perhaps I have worked so hard at trying to maintain a sense of normalcy for myself and my family that I have not taken time to think about this.

I found myself with the question, "Do I quit what I am doing and hide in a cave, or do I fight through this and find my way to live?" It did not take me long to realize that even though I sounded differently, I was the same person with the same responsibilities in life and I could not afford to sit back and let life pass me by. I still enjoy all of the things I used to. Oh sure, I have to speak slowly at times, and repeat myself with people that may not be used to my speech. I experience my "accent" shifting from 'British' to 'Scottish' when I am very tired or upset. I even have gotten used to explaining myself and telling people in my hometown that I am one of their own. Despite all of this I am still here, I am still enjoying life, and I'm still me.

Kenley Byrd
Lucedale, Mississippi

Gretchen Daniel again reminds us poignantly that FAS affects a whole family, not just a single person. We also understand what important support a loving family can offer to mitigate the devastating suffering that often accompanies FAS, as well as the enormous struggle to explain to the children what is happening. Gretchen's husband **Mike** offers his insights into his wife's condition from a family perspective. He offers us wise words of what a family should offer their suffering loved one.

My story of dealing with FAS

GRETCHEN DANIEL

My name is Gretchen Daniel. I am 45 years old. I have four children, one daughter and three sons. I also have two stepdaughters. I am married to a wonderful man named Mike Daniel; we live in Lexington Kentucky. This is my story of dealing with FAS (Foreign Accent Syndrome) . . . . It all started on September 21, 2010 when I suddenly passed out while driving on New Circle Road (a four-lane loop around Lexington). As I was driving, everything around me went completely silent then completely black. Fortunately, my 22 year old son Joshua was in the car and screamed "MOM" as loud as he could. Fortunately, I regained my bearings and was able to get the car pulled over before I wrecked. Joshua was very upset and scared. I remember telling him to relax and calmly drive us home, because I was not feeling well. I felt like I was having a heart attack in the car. I was in major denial that this could be happening to me.

It only took about 10 minutes to get home. I got out of the car and into the house where I started to feel very strange. My thoughts were not clear, my face began to feel tingly and my lips felt numb. I ran into the bathroom to look in the mirror. I was in total shock! I saw the left side of my mouth drooping, as if I was having a stroke. I tried to yell upstairs for Joshua, but I could not get any words out of my mouth. I thought, "This cannot be happening to me". I started crying and picked up the phone to dial 911. I could not stop crying or speak to the operator. The operator remained very calm and tried to calm me down. I was finally able to say, "Stroke", not well, but she was able to understand me. The next words I heard her say were comforting and they will stay with me forever. She said, "Honey, the angels are with you and watching over you. You're going to be OK. Just hang on the line with me. I have the Police, Fire and Rescue on the way. Don't be alarmed when they run in the house." I have not been able to tell her, "Thank You", but I believe she was my angel that day.

They ran numerous tests while I was in the ER, but nothing showed up. They decided to admit me in the hospital for further test and observation. I spent 8 days in the hospital. The doctors said they believed I was having "complicated migraines". I thought, "No way! This is crazy." I have had a headache ever since that day; it never goes away. After my release from the hospital, I was sent to a neurologist for a spinal tap. As with all the other tests they ran in the hospital and every test since, the spinal tap come back "normal".

Then one faithful day October my life was turned upside down. I was extremely frustrated while leaving my neurologist's because he said he didn't know what to do for me. I was in the elevator leaving his office building when I began shaking tremendously. I felt like I was having a seizure and was going to faint. I stopped, took some deep breathes, and began praying it would pass. By the time I got to my car I was shaking uncontrollably. I called my husband hoping he could talk to me until the episode passed. I was stuttering so bad I could not complete a sentence. Being the hardheaded person I am, I started the car and drove home while trying to talk to him, hoping the episode would end. The stuttering stayed with me for two weeks; then out of nowhere, came my very thick French accent.

During the two weeks I was stuttering, I went back to the neurologist who had no answers as to why I was speaking that way. Frustrated, I never went back. By the third week, I began having memory problems. I thought I was literally going crazy. My spine hurt, and I was having trouble walking. Sometimes when I would get out of bed, I would fall or stumble; running into walls from the dizziness.

I was at my wits end, when I decided to begin an internet search to find anyone who could help me. After days of searching, I found a speech specialist at the Cleveland Clinic in Ohio. I scheduled an appointment hoping that a specialist could explain my sudden speech change. We drove up the day before to ensure I was rested when I saw the doctor. We meet another couple at the hotel pool and of course, like all others I have met since my faithful day, they ask, "Where are you from? You have a very interesting accent."

I told them my story and decided to go to my room and take a nap. I woke up after a short 45 minute nap and felt WONDERFUL! It was amazing. I had no pain and my head felt clear. I went back to the pool and guess what? I had my normal voice back! My husband and the couple we had just met a hour ago were astounded, but as fate would have it, 15 minutes later, the pain and accent returned. We went to Cleveland Clinic the next morning. After in-depth discussion with the doctor he stated, "You have Foreign Accent Syndrome".

I was shocked. I didn't know what to say other than, "Thank You". Once we got back to the car, I realized Mike was very upset. He said, "You mean to tell me we drove 5 hours for him to make up a diagnosis like that! I could have made that diagnosis up". Of course, as soon as we got home, I started another internet search for Foreign Accent Syndrome. Sure enough, the doctor did know what he was talking about. I lay in bed for about a year. I was very scared! I would only get up to use the restroom. I would just cry because the headaches never went away. They would alternate between ramping up, and being a dull headache; no medicine would help.

I have made numerous trips to the ER due to the migraines and my mouth drooping. I was told by another doctor to always go to the ER when my mouth started to droop, because I wouldn't know if it was a real stroke. The pain has gotten worse; I would be in bed screaming for God to take me to Heaven. I finally found a neurologist who tried to help me with new medicines. As luck would have it, they didn't work either. She told me she wanted to try Botox. I have had 5 rounds of Botox. It has not stopped the headaches, but the Botox has calmed down the tightening in my shoulders and neck and the sensitivity to the scalp. Before the Botox, I could not move my hair without it hurting terribly.

I have what I call "dark periods" or moods that come over me. I have no control over them. I can get angry, mad or cry. I just go to my room and hope the pain will pass. I don't want to act like this, but it just happens. After 2 years of these fits and going into my room to isolate myself, I learned that when I get like this, I'm going to have a major migraine. It may be within an hour, or it may be three days, but a major migraine is coming. My husband says he can tell when a major migraine is coming, because Satan visits two days before the migraine visits. That hurt my feelings the first time he said it, but I soon realized he was right.

Since September of 2010, I have hid in the house. I do not want to go anywhere. I don't like to talk very much because that makes my headache worse. It's a struggle to speak. It's actually exhausting.

Stress makes everything a lot worse. I could have a seizure, or just get a worse headache. So I try to not do or get around anything stressful. I am not the same person I used to be. When I look in the mirror, I don't recognize the person I'm looking at. I know she's in this body somewhere. I hope she's not gone forever.

There are days where I don't want anyone to talk to me at all. I don't want to do anything but stay in my room. I have trouble sleeping; only getting 2–3 hours per night. I don't even like to be touched or hugged anymore. When there's a lot going on around me, I have to escape to my room to "decompress".

I have days where I can't speak very well. People just can't understand very many of my words. The pain in my spine and legs hurts so bad that I have to stop walking and just stand for a while. Going to bed only makes the pain worse. To sit in a chair is a challenge because I have trouble getting up.

My short-term memory is terrible! I literally do not remember hardly anything. It's scary, 2011 is just a huge blur. I go the ER when my headache is really bad and my face drooping, only for them to look at me and say, "Well you haven't had a stroke, and we don't know what to do for you." I am so very tired of that! I try to medicate myself when I feel a big one coming hoping I can get on top of the headache before it is too late.

When I try to have a conversation with someone, I lose track of what I am talking about and jump from one subject to another. Consequently, I really do not want to interact with new people. It is sad because before this, I used to love to talk to anyone. Now I fight to just get out any words.

I am surprised I am still married. All I can say is that he must truly love me. I have tried to tell him to let me go and go live his new life. I feel like I am a liability and not an asset any longer. I was a very independent person before this, and now I rely on him for so much. He has had a lot thrown on him in the past few years.

The doctor bills just keep coming in, and piling up. The bills have caused me so much stress only to be told by the doctors they don't know anything about what is going on with me.

Now I have noticed when the weather changes, BAM!, I get a migraine. I may have one to two good days a month. I don't drive anymore. I'm scared to, and it causes me to get stressed out. The last time I drove, I looked up and nothing looked familiar. I just kept telling myself you are ok and kept driving till my brain came back and I knew where I was. There were other times I tried to drive and I would forget where I was going. I would call my husband and ask him where I was going. My son told on me and said, "She made three wrong turns, but we finally got to where we were going." I just can't drive it; is too stressful.

I don't cook anymore. My husband said it is best not to cook when no one is home because I simple will forget I am cooking and walk off to do something else. He's afraid I will burn the house down. He calls me every day from work to check on me. I am having trouble walking and getting up from sitting down. I don't tell anyone, but I'm seriously afraid I will soon not be able to walk. I am still lost. I don't understand why all of this is happening.

My kids do not understand all of this either. Two of them are still living at home and I feel as though they babysit me, instead of me being a mother to them. If they have something important going on at school they have to constantly remind me. They will even remind me of my doctor appointments. I simply forget. It is as though I have lost sense of time.

I lose track of days and have very poor short-term memory. I was crying the other day and my husband asked, "What's wrong?" I said, "I am afraid I will wake up one day and not know my family."

One morning Devin, my 13 year old son, yelled and came running to my bedroom saying, "Hurry, hurry come watch TV. There's a person on there just like you." I said, "There is?" I went in there and, sure enough, there was a person being interviewed that sounded like me! I just started crying. I felt a little more at ease knowing I was not alone. For a long time I was in denial. I thought everything would go back to normal. I've dealt with FAS for two plus years now and the old me is not coming back.

I recently got the courage up and wanted to meet people like me. I wanted to see what they were going through. Now I feel I have found a whole new family. They understand what I am saying. They don't care if I don't put my words together right. I have spoken with a few of them on the phone. It is scary how we can understand each other. We understand what each other is really talking about. I cannot describe to you what I am going through some days; I can't believe it myself.

I got the courage up to Skype with Curls which was fun, but at the same time, hard for me to relate to her British accent. I have also spoke with Karen on several occasions and I more relate to her because she has the same accent and we both talk with our hands. I Skyped with Karen on 14th of August 2012 and I let her see me at my worst. She was able to see the swelling in my face and the drooping of the mouth. Karen said, "You no feel good do you?" "No" I answered. She said she could see it in my eyes. We didn't talk for long, because I knew I had a long day of travel the next day.

August 15, 2012, I am going to Diamond Headache Clinic. The seizures are coming more often and I can't get control of my headache pain. I am hoping they have some kind of answers to deal with the pain. I would love to have more good days than bad. Diamond Headache Clinic was able to diagnose me with Hemiplegic Migraines (stroke-like symptoms, including drooping face, weakness on the left side, stumbling around, dizziness, slow, and slurred speech). I stayed at their inpatient clinic for 2 weeks. During my stay they found three bulging disks in my neck. They performed a nerve block which has relieved some of the stiffness and pain in my neck.

It is now February 5, 2013 and I am doing a bit better. I still have daily headaches I now have medications that knock them down to where I can tolerate the pain. I go through periods where I sleep for hours on end, days at a time. Then something will change and I am up for days with only a few hours of sleep a night. I don't know what lies ahead for me, but I just have to take it one day at a time. At times, even an hour at a time. My short term memory is still bad.

The accent is here to stay; I have finally accepted that. This has been an emotional rollercoaster for me and my family. It's amazing how your life can change in a second. My FAS friends have helped me more than I could have ever imagined. I suggest that anyone who feels alone in dealing with an illness should do an online search for a support group that can help them in dealing with their illness. You do not have to be alone. Summon up the courage to reach out for help.

F.A.S – A Family's Perspective

MIKE DANIEL

My name is Mike Daniel and my wife, Gretchen Daniel, suffers from Foreign Accent Syndrome. By now, you may have read stories of individuals who are personally dealing with Foreign Accent Syndrome (FAS). I want to help you understand its effect on the rest of the family. While FAS may not be 'life-threatening' like other chronic illnesses, such as cancer; it is 'life-altering' for the affected individual and other family members.

My story begins on July 13, 1996. Even though Gretchen has only been suffering from FAS for about 2½ years, to clearly understand its effect on a family you have to understand how this disease changes the individual.

On July 13, 1996, I had my first date with the amazing woman I would later have the pleasure to call my wife. I found myself impressed with her strong willed, compulsive, spontaneous, and fun-loving attitude. We both worked for the same company, so we were together 24/7. Every day with Gretchen proved to be a new adventure. We were constantly on the go looking for our next adventure. We could be sitting at home one minute, and then the next minute in the car heading to Florida. There was never a dull moment with Gretchen, anything was possible. Everywhere we went we would meet new people. No one was a stranger to Gretchen and I, we would talk to everyone and anyone.

We were married on February 20, 1998 and have six amazing children. Each of us had two kids when we met, and we had two together. We've had a wonderful marriage full of all the highs and lows every marriage experiences. Regardless of how upset we may get at each other from time to time, we still stand strong.

We've all heard the saying, 'Your life can change in a second', but few people have ever experienced it. Our experience with FAS has proven this statement to be true. I'll never forget that fateful day in September 2010 when Gretchen called me at work crying heavily, unable to tell me what was wrong. All I could do was tell her to hold on, and that I'd be there as quickly as I could. I jumped in the car and raced home. It only took me about 15 minutes to get home, but as I turned the corner onto our street I could see an ambulance sitting in front of our house. My heart just sank. 'What in the world is going on?', I asked myself. As I slammed the car into park I saw them wheeling her towards the ambulance. The left side of her face was drooping and she couldn't talk. I was shocked!

'Holy cow, she's had a stroke!' was all I could think. I followed the ambulance to the hospital were Gretchen was admitted. While in the hospital Gretchen told me that she blacked out while driving on New Circle, a four-lane bypass around Lexington. Fortunately, our eldest son was with her and was able to get her to the side of the road and drive her home.

Eight days and many, many tests later, we were sent home without any answers to what happened that day to cause her to pass out. Gretchen has had a headache ever since that fateful day on New Circle. It's not a question, 'Do you have a headache?', rather it's 'How bad is your headache?' We have spent numerous days in doctors' offices, hospitals, and emergency rooms, and thousands of dollars seeking answers.

I found myself continually irritated with the inability of anyone to find answers. About once a month we would be in the emergency room with her face drooping and us wondering if she was having a stroke or not. Every time her face would droop, we would spend several agonizing minutes trying to decide if we should go to the ER or not. We knew if she was having a stroke, every minute would count. So every time we ended up making the decision to go to the ER, only to hear that they didn't know what to do. The doctors would fill her full of pain meds, stop her face from drooping and send her home. Over time we became pretty good at predicting the onset of the face-drooping episodes.

In my words, Satan would visit about two weeks prior to the face-drooping episodes. Gretchen would suddenly become extremely irritable for no reason, basically locking herself in her room, so she wouldn't take her anger out on others around her. Then, sure enough about two weeks later, she would have a 'drop you to your knees' headache, her face would begin to droop and off to the ER we'd go.

About two months into her ordeal with headaches, Gretchen began to stutter uncontrollably. A few months later her speech took on a heavy foreign accent. At times it sounds German, but at other times it sounds French. I think the accent is pretty cool, but Gretchen is embarrassed by it, and avoids speaking when she's around people she doesn't know.

We were very frustrated that none of the doctors in Lexington were able to find the root cause for the headaches or the sudden change in speech, but we knew they were related. We decided to take a different approach to finding the solution. Rather than go to a neurologist to find the source of the headache, we decided to go to a speech specialist to find the source of the change in speech. We found a speech specialist at the Cleveland Clinic in Ohio and scheduled an appointment. I remember my shock when the doctor said, 'You have Foreign Accent Syndrome.' My first thought was, 'What a quack! I could have made that up.' Once we got home, Gretchen began researching Foreign Accent Syndrome and found out that the doctor I had originally thought was a quack, was actually brilliant. All of Gretchen's symptoms fit the diagnosis of FAS.

In 2012 the episodes with the drooping face and intense headache became more frequent, happening two to three times per week. These episodes triggered further research and a visit to a migraine specialist. During our trip to Diamond Headache Clinic in Chicago, we finally learned that the drooping face is caused by a hemiplegic migraine, not a stroke.

Now fast forward to 2013. Remember the strong-willed, compulsive, spontaneous, fun-loving women that I married? My wife says she is not that person anymore. In many ways she's correct, but in my eyes, she's a hero for dealing with the daily pain. FAS and migraines have totally changed her. The person I married is still there in her heart and soul. Every time she has a good day I get the pleasure of enjoying her. She's very reluctant to go out in public and seldom gets behind the wheel of a car.

She's hesitant to drive because she's afraid she'll black out again and hurt someone or maybe get lost. Her short term memory is very bad and at times when we're driving she doesn't realize where we're at or where we're going. We used to drive 15–16 hours in a car without hesitation; now a 20–30 minute ride in the car is so stressful for her that she hates getting in the car. She's unable to go to the kids' school events. We used to have friends over at our house daily and would have groups of 15–20 people over every weekend. Now the people we see the most work at our local pharmacy.

The kids and I worry every day what kind of day Mom will have. Will she feel like spending time with us? Will I need to give her shots to help control the pain? Will we have to go to the ER? What exactly should we expect today to be like?

It rips my heart apart to see the woman I love struggle daily. I would do anything in the world to take her pain or to trade places with her. Imagine for a minute how you feel when you're in pain. Are you irritable, maybe a little cranky? Do you want to spend time with family and friends or do you just want to be left alone? Now imagine yourself with chronic pain EVERY day of your life! The people dealing with FAS are the strongest people I know.

I find myself increasingly impressed with Gretchen's ability to handle the headache pain she deals with daily. She has become a member of an online group of people dealing with FAS. This group has helped her to accept her condition and to know she's not alone in her battle.

My advice for husbands/wives and children of people dealing with FAS is love the person unconditionally for whom they've become. Support them as they struggle through their daily trials and tribulations of dealing with this disease. Celebrate and embrace the good days they have, and stand beside them and support them through the bad days. Pray daily for more good days than bad, remain hopeful that a cure will be found and find a support group.

God bless and good luck!

Julie Dieschbourg offers us her highly personal journey of recovery from a debilitating automobile accident. She emphasises how, far from being a simple change of accent, FAS was accompanied by a whole new personality. We come to understand why so many persons with FAS describe themselves being replaced by a whole different person. Julie relates how her deep faith allowed her to persevere and establish a company dedicated to serving those with brain damage.

My FAS journey

JULIE DIESCHBOURG

My story started in 2004 on March 26th. It was a beautiful day. Two weeks earlier I had just received a 2005 GMC light pickup truck from my husband. My husband was supposed to drive my brother to work that day. My husband was on the phone and I decided to drive my brother. I believe I wanted to show off my truck to my brother, so I took him to work that day. I dropped him off, and proceeded to drive home.

I was driving across the median to make a left hand turn. I heard a crunch of metal. I was thinking to myself boy that person was really in a bad crash, not realizing I was the one hit! It was over in a matter of seconds, my glasses were on the floor and suddenly a lady appeared asking if I was alright. I was right in the middle of oncoming traffic as it was the busiest time of afternoon. The lady stopped all traffic from hitting me further. (An Angel perhaps, because no one found her, or saw her except me).

The ambulance pulled up and tries to get me to go to hospital but all I can think is I need to ask my husband first. They talk me into going to hospital. They had seen the outside of the truck and did not know how I survived the crash. In the ambulance, they asked me if there is any pain? I tell them my head feels as if there was an elephant on top of it– the pressure was so intense!

My stomach feels pain. My husband met me at hospital I start to throw up and feel very nauseated. The police come and try to figure out what happened. An older man hit me dead on pushing my truck clear across the median, almost into a retention pond where I could have drowned. The curb of the pavement stopped my truck from crossing over into the pond. Tests were done to see if there was any damage, They did find my grey matter was off center in my brain but decided it was from sinus infections, which I never had. After a week they sent me home feeling I was stable to recover there. About two weeks after accident I was still dealing with nausea couldn't eat felt and like every muscle and bone was in agony. I had extreme Migraine headaches, and then something unusual began to happen. I could not talk at all. My speech completely left. I was using hand gestures or writing things that I needed. We went to the Pain Clinic where I was receiving hot pack treatments, Chiropractic adjustments for neck and back pain and told the doctor of my unusual symptoms.

He felt I needed neuropsychological testing. We went home and my husband prayed. He said God you did not give me a wife to be a vegetable, fix her please! After that prayer, I started acting strange. This in words of my husband, and my two boys. I took every picture of me down off the wall and said I do not know this woman.

I did not recognize any of these clothes in the closet, and by the way, who are you people? My brain had been completely wiped. I was acting like a child, a new-born with no memories, no bonding, emotionally unattached to anything. Then the strangest thing happened. I began to talk but it was not in a voice my husband or children recognized. I sounded foreign to them and I was not the wife, or mother they knew. I was a strange foreign lady, my personality was different. All of a sudden, I wanted bright florescent clothes, the brighter the better. Whereas before I dressed conservatively blacks and browns. I could not stand loud noises, or music of any kind. I couldn't understand people because they talked too fast. I couldn't dress myself, everything took so much effort. I was fatigued and tired all the time. I slept 16 hours a day and woke up, still tired.

I talked in Spanish, Irish, Scottish, and Russian accents. I could not say whole sentences, just one or two words. I thought I was insane and going crazy. My husband and kids did not know what to think. I knew I was different. I couldn't cook. I couldn't lift a knife to put into a peanut butter jar to make a sandwich! I knew something was wrong with me. So we went and got every test done from MRI's to Psychological testing, CAT scans, every brain test that the doctors could think of. Surprisingly every test came back normal. How could it be? I was not normal. The doctors had never heard of this condition before. They said it would probably go away on its own. I began to feel like I was of no value. After all, I couldn't do anything, but talk strangely. I began to get depressed what was my life but to sleep all the time. Before, I was very active in Church, Music was my thing, I loved sermons, but I didn't know this Christ they said I had a relationship with. He was like all the rest, someone I did not have memory of. I felt like I was in a deep dark box, no connection to anyone, I was truly alone.

I no longer wanted to even get out of bed to wash my hair or prepare for the day. No one could reach me and all I did was cry, cry, and cry. Cry a lot with no comfort coming from this strange family of people who said they loved me, no matter how weird I sounded. My Family rallied and said we are going to beat this thing no matter how long it takes. My family made a commitment to me to stand by me. My husband never left, although he could have. My Kids adjusted and began to call me their cool mom because no one had one like theirs.

Through a process of years today I feel like I am about 85% back. The last time I heard my accent was June 2011. I still have some cognitive issues, but nothing like I had. The connections have been made in my brain to rebond with my family. My husband and kids say I am a better mom and wife than I ever was. Was it difficult? Yes! Was it Easy? No! Did I struggle? Of course! But I made it over to the other side, and so can you.

Esther Crown of Beauty LLC
jdiesch@yahoo.com
Julie Dieschbourg

Joy 'Curls' Garcia, in her insightful perspective, assists the layperson to understand what it feels like to experience FAS. She has a remarkable ability to relay the complex existential experience in simple terms that anyone can grasp. Her remarkable faith allows her to persevere.

My new beginning

JOY 'CURLS' GARCIA

In September 2006 I was taken to the hospital by my husband because I was not speaking or moving and hardly could use my right leg. I hadn't told him as I tried to walk normally hugging walls when he came in from mowing the lawn. At the time we had no idea what was going on. My daughter was delivered almost 2 months earlier preemie and there was alot of stress going on as well as high blood pressure. Let's go back now . . . Just before all of this I had what I thought was a nervous breakdown . . . After I calmed down he went outside and I lay on the bed. After wards, while my husband was outside I called my Pastor's Wife and she prayed for me. I then called my mother and she talked to me. I had started stuttering. I had never done that in my life. I didn't know what was going on. After wards I thought I should eat as nursing made me weak and we needed to go to the hospital at some point. I made some toast with peanut butter put it in my mouth and froze. I sat there as if nothing was there and didn't eat it. I walked around and my leg on one side wasn't working well but i didn't want to worry my husband so i didn't say anything and pretended to be ok. Later he came inside and there he caught me and asked what was wrong with my leg? Uh oh, I was caught so we went to the hospital..

At the hospital they tested me said my blood pressure was high and left me there laying with no food or drink for hours. My head was throbbing and I felt sick. Eventually I was able to walk better and they moved me to the Neurology floor. They had me do the regular tests MRI and CT scan and so on . . . Everything came back negative but I got to see my daughter in the NICU. My stuttering they didn't think of much. Once the scans came back normal they released me and my baby thank God!!

I went to my follow up Nero appointment only to find out It was nerves . . . basically she told me I had not had a T.I.A which was believed by my Regular physician at the time and she told me the stuttering was nerves even though I had never had them ever!! I had read if you had them as a child they come back. So out the door. $40 co-pay and out the door feeling hurt and basically treated rude . . . That was the end of that . . . I had the stuttering for quite some time especially with thinking about numbers, reading, adding or games.

Over the years I had migraines where I used Excedrin Migraine 24 hour and it worked for me. I would take two and never noticed any more symptoms besides light and vomiting . . . I did notice however after the 2006 incident at time my brain would shut down where I would become un responsive and catatonic and in about 15 minutes I would be back.. I Figured my body could not take any more stress from my preemie and my husband who travels for work..

In last year of 2011, I was just finishing teaching the children at church. When I went out to the car and went to eat. Everything seemed fine and we went to eat. After lunch we were on our way home and I had my drink in my hand which had become frozen. I was holding it. My husband watched me and I could see his concern. We arrived home and I was frozen. My husband was trying to hurry to get me in the house and he tried. Both of my legs were not working! He tried dragging me to the couch where he called the ambulance. I Sat on the couch barely able to see and couldn't move. Eventually I told my husband as I fell over that I felt I was going to have a stroke. He said the team was on the way. They arrived in sat me up and took my sugar and it was ok. I was relieved. They asked me can I sit, lift my legs and smile and say something. At that moment I realized I could not smile. That was scary for me. Then the one man asked me to repeat a phrase every so often and it was bad. They took me in as a stroke patient. In the ambulance on the way I improved and the paramedic was stunned. I even started talking better and I said, "Hey look I can smile now."

This time I had a good neurologist which found out all of this had come from complex migraine which can mirror strokes and give me spells he calls them. So I am on medication for non-epileptic seizures and migraines, plus Botox and some natural vitamins. My neurologist is wonderful and has helped.

But in Jan 15 2012 I was given an even different surprise . . . FAS my new accent . . .

I had watched some cooking shows with Curtis Stone from Australia. My husband and I loved him catching shoppers on Netflix. Well I would cook and started sounding like him. One day I was real upset about something and phased out I guess and my voice changed. I was like that for overnight until at a party with friends for games. Then it left. It was weird but they understood and didn't say much.

Not to many days later I must of been having migraines as my Topamax wasn't up to speed yet and had a seizure . . . I woke up speaking with the accent again! Well I just went along with it. My husband thought it pass but it lasted for weeks and then months and the neurologist. He said it passes after a month or two. They never had cases worth keeping books on. But he said its migrainous for sure and not to worry. So we didn't worry. I embraced it as a new life adventure and a new fun way of being me.

I like having a new voice I don't miss the old one although family does sometimes. I do have old videos. But weeks after I started to see myself as who was I. I wasn't that silly girl who pretended to rap, or the silly girl who just talked funny and so on. Now I turned into some other person I pictured and wasn't me. I don't see me now. I see someone else because looking at videos my speech is different and my teeth show. I don't hear my mom when i speak either and probably won't.

When I found out I had an accent it was weird because you wondered if this voice was going to leave. Each day you weren't sure if you opened your mouth when you woke up what you would hear. At first my husband was worried and wanted it to go away and return to normal. He was worried something was wrong and didn't understand. Then his researched and found about FAS and was somewhat relived as long as I was OK with it. I always had peace about what was going on because I know God had a plan for my life and if that was this well then I am happy with it. My husband smiled so much when he heard me speak it was Joyous in our home. He never smiled so much. Most people that I spoke to from Church that knew me loved it. My Pastor couldn't help but laugh it was such a shock. Does laughing bother me? NO not at all. IN my mind my accent is bringing others Joy and that is what I love to do.

When I am out some people have made a comment about how they love my accent . . . I remember when I first had it. . We were at Applebee's, this waitress came up to get our drinks and says to me, "I really like your accent." I responded with excitement. "So do I!" she asks where it from and I said, " I don't know." and we laughed. At the time I didn't know so my husband and I explained it was complex migraines. Most people don't ask me but if they do they think I'm British and I tell them I'm American and it's actually from migraines. Whether they believe me or not it's up to them. My husband travels and he also talks to people about me.

With both of us people have heard about FAS and a lot about the effects of Migraines. There was a coworker of my husband's so interested at his work of my voice so I made him a voice email saying Hello and my husband said he almost fell off his chair.

Since I had no idea how I sounded, or which accent I had I had a chiropractor appointment and my doctor there is South African. He had roommates in College that were from different places. I knew he could help me out as I had no idea what I was speaking and knew it wasn't British. When I saw him he said to me, "Hello." I said, "Hello." he replied with surprise." What are you doing talking like me." as he had heard my old voice. I talked back and told him in the room later what happened and asked what i sounded like. He said, "Well you don't sound like me. Yours is Australian. ". Finally relieved and trusting him I had the name of my accent. On the way home my husband wondered if it was from Watching Curtis Stone the night before and if it was on my mind when I had these seizures. Of course I had known idea. But I did think I sounded like Dorothy from the Wiggles– an Australian Broadcast Kids show. We watched it when my son was little. We loved it. Those cooking shows ran out and we watched lots of others but accent still stuck. I saw other shows though. There was one with an Oceanaruim I watched with my daughter. I said, "Hey they sound like me . . . " then I saw it was an Australian show . . .

Having a different accent made me feel bolder I think. It hadn't changed my personality because I already was my own person and different so I kind of fit it–wearing big hats, colors that stand out. Ribbons, long boots, weird boots, and so on. I think having the accent I stand out more and I am noticed when before I would hide. In high school I hated for people to look at me. All worried about what I wore past 27 years I came into who I was and thought who cares I will wear what I like for me. When my mom and I talked she and I laughed because I already was like that personality except I'm not into being outside and the earth yeah . . .

After time went on though you start to wonder if you still have the accent maybe it gone or went away . . . I would video tape myself on the Ipad. I could tell even though my family thought it was lighter it was still there. Or I could just randomly say the alphabet and know. My vowels had severely changed. It was curious once I went on you tube to still see if I was Australian sounding. I found a YouTube site, perfect one, with a lady doing vowels and I was agreeing with her. And yeah that was me. So no change . . . After a bad migraine seizure the accent would increase, now I think it's pretty much stable. I sound the same all the time now at 10 months and I don't hear anything else in my ears. FAS doesn't bother me at all. I am not bothered by it. Just see it as a change in my life that makes it exciting. How many people get changes almost have way through life right? The migraines just need to be under control and my neurologist tries to do the best he can. My husband and I are not worried about finding why I sound this way. But when I die I want to have my brain dissected so we all can say. "I see here. This is it . . . "

I know some people struggle with their accent change but as you can see I just accepted it as Gods plan for me. He knows what he is doing and I wasn't going to let it beat me down. Do I get paralyzed sometimes? Yes, do I have migraines and other symptoms? Yes ... Do I even sometimes lose my ability to speak and can't talk and just speak syllables? Yes but I in his hands..That is what keeps me stable ... There are a lot of worse things that could be them just a change in my voice. There's things like that we can't change, but hey that FAS and God has a new plan for me, I am walking in it so I rejoice in what he Gave me. This is my story thanks for letting me share it with you.

For I know the plans I have for you," declares the Lord, "plans to prosper you and not to harm you, plans to give you hope and a future. (Jeremiah 29:11 NIV)

With FAS or accents sometimes you feel like you're an alien in your own town. You like to hear someone who sounds like you.. There can be an up day and a down day and that's why I am glad to have the FAS group my friend pointed me to. They are very comforting and they lend support. With this you need support and comfort from someone who understands. Just like with AA or some other group you're in. You cannot walk alone with this. So find others that have this. Only the ones who live with it can understand you pain and frustration. Find us on Facebook.

Have a joyful day!

Nancy Haller delineates poignantly just how FAS changed the arc of her life, and she includes insightful observations of healing strategies. We feel the strength of a powerful woman and gifted author, coping with the debilitating effects of brain damage with alacrity and wisdom. She offers us a vision of hope in overcoming life's most difficult challenges to educate and ease the suffering of her fellow human beings.

In their perception

NANCY HALLER, M.A.

Guild certified Feldenkrais practitioner, author of *I Don't Know How Long My Short Term Memory Is: Strategies for People with Brains*

We spend most of our lives speaking and listening to people in conversation. It is through our own life filters that our perceptions of people are formed, including the speaker's land of origin. Then there are the few who speak with Foreign Accent Syndrome and the listener's perception is jarred by the sound of the accent, cadence, and word placement or order. Most listeners politely respond with a nod, ask a clarifying question or stare blankly, wondering what to do. When a person with Foreign Accent Syndrome (FAS) speaks, it is the perception of the listener who is challenged while looking for a common ground in language. People with FAS may not even hear the differences in their own speech patterns.

My experience with Foreign Accent Syndrome has changed my life and the path I now follow.

I had a single incident brain trauma as opposed to those with multiple incidents of continued damage to the brain. In March of 2000 I had an elective Maxilliofacial surgery to adjust my class 3 malocclusion. My lower jaw was 14mm wider than my upper jaw. During surgery, 21 plates and screws were placed to hold my jaws together. It was during the surgery that something occurred. After the surgery, things were different with my speech, my memories, and my ability to process inconsistent patterns of balance or movement. My speech had a new cadence, word order and it sounded like I had emigrated from Eastern Europe, Asia, or was basically unintelligible. Most people thought that my speech pattern was a result of my jaws being wired shut and I was talking through the wires.

At the time of my surgery, in my professional life I was President of the Feldenkrais Educational Foundation, Vice President of the Feldenkrais Guild of North America, partnered with an equestrian trainer providing clinics for equestrians, teaching continuing education seminars to massage therapists, meeting a schedule of speaking engagements, flying over 75000 miles a year as a Northwest Airlines platinum elite traveler and running an active full time Feldenkrais practice. My personal life was filled being a single mom raising two gifted children and running the household.

My calendar was full and I began working 10 days post surgery by driving over 300 miles across the state of Washington to participate in a four day ferrier symposium. Life resumed the same rapid pace from prior to surgery and there was no time to consider the situation. There was no discussion, evaluation or assessment of the damage. It was as though nothing was wrong or different. I had a couple of follow up appointments with the surgeon who looked at the structural recovery of my jaws with satisfaction of a job well done. When he listened to my speech, he suggested I keep talking.

Life continued without knowing what was wrong and what to do about the changes. I didn't hear the differences in the speech. I was more likely to notice the difficulty finding the correct word and at times, any word. I did not answer the phone with the difficulty of being understood. Even this was not impossible. I had help to schedule appointments and used email. Everything kept moving forward. Accommodations were made and the pace of my schedule kept me moving forward. A simple statement about jaw surgery and all was accepted.

There were several incidents that led me to my "Pseudo Foreign Accent Syndrome" diagnosis. I was having dinner with a friend, part way through the meal she turned to me a said, "you sound like you learned to speak after being born deaf and your words are in the wrong order or you use the wrong word. This makes you sound illiterate and stupid." Within a couple of weeks I was working at an equestrian clinic in California when one of the people said, "You have so much to say, but your accent makes it difficult to understand you." The third incident

I was in a FGNA Board meeting and the woman across the table from me said, "You do know you have a brain injury don't you." To which I replied, "Everyone thinks that I am brain injured." She then responded, "Oh my God, You don't know."

And to be honest, I didn't. In my perception, I was functionally fine.

At about the same time I was preparing to teach a couple of new seminars, and with the recently discovered information, I sought further assessment. I made an appointment in 2002 with Deanna Britton, PhC. in the Speech Department of Harborview Hospital in Seattle, Washington. During the initial appointment intake, Dr. Britton did a bank of assessment tests. During the session she noted, "I deal with very difficult cases. She suggested that I was one of the few people to walk into this clinic from the street with the depth of speech issues I presented. Most people come from neurology. She sent me to my primary care doctor for referrals to neurology for brain scans. It was the suggestions that I might have a tumor or a lesion causing my speech patterns. It was at this time that I was diagnosed with the common description "Pseudo Foreign Accent Syndrome". This is the terminology of the Mayo Clinic tradition and close to the French neuropsychology tradition which calls FAS 'pseudo-accent' in recognition of the fact that it is not a true Foreign Accent. [Please refer to Chapter 2 for more information on history and terminology.]

My drive home from the clinic was an auto pilot experience. I was shocked and in total disbelief. I was just told that I might have a brain tumor that was causing my speech patterns. This was not what I expected to hear. In my perception, I thought I sounded like myself prior to the surgery. I couldn't hear the accent. I didn't know that my word order was incorrect. How could all this be going on and I was so deaf to it?

Hearing the words, "Brain Injury" shocked me. Brain tumor . . . that was not me. I did not look or feel like a brain injured person or match my image of a brain injured person.

I went home and searched the internet for any information about Pseudo Foreign Accent Syndrome. At that time, there were a couple of men and a handful of women that had been diagnosed and very little research or information to be found on the subject. Very few people in the world had this rare speech disorder with the first case being a woman from Norway shortly after WWII. It was a lonely and scary place to be. When I told people about FAS, there was total disbelief that there was such a diagnosis.

My second speech therapy session included more assessments to determine the intelligibility of my speech. At that time it was determined that I was approximately 52% intelligible in single word and 70% intelligible in my sentence structure. I asked what was normal for the public. It was not easy to hear that most people hear and speak with close to 99% intelligible speech. This information was overwhelming.

My third and final session ended with a referred to the University of Washington Speech Dept. to potentially work with the MA students for rehabilitation. I went for a day of evaluation and with the testing. The students wanted me to come to the department as a research subject several mornings a week and they would provide parking fees. At the end of the day, the director of the department suggested that I "talk like a Texan." With all the new information pouring in, the adjustment to becoming a research subject was too difficult .

I did not return.

Observing functional life patterns, recognizing the issues and then making strategies for change became the focus of my time. Being trained in changing movement patterns assisted in my discovery and actualization of building the repertoire. Understanding the need to build a *greenhouse* situation, planting ideas and slowly installing information for use required tenacity and patience. Developing safe, secure and supported challenges in posture and balance involved working outside of any box I knew.

My discoveries for healing

One of my great fortunes was being included in the equestrian world, both working with riders and horses. I would never say that I am an equestrian and have never owned a horse. It was a process of events that lead me to work within this world. Meeting Wendy Conner and Carl Longanecker opened doors to participation on and around horses. Working with balance while riding on the horse assisted in a subtle and challenging ways to repair and replace missing pathways using an organic neurological recovery of the sense and ability that balance provides. Being in the presence of animals with the capacity to feel and hear, always within the framework of the *"fight or flight response"* trains the instincts and responses to posture, balance and movement to a different level. Each stride of the horse is relative to the rider's posture and balance. If the desired goal is to have the horse turn left, the body of the rider must be in position to create the opening and the directional force to initiate the movement and when ready stop the action. Walking next to or riding upon the horse requires clear communication by the human in order for the horse to respond. It is when subtle differences create incongruent messages that the expectation does not meet the outcome.

Learning to communicate with FAS uses the same principles. When someone with FAS speaks, the desired sentence may be totally different than the actual spoken words. It may only be the word order within the sentence, a totally wrong word, or consonants improperly enunciated leaving the listener having difficulty understanding. The speaker may move on to the next idea without the input feedback of imperfection. Working with animals and observing their reactions to the human's actions, clarifies the necessity to work at the pace and pressure that allows the brain to react and respond. I believe there is a difference in the brain's ability to focus and respond when the posture and balance are clearer.

Observe the speed of your expected input and response. When is it easier? What is the environment that makes things easier? When is it more difficult? What are other factors that reduce the ability to speak in a clear and concise manner? At a time where clarity is at the highest and assessment is easy, observe, when does the sense of safety, security and support predominate? Find environments, timing and stress levels that allow working at the highest and most efficient level.

In 2010 I completed a MA in Somatic Movement Studies, at Lesley University in Cambridge, MA. Writing my thesis was an enormous challenge. The initial drafts were written as I spoke, incorrect word order, lack of connecting words, and concepts without sequence. Completing the final draft involved projecting my thesis onto the wall and sitting with an editor so that I was able to see the imperfections and make the necessary corrections. This process was huge in the formation of correcting my speech patterns. By completion of my degree program I experienced a huge relief and total brain exhaustion. Personally, the outcome to clearer speech patterns was worth all the time and effort.

Spending over a decade with Pseudo Foreign Accent Syndrome has provided an opportunity to assess, comprehend and articulate, or not. It may take years to heal brain injuries and some areas may never heal. Having a single incident occurrence has made my healing easier. In the process of writing my book I went for a follow up evaluation in 2012, a decade after the initial session with Deanna Britton. This session provided insight into the improvement I have made. My speech is now about 91% intelligible on a good day. The accent is still present and there are still difficulties in word order, consonant pronunciation that are exacerbated by stress and exhaustion.

It is always a point of awareness and a constant reminder to find that, over a decade later, people still ask where I am from, where is my accent from, and how long have I been in America? There are people who I have not seen in years who wonder why I still speak with the weird accent. My status as an American dates back to early ancestors who were in Jamestown and many more immigrated through Boston starting in 1635.

I am fortunate to have an isolated incident as the onset of my FAS. There are other people with FAS that have reoccurring brain trauma incidents potentially making the recovery process more difficult. For these people there are ongoing assessments, building patterns, damaging patterns, more assessments of the new areas of dysfunction and starting to the rebuild patterns again. Some people with FAS notice other differences including personality changes to fit the accent, memory loss and loss of speech for periods of time. Over the process of time, I have sounded as if I had learned to speak being deaf, outbursts of language similar to Tourette's syndrome, stuttering and unintelligible gibberish speech. People listening through their perception have placed me from somewhere in Germany, Eastern Europe, Asia, and most recently northeast coast of the United States.

Along this pathway in 2010, I requested the genetic "Methyl Tetra Hydrate Folic Reduction" (MTHFR) blood test. Having this genetic factor increases the propensity for heart problems, strokes, thrombosis, and women might be more likely to miscarry. The liver doesn't methylate into the renal system as designed, instead into the bloodstream to the brain and muscles.

It is difficult to find oneself in a medical situation where there are very few people who have a specific diagnosis. With so few cases to assess, FAS survivors have little help or direction to heal. Many report the medical community does not have answers to assist in the healing and recovery of this rare brain and speech dysfunction. Time, training and tenacity are required with no guarantee of any change. There have been doubts as to the validity of the accent and my sanity bringing forward this change in my speech patterns. My brain MRI's showed unremarkable damage, none that would relate to this issue and yet the speech had changed. With all the testing and evaluation, the process divulged very little information and few resources as an individual case.

Making contact with a group of people dealing with this rarity, many of the oddities were shared by the whole group at some level or another or during some period in the recovery. The sense of being alone has begun to reduce and the sharing of information makes the process more tolerable. It would be wonderful if the medical community was primed to heal all the ailing people. Not as simple as it appears or as one would hope.

Healing is a time consuming and a constant daily process of building awareness, speaking, listening and patience with the mistakes. Having a supportive group of people integrated into your work, home and personal life makes all the difference. Finding peace in the facts as they are reduces the stress and resting when exhausted gives the brain opportunities to make the best decisions possible. Speech takes longer for the brain to produce when there is damage to the areas in the brain related to speech, word order, word recognition and cadence. Finding a team of people with the necessary skills to assist may take time. Instant healing does not happen and most suffer for years without appropriate rehabilitation or self-sustaining education.

Working with the difference between the reality of the language spoken and the perception of those who listen leaves a ravine of experiences.

A few additional anecdotes

Conversation with people is usually interrupted with the infamous question, "Where are you from?" I reply, "Seattle". This is usually followed by a long silence and the look of incongruence from my statement to assumed reality spread across their face. Question two was, "No, where are you from originally?"

As a representative of the Feldenkrais organization, I was in Washington DC, speaking at the White House Commission on Complementary and Alternative Medicine. It is fortunate there is a written copy made of all the speeches given. During a break in the sessions, I met a woman from Asia who asked me about my accent. After explaining that I acquired the accent during a surgery, she asked if my doctor could do surgery on her and give her an American accent.

At a school parent – teacher conference with my younger daughter, I met the Spanish teacher. Upon introduction she immediately began speaking to me in

German. This type of circumstance is fairly common. I have been spoken to in many languages. I reply in my English and explain my situation.

There have been many instances where it was suggested that I tell everyone that I was from "somewhere". I have had people from many countries speak to me in their native language.

I was on a plane to Seattle, Washington from Nashville, Tennessee. I was talking with several people on the plane when they asked about my accent wanting to know if everyone in Seattle spoke like me. I said, "Yes."

Sitting at Thanksgiving dinner with my family, I noticed that there was a total lack of understanding of my input into the conversation. I looked across the table into blank stares and shock of those who have known me all my life.

During my travels to Europe and Asia, my accent was both a benefit and bewilderment. I just didn't have a box that fit the image. I didn't fit the average American image. I believe that I could stand in the United Nations and not one country would claim me as their citizen. The illusion of speaking a foreign language or having a true accent was shattered.

It is always a point of awareness and a constant reminder to find that, over a decade later, people still ask where I am from, where is my accent from, and how long have I been in America? There are people who I have not seen in years who wonder why I still speak with the weird accent. My status as an American dates back to early ancestors who were in Jamestown and many more immigrated into Boston starting in 1635.

I wondered what happened and why all of this occurred. It was years later when I heard of the Methylenetetrahydrofolatereductase (MTHFR) genetic test. I took the test and was found heterozygous for the A1298C factor. Research on this genetic factor is fairly new and findings include the propensity to heart, stroke, thrombosis, a wide variety of auto-immune and neurological diseases and miscarriages in women. There is new evidence of an association to many autoimmune diseases. Knowing that this factor carries increased difficulty with exposure to anesthesia, I consider this a portion of the outcome of FAS as a result of the anesthesia during my surgery. My suggestion to everyone is to take the simple blood test and have confirmation to continue researching this factor and the effects in their personal lives.

As a result of my life experiences with FAS I wrote the book, *I Don't Know How Long My Short Term Memory Is: Strategies for People with Brains.* Working for over a decade with my brain issues, I looked around to see that there is a common ground for everyone. We all have brain issues at some point in our lives. We have experienced brain injury, are brain tired, we find ourselves living in the brain fog or you know someone who is experiencing one of these categories. I would like everyone to know how to begin to assess the subtle changes and create strategies to make life more tolerable as the dark pathway unfolds in their lives. You are not alone, Join the club!

Kimberly Martens' compact account reminds us how a person with FAS struggles to handle all the myriad activities of daily life in the face of new challenges. She places her story within the larger compassionate context of how much worse it could be. Her resolve and calm in the face of adversity are inspiring.

Thoughts on foreign accent syndrome

KIMBERLY MARTENS

"Where are you from?" To me this question has become like that annoying mosquito you just can't swat. Prior to October 31, 2011, I was a typical thirty-seven year old woman. I was a multitasking mom who had just graduated from updating her education for a new career. My days consisted of juggling kids, home, work, new job searches, studying for certification exams, and partaking in social activities.

Since my event, my days consist of trying to remember basic tasks such as taking my meds, my kids' school open houses, doing puzzles, quizzes, and games to improve my memory, trying to figure out how I could do a job again since my multitasking skills are practically non-existent and avoiding most large social events.

I have been lucky enough to have family and friends who are just happy that I am here, and understand that I have good days and bad days. Sometimes I think they have accepted the accent more than I have. I have been told by most of them that they don't even remember what I sounded like before. Sometimes this makes me sad, like who I was before has just disappeared.

What people need to understand about foreign accent syndrome is that it is not just a change of voice that occurs. It's a change of life. To this day, I suffer depression, anger, confusion, and just an all-around sense of being lost most days. Don't get me wrong, I am very happy to be alive. To be able to talk, (even with an accent), to think, to move, to be mentally and physically a person in whole, is something I am grateful for. However this syndrome has taken a lot away from me too.

I avoid social gatherings except with those people that know me well and don't mention the accent. I have made a game out of going to areas where I don't know people. On the very rare occasions I can get in and out of someplace without anyone asking where I am from, I consider it an accomplishment. Other days when the question is asked, outside of taking all the time to explain it, I have come up with some fun ways to answer. Some of my replies include answering "I am from Illinois" which spawns "no where were you born?" to which I reply "Iowa." This gives me a mental chuckle, as I watch them try to figure out where in Iowa a person talks like an Eastern European.

Other responses included asking where they *think* I'm from, and just agreeing to whatever they guess so I can get the hell out of there if I'm in a hurry. My cousin (who by the way is from Boston and nobody asks him about his 'accent') will tell people I was 'mail ordered' from Russia, or that I had a brain transplant and the donor was foreign. One of my favourite responses comes from my friend Gus who told me when I'm asked to simply reply "my mother."

I have also had some personality changes to accompany my speech and memory issues. Some haven't been so bad. An example being that I used to be a 'chocoholic,' but now I really don't like the stuff. I can eat it, but it's not the same. I have figured however my butt would benefit from this change, so I'm not going to dwell on it. Most others are hard to describe in words. I have been told though that my outlook on life seems to have generally improved, despite the depression. Some of the things that used to stress me out, don't seem that important anymore. The time spent with my children is far more important to me.

Despite the problems I had immediately following the event, and despite the difficulties along the way, I am recovering and thankful that the outcome of this was better than it could have been. While I still struggle with the accent, I am at least still here for the struggle.

Perhaps **Karen Mullinix** has the strangest trajectory to FAS: from a spider bite. We are reminded just how vulnerable our precious brains may be to the smallest but ultimately most dangerous of creatures. We come away from her story with a much broader perspective and a sense of awe at the intricacies of the human mind and the fragility of human existence; but also with a sense of wonder at our place in the complexity of nature.

My story

KAREN BAILEY MULLINIX

I woke. It is early i could feel something biting my neck. I swipe it only to see it on my arm. Yuck! A spider! It looked hairy and brown in the sun light. But i could see a red mark on it. And it would be later when I remembered it. I hit it off, an jumped up. It was burning on my neck and i could feel my breathing hard. I was scared, and i told my son something was wrong . . . I thought the spider scared me to have heart trouble. But I begin to break out from head to toe with rash. I live very far out, so I have to have my niece take me to hospital. My nephew told me to take Benadryl. I toke them 3 within hour to help me breath. He said you're having a reaction from the spider. Little did i know, my life was changing that minute . . .

I went to hospital. Breathing was bad. I told them it was spider bite. I showed them my neck and rash. Nurses said to be quiet. They check my heart and lungs and said i think u have asthma . . . My niece and my son told her again please I was bitten by a spider. But i was sent home.

They say take some inhaler and Benadryl and I did. I began to lost my voice as day went on. By next day i could hardly speak. My head hurts and trouble breathing still. My doctor sent me to breathing doctor and throat doctor. My throat was almost closed and they did not know why. They sent me then to a brain doctor right away and he ran test on spine and blood, CT and MRI scans. The venom had set into my brain. He was at lost. Never had this happen before, so he talked to doctors all over and they did not know how to treat it. So i became a guinea pig. I was not upset, but my husband said I was scared by then, my memory was gone .i did not know where or who I was . I began seeing bits of my life in flashes.

i did not know myself anymore. And i could not do some small things like drive or know were i was. My husband said i would not come out of my room, most of time. And talking was gone. So i went to learn to talk again. At first i would have many days were I could not get sounds out. Then when i could, it was with Arabic sounds, my husband said. But i was blessed to be alive. I worked with my speech teacher Donna for almost year, maybe more. I was not able to write. I wrote backwards– left to right and spell like that also . . . To read, well I could if I placed in mirror. My doctor tried many medications and tests over the next few years, always saying I had foreign accent, and that I should be on CNN. Because of one spider, no more speech. He treated me for few years and I learned to speak again and use a hand held computer to help me speak when i could not . . . It helped so much over years, i stayed in my room most of time. Only to sit with my husband and mum, as she was sick. I began to draw when i could not speak. People as they set in my mine. I think I was trying to find one face that i could know or feel something. I had become lost in mine and locked in my room. Even if I could leave it I never left it on my own.

It became my safe place. Where I sit watching the world looking for a spot were i would fit in, or a place i could find me. Who I was before? Or a feeling i would feel belonged to me. I never become mad at the world or anything. But I found peace with the thought that I was somehow picked by God to help doctors and others so they would live. But still the loneliness was overtaking at times and still can come over me like a wave. If out I become scared and would become confused and speaking would become harder for me. Driving to town i would be lost and my husband would have to tell me over and over again. He said where we were. I remember sitting in an office people, coming in and out, and i felt like I was floating in a sea alone and i was scared. I was drowning form fear, loneliness and I could not breathe. I yell, but no one can hear me or understand me.

I would go to the mirror and look in and did not know who that was. It was like I was in someone else's body, and the memories I have, or I should say 'flashes of memory.' Well I have no feeling from them. One day sitting I began to cry. And I could not stop. It was like water was running form my eyes and I did not know why. And I would have water eyes many times still. I was told by my heart, I was mourning my lost self and like child learning over again. People say I wish I could start over. No you don't. I say some days I remember better, and some days, no I don't remember. One day over at first, then I can almost get through two days.

Now after 5 or 6 years and, I know it sounds crazy, but it is almost to me if I can get up and remember something. Long term comes in flashes something well set it off–a picture or a smell. I will remember her life before. And I now make my thoughts and dreams. I cannot live the life she had before. See, there are two of us– me before and me now. And she lived through a lot. But I must live now.

Some 'LOL' at me but i know it sounds crazy, but it is what it is. So I sit in my room learning to read and write again missing my love of words.i have before the one thing i do remember. And trying to make peace with who I have become and who I was . . . My doctor was moved, telling me to please go on CNN and tell them about my story. And I become more alone . . . It is hard for people I find to understand . . . And I start to see people LOL at me and some well, they mean well. But they think oh coo,l talk more . And I want to sit and have you talk. You say i was born in? But they don't believe you. And you feel more alone. The sea becomes larger as you go alone. No lifejacket to save you, no one to understand you. I went to a new doctor for my headaches. At UAB where I live close to. And I saw a new doctor. He came in and was so mean, told me I was crazy and to stop talking like that. It must be I want to be a baby. And he had no time for me. He never looked at my records– just sent me away. I was crushed. I would not go back to the brain doctor or think of it for long time. Then one night my husband asked me to turn on the tube and there was my lifesaver—Kay! And behind her was another show with a Dr. Ryalls on it. I was begging to go on the computer looking and found the Foreign Accent Syndrome group and Kay. It was like I was in my room and someone opened a window and I could breath. i could feel the soft breeze blowing in all round me. Like i was being saved. No more waters drowning in that sea alone, my window was open and i was found. No it was not the old me found but me who i am now. A feeling of what a child must feel when they are lost and their mother finds them safe. I know my window is open now and I will have some bad days still. But i have a name now and i know I'm not alone anymore. And I can swim and I can fly through that window and reach out to know there is someone there who, like me, has found themselves now. In some ways I found a family. And no matter what happens or how I feel I can come to that spot, and they well know what I fee. No one can take that away from us.

HERE I SIT LOST IN MY OWN WORLD.
LOCKED INSIDE A BRAIN WERE THERE IS NO DOORS.
WORDS ARE AT A LOSS STREAMING OUT WITH NO PATHS.
ONLY TO BECOME JUMBLED IN THEIR PLACE
LOST IN TRANSIT. IS MY MIND A MESS?

REACH INSIDE AND SEE MY SIDE.
EMPTY IS MY MIND.
MEMORIES ARE OF SOMEONE ELSE'S TIME
NOT REMEMBERING WHAT IS MINE.

I SIT LOST. LOST IN THIS PLACE
THEY SAY IS MINE
BUT NOTHING LASTS.

MIN BY MIN PASS BY MY MIND
CIRCLES AND CIRCLES OF DREAMS
OF ANOTHER'S LIFE IS WHAT I FIND.
IN ITS PLACE . . . .

I CALL OUT IN TIME TO REMEMBER WHAT IS WAS
BUT NOTHING . . . RUNNING IN IT'S PLACE IS SOMEONE ELSE'S
     DREAMS NOT MINE

Karen Bailey Mullinix (FAS from a black widow spider bite)

Alice Murphy highlights the fears involved with FAS. She brings the unique perspective of FAS as a result of what medical authorities have diagnosed as 'psychological'. Alice relays her experience in terms that vividly portray the experience, and with humour. She reminds us that FAS happens to a person, to a family, a delicate system; and she relays her insights on how to cope.

'The part of my brain that controlled a minor part was left in charge of everything and could not do the job thus everything shut down'

ALICE MURPHY

My experience

My Name is Alice Murphy. I grew up in a small town in Nebraska. I am one of a family of 6. I am the youngest child and fear has been an issue for me since I was young. Fear of the dark, or fear of being alone, or anything that fear can touch in one's life. So, psychological issues have been with me for many years. But the speech issues did not begin until 2 years ago when I suffered a complete mental break down. I spent 3 days in the hospital seeing a variety of doctors.

At that time, I displayed all the symptoms of a stroke as I could not speak, or when I did it was not understandable. I became paralyzed in my limbs at different moments, I had a headache, and my vision was gone as I could not open my eyes. My eyes would stare off and I could not move my head, but through the whole process I knew what was going on but could not get my point across. While in the hospital the doctors ran every test possible on me from blood work, to MRI's, to head scans, and spinals.

To me it was all as if the inside of my brain were a factory. One part controlled the legs, one the arms, one my sight, etc. Then one day all the workers went on strike and the part of my brain that controlled a minor part, say the cleaning, was left in charge of everything and could not do the job thus everything shut down.

Now I am still trying to piece everything back together again. When I was released from the hospital my speech pattern changed. I went to bed that Friday night and woke up to the sound of a Swedish person. (The doctors felt I have this accent because as a child my grandfather had a friend who would come to visit and he was from Sweden. I loved hearing him talk and would just sit and listen to him tell stories.)

I still have the accent after 2 years but it is not always present. When it does affect me I don't know it because what I hear is just me talking. I often know the accent is present by the look on the other person's face to whom I am talking. My friends prefer the accent as it is unique. When it is present everyone else still sounds normal, but then so do I in my head. It seems to come on when I am under stress, or meet strangers.

I am glad to be a person with a sense of humour as one needs it when faced with this kind of challenge. There is one thing that is hard and that is when someone asks where I am from, I tell them Nebraska. Then I tell them my family came over from Europe over 200 years ago. Some catch the joke others do not. Then I try to explain F.A.S. Every day is new and I never know what to expect. I still have bouts where I have trouble walking, writing and using my hands properly, where my eyes wish to remain closed, I have unusual headaches and my scalp is very sensitive to the touch. There are times when I feel as if my head must be bruised but there is nothing there. I have had numerous tests over the years run but when they come back there is nothing wrong.

Some people ask about the Swedish accent, I have no clue where it came from. I have always had a fascination for the way people from England, Ireland and Scotland talk. The doctor assumed how I speak when I have an accent came from the memories I have locked away in my brain (as they put it). But, please remember, we are in Wyoming and have little contact with any foreign accent except on television. The accent does come and go and sounds different to my friends; it is not always Swedish like.

I now at times feel it coming on, or have a clue when it is going to come on by the symptoms I feel in my body. I get muscle spasms all over, I become very tired, being able to sleep all night for a period of 8 to 10 hours and then take a nap during the day of 1 to 2 hours, my regular speech becomes odd with words missing and I have a hard time remembering what to say, my eyes seem to have trouble adjusting at times, my balance is off, my speech and motor skills become slowed down.

All this can happen in a period of 1/2 an hour or more making me lay down or not be able to walk, or function. I try to get rest every day as that seems to be the key for me, but I cannot make stress go away. It faces us all every day so I have some form of trouble every day. It is just that some days are slight; others are extreme and make me take rest and stay home. I am on disability at this point. I do have the support of my husband, friends and family. My husband usually knows when things are changing for me before I even do and does his best to help me stay on an even keel. I am 57 yrs. young and try to keep a positive outlook on it all. However it is hard when all problems that seem to plague me have usually tested out to be a figment of my mind, no matter what tests or scopes the doctors do to me!

I neglected to write earlier how I speak Spanish but for a period of 4 to 5 months I could not remember any Spanish. My family and I lived in Central America for a period during my teenage years and that is where I learned what I know. There was one evening about 4 months ago where I could not remember English only Spanish. This only lasted one evening though. Too I have trouble swallowing at times and I cannot sing when I am having trouble, something I never had trouble with before. I am not a professional singer I just like to sing. I am and have been treated for depression and have been on a number of different medications. When I was a child the doctors had me on tranquilizers which were not effective. I don't allow my problems to stop me from living my life but I am more limited than I used to be. Loud noises also really bother me thus I watch calm shows or listen to easy music. I do tire easy so I try to remind myself daily that my brain needs rest. If I overdo it I know I will be in bed or using a walker, or my cane, or needing help with mundane things.

My brain does not cope with stress thus when it faces stress, as I have been told, it converts the stress into physical symptoms. As such I feel ill and then I know I have to rest, go for a walk, journal my feelings, whatever it takes to relax myself. I do a lot of relaxation thinking and that centres me. Plus I must say that as one of Jehovah's Witnesses I have great faith in my God, Jehovah, and appreciate the help he gives me every day. Too I have a lot of support from my husband, and family, and friends. These things help me get through the difficult days.

I hope this information will be of help to someone else.

Cindy Neely-Langdon's story combines her daughter's perception of her mother's bewildering condition with her own personal observations. Deeply insightful of what it feels like to have FAS, Cindy places the reader squarely in her own shoes and body. We feel the beginnings of a nascent novel, so vivid is her portrayal. There is a kind of cinematic quality to her writing which surely echoes her career as a successful video production and graphic artist. We are reminded of the triumph of the human spirit despite the debilitation of the body.

My stroke. My recovery

CINDY J. NEELY-LANGDON

10–28–13

My Daughter Morgan's Journal ~ May 29, 2002
"This is Mom's first night out of the ICU. Her stroke has affected her right side the most. She can move her left arm pretty well so far, and seems to understand when you speak to her. She still isn't speaking; this is probably the most frustrating part. Not only for us, because we don't know what she needs, but for her because she doesn't have a lot of ways to show us what's wrong. You can see the frustration in her face. She may not know exactly what's going on, but she does know what she likes and dislikes! I noticed that our family is starting to get a little frustrated with each other as well. We've never been in a position where the one person who always takes care of things is not well. It's hard for me to look at her in this condition, especially when she was always the one that took care of me. For the next few days, there's not much we can do but see what kind of progress she makes. I think it will help to have family here always, so that she knows she's not alone."

The year was 2002; I was 51 years young, a single parent of three awesome kids, Dillon being the oldest at 25 and the twins, Beau and Morgan at 21. I was self-employed in graphic design, marketing and advertising, working out of my home, very active in tennis, among other sports, and loved getting together with friends. Enjoying life.

It all started Monday, May 20 when I was putting on my makeup at the mirror, sitting at my vanity when I noticed something wasn't quite right. My eye-hand coordination seemed to be off as I looked up to the larger mirror on the wall, back to the smaller makeup mirror and above the vanity, trying to see if I could shake it off. But it seemed no matter what I did the feeling of 'spaciness' would not go away.

I had been fighting a migraine headache and still was suffering with it when I woke up that morning. My accountant, Jean, had come over and was downstairs at the computer working. I started down the stairs to talk with her and explain how I had been feeling. But when I reached the bottom of the first flight, I stopped, then turned around and headed back to the landing, feeling as though I was going to pass out. I was afraid I would fall down the stairs if I continued. So I started back up the steps and when I reached the top, I collapsed. Jean called out and asked me if I was all right. I only managed to say, 'no.'

When she came upstairs, she found me lying on the floor in my bedroom doorway. She later told me that I was shaking, but never lost consciousness. I felt paralyzed for those few moments and didn't try to get up. After a few minutes, she helped me up and I sat on the bed.

She called my son, Dillon, who immediately left work and came over to check on me. I was sitting on the edge of the bed and I was thinking that I should take my one contact out. But as I tried I put my finger at my nose instead of my eye to remove the contact! He eventually decided to take me to the emergency room. Jean followed us to help explain what she had observed. In the ER, the doctor ordered a CT scan of my head to try figure out what caused the collapse and the disorientation. He tried several drugs for the migraine. But nothing worked, except giving me morphine to ease the pain, and he sent me home.

Four days later, Friday, May 24th, I was back in the ER. My two sons, Dillon and Beau, took me there again because I was having a tough time putting my thoughts together, still feeling 'spacy' as before and having trouble just making sense of pretty much anything. And I still had the migraine headache!

Beau, my younger son, was living with me at the time and we were having breakfast in the kitchen. While we were talking, I was having trouble coming up with very simple words like "orange" and "faucet." We were laughing about it initially, but combined with the headache and other symptoms, we decided to go back to the same hospital. This time the doctors did about the same things as before, less the CT scan. They gave me morphine and sent me home. For the next few days, I stayed in bed with pain medicine.

If I only knew what was about to come.

The following Monday, May 27th, which was Memorial Day, Beau came home after a soccer game and checked in on me. I still had the major headache and was in bed. He called the doctor, concerned that I wasn't getting any better, and was told to bring me into the ER at a different hospital.

By the time we got there, I could barely speak and was really tired. In the ER the doctor asked me my name and I just replied, "Okay" and never said my name. They decided to admit me for observation. By the time I had settled into my room, all I had was a one-word vocabulary: "Yes."

When my doctor came to observe me and was speaking to me, I knew he was talking to me, but I couldn't put everything together and didn't understand what he was asking me to do. I didn't feel stressed, I could hear him, but just couldn't make sense of it. I finally sat up on the edge of the bed, as instructed, as the doctor continued to talk. I was looking around the room at the people there when I noticed my son was motioning with his head to come over there or come here. I must have gotten the right idea because I got up and walked across the room and back to the bed slowly, not really knowing what I was exactly doing or why. I believe that my brain was still putting bits and pieces together at that time, or why would I have even got up and walked? Several weeks later, I was told by my family that the evening hospital staff was off for the Memorial Day holiday, so they were going to give me the tests they needed in the morning to try and understand what was going on with me.

In the hospital that night I slept soundly. Unfortunately everything changed dramatically by the morning. I had a severe stroke while sleeping and was in bad shape. My entire right side was paralyzed and I couldn't speak at all. Now, I can thank God that Beau came home and checked in on me the day before and, with the advice of the doctor, decided to a take me to the hospital for the third time!

That morning the nurses seemed to be racing around getting me ready to go for tests, that I didn't realize I needed. Although I still didn't totally understand what was happening to me, I felt the urgency of everything.

At one point, I was lying on a gurney in a darkened hallway waiting to be transported between tests. I was alert, somewhat anxious, unable to speak, unsure of what was going on . . . but amazingly calm. I had been left all alone in the hallway and waiting for what? I didn't know.

I was slightly worried about what was going on around me, but I remember trying to reassure myself that the doctors and nurses would surely take care of me. And hoping that there would be no pain. Now, I realize that the test I was given was an MRI, because they were careful to pad my ears so that I wouldn't hear any sound. Not being able to talk, ask questions or even think of what I would say and not realizing what was really happening to me, was a weird place to be in. Prior to the test I could see that they were watching me through windows at the other end of the room. Then I was moved inside the MRI machine. Even though I had worked in hospitals before, I had no personal experience with this type of test. This situation was a bit frightening.

The next thing I remember was being in a darkened room and seeing a lighted image of veins up high, like a slide show, which I now recognize as a projected image of the veins and arteries in my brain, a cerebral angiogram. They then rushed me into surgery where the neurosurgeon began the serious task of repairing a tear in my carotid artery that had constricted the blood flow to my brain down to 1% of the normal flow . . . medically defined as a Carotid Artery Dissection. In surgery, the surgeon had to skillfully place two stents into my artery, while also managing to remove a dangerous blood clot before it broke loose and went to my brain, which would have been fatal. Fortunately, surgery was successful. Yet I was still left with the effects of the stroke: right side paralysis and no voice. My family asked the doctor what he thought my prognosis would be and he told them that at about 3 months into the recovery process is where I would be . . . implying, for the rest of my life!

The recovery begins.

There was one more test after I got out of ICU and into a private room. It was the swallow test and it was a strange test! They took me to a darkened room, handed me a cup of what seemed like crushed Oreo® cookies in milk and told me to swallow it. After just having the stroke, my swallow reflexes were a little slow! I remember holding the mixture on my mouth while they are instructing me to "swallow, swallow." I sensed the frustration in their tone, but that wouldn't force my brain to react immediately or any faster. Finally I did get it down. I passed.

That meant I got to eat solid food, although my swallowing skills were minimal at first. I could only use my left hand to eat, due to the fact that my right side, arm and leg were now paralyzed. And, I could not speak.

I remember that my daughter, Morgan, would never leave my side and spent nights in my hospital room in a chair by my bed. I think she realized the severity of it all and what was to about come. But I didn't.

Within a couple of days I was transported to the rehabilitation hospital. There I would get the therapy that I needed: physical, occupational, speech therapy, and to work with the memory group. Little did I know that memory would be a bit of a struggle from then on. To this day I still use a recorder to help me remember what was said in conversation. I struggle to write notes down as reference and use my smartphone to record or type notes for recall in business and my daily life.

I thought I would be home in a couple of weeks. This was before I truly understood why I was there in the first place. Learning why I was there was quite overwhelming. Up until I was in the rehab hospital, I was in some kind of a euphoric state, like I was on vacation, no work and everyone taking care of me. Not even questioning it. Surreal!

It was summertime and one evening my kids wheeled me outside in front of the hospital to enjoy the fresh air. Why the question came to mind at that time, I don't know. Still not able to speak, I scribbled a note, barely legible, with my left hand on the pad that I kept by my side for times such as this. "What happened to me?" No one could have prepared me for the answer. That evening Dillon stood in front of my wheelchair and proceeded to explain to me what had happened: surgery, the stroke, how the surgeon described what was happening inside my head, the risks and all. A stroke? What? I was in a state of shock. I couldn't believe what I was hearing. I'm not sure of what specific thing put me in that state of shock … hearing the details of the events that occurred or how I had put my family though all of this without even realizing it! After my initial shock sank in, I immediately had them take me inside to my room and to bed. I was done for the night, alone, and trying to make sense of it all. Devastated, to say the least.

The next morning I continued my therapies. I felt comfortable in the gym with other people in similar situations struggling to get their lives back. I was in the rehab hospital for over three months and then commuted to outpatient therapy a few days a week for a couple of months, with the help of my family. The physical therapy process I went from just being able to stand, to walking with a walker, a cane, and then by myself. This was all accomplished with the help of my therapist encouraging me and giving me confidence along the way.

"Don't look down," they'd tell me as I walked the halls of the hospital and practiced going up and down stairs, outside over rocks, grass and up and down curbs. I also did water therapy while in rehab. They would wheel me to the pool and put me in a hydraulic chairlift to lower me down into the water. One therapist would float me on my back, while another therapist would do range-of-motion exercises by moving my arm around in circles. Later on we would walk around in the warm pool and do various other exercises.

One of the therapies that I went though was occupational therapy. This is another therapy for brain stimulation to reroute nerve connections or create new pathways to and from the brain for basic motor functions, reasoning abilities and to compensate for permanent loss of function. This would help improve my dexterity with my right arm, hand, and fingers for day-to-day tasks both in my personal and professional life. The therapists would play games with me, such as 'Hangman' on a chalkboard, to improve my concentration, and arm and hand movement. To improve the sense of touch I would play, with much effort, in a tabletop sandbox . . . picking up and moving objects around. There were clips on a rack that I would have to squeeze off and on. There was Thera-Putty® that I would play with to help regain a sense of touch, strength and feeling back in my fingers. And there were tedious exercises such as buttoning and unbuttoning a blouse, folding clothes, among other daily skills that I would need to be able to do again.

I became very conscious of weight bearing and remember the therapists having me do it on regular basis, everyday. It's my understanding that weight bearing can stimulate brain connections or create new pathways that control muscle movement. While standing, I would focus all of my weight on the right side of my body or my arm and right hand with fingers extended –my therapist would spread them individually for me when I couldn't in the beginning. I also used a portable functional electrical stimulation device (FES) that worked by attaching electrodes to my right arm and shoulder. It would send electrical impulses to the muscles and nerves, not only improving the muscle function but also helping ease the pain in my shoulder. In memory group, I remember answering questions by scribbling my answers with my left hand as I was trying to get my memory in focus when I couldn't speak.

And then there was computer lab. That was by far the most frustrating for me to have to relearn, since I used the computer everyday and it played such a large part in my business. I have been self-employed since 1992 and had ongoing projects at the time of my stroke. My work included various types of production in the advertising and marketing business, such as graphic design, video, websites, event coordination and production of which projects were in different stages. I definitely needed all of my faculties to proceed with them.

My oldest son, Dillon helped with the financial side and communications of the business to keep things going, such as getting power-of-attorney for writing checks on my behalf or making legal decisions and contacting clients who weren't aware of my situation. Some of who, after learning of my stroke, decided to wait for me to recover and finish their jobs. Beau, my other son, who had experience helping me with coordinating video production projects and expediting media to various suppliers, had taken on that responsibility and was extremely helpful in keeping that part of the business moving forward.

I specifically remember a graphic design project with printer's proofs that needed corrections made to them before it could move to the next stage. Again I wasn't able to speak or write with my right hand, which made it very difficult to get my point across for those corrections that I knew needed to be made, prior to the stroke. My kids didn't have any idea what I was trying to tell them, or show them what needed to be done. Because of my stroke I couldn't talk to explain, or even come up with any way to show them what needed to be done. It was like playing a game of charades, but no one got it! That was frustrating for me.

After that experience not getting anywhere, they called my ex-husband Tom who's also in the graphic design business to help. The typesetting term 'leading' was the mystery correction that I couldn't say or actually remember the word used, but I knew it needed to be corrected on that proof. So when Tom said that magic word, we all breathed a sigh of relief. It was a lot of work, but we got it! That was the beginning of how work was going to change for me, and getting back to my life as it was.

In my first meeting with the speech therapist, I couldn't make a sound. My daughter had to speak for me. It was about 2 -3 weeks before I was able to make any sound at all. At that time my speech therapist started me out with simple one-syllable words. Some letters were harder than others to say, such as 'R.' With more sessions I learned to form words, one syllable, two syllables, three syllables, then sentences and finally paragraphs. To this day it is sometimes hard to get the words out as fast as I can think them. And there's the short-term memory that messes with my conversation every now and then! It is still difficult for me to stay focused on the subject when, at any given moment, it can be lost somewhere in my brain. So, I have to be quick to make a note or scribble something that will hopefully jog my memory when the time comes to communicate that point. And then there is the brain overload . . . I hate when that happens! So much for multi-tasking!

It was when I was able to read paragraphs that one day my therapist said, "Today we're going to work on your accent." Of course, I didn't know why or even thought to ask. I was only trying to get back to my former self as soon as possible. So, she tried and tried to get me to say the words with a typical Midwestern accent. But I never did.

It was at one of my future visits that she told me about Foreign Accent Syndrome (FAS) and how she had read about this rare occurrence in a speech therapy newsletter. She then told me about the article and that she had contacted Dr. Gurd at the University of Oxford, in England, and asked her about my case. That is the only reason I would have ever known that I was speaking with an accent. Not only because I didn't hear the accent in my voice, but that I was just happy to be talking at all!

When I would go home for visits I would search for FAS on the Internet and found nothing but Dr. Gurd's documentation. So, I understood what was going on with the whole accent thing at that point and that it was a rare phenomenon that most people were not aware of. I would soon begin to hear the accent myself when in conversation. While my brain was making new pathways to connect my thoughts I was talking much slower and very often I would hesitate before speaking certain words. Quite frequently I would say, "How do you say . . . " which gave my brain time to think of the word or phrases to catch up with what I was trying to actually say in conversations! This made me sound even more like a foreigner.

There are more than a few funny stories to tell about this accent of mine! Like when my family would hear me say a word or a phrase that definitely isn't Kansan style. They'd repeat what I said with an accent as closely as they could to mine, and smile at me. That would make us all laugh . . . sometimes hysterically!

And then there is the proverbial, "Where are you from?" When I would tell them, "I'm from Lenexa, Kansas," they would ask, "No, I mean originally." At that point I knew they were fishing for a country other than the United States. Different people would hear different accents . . . French or Spanish or English or even Croatian. Primarily, I think I sounded more like a French speaking person, but some say like a French Canadian.

Which brings up another point. Within the first three years, when my accent was the strongest, my friends tried to help me to come up with a country that I could be from somewhere else in the world. That way when people would ask me "the question," I could tell them a country to quickly to appease them. At one time, I'd use the country Réunion, a French colony off the coast of Madagascar, east of Africa, far enough away from America that most people wouldn't have heard of it!

I tried using that angle a few times, until someone knew a person from there or sensed that I didn't actually know the language! Usually I just say France. But that too has been squelched, when they speak the language to me or ask me to say a few words! In my neighborhood some of my good friends and little kids call me 'Frenchy.' Over the years I've gotten used to that nickname, especially with the little kids, and it doesn't bother me so much . . . whatever works.

Something interesting and amusing that happened, occasionally, was when I would be talking to someone in a conversation and they would begin speaking with a spontaneous accent similar to mine! I always thought that was weird.

Another time out in public, a young man asked me where I was from because he noticed a bit of an accent. I tried the usual countries, but nothing seemed to work with this guy. I thought, "How was I going to avoid telling the whole story?" After much prodding I eventually admitted that my accent was called 'Foreign Accent Syndrome' and was the result of having a stroke. To my surprise, he told me he was student of linguistics at the University of Missouri at Kansas City and was extremely excited to hear and meet someone with this syndrome and better yet, to become face-to-face with it! To say the least, it was a refreshing experience to meet him . . . again validating my newly acquired accent. So it's not all bad, once in a while, to be a perceived foreigner! This would all become frustrating to deal with, but now I have finally come to accept it. It is just going to happen, anywhere, anytime and with anyone.

The first three to six months, and at different intervals throughout the course of my recovery, spurts of drastic change or improvement would show up. I would say in the first three years of my recovery, my accent and voice overall had changed dramatically from when I first started speaking. I did realize, over time, that I was improving the speed of my conversation as well as the diction; inflection and enunciation were also changing.

Another interesting part of my therapy was when my speech therapist had given me facial and tongue exercises to do daily. Some examples were: making American English long vowel sounds forcing my mouth to take the shape of each a–e–i–o–u; trying to touch my tongue to my nose and sticking it out as far as I possibly could; touching my tongue to the roof of my mouth and running it from back to front to back. I realize now how doing those exercises had helped strengthen the muscles that I used to form the words and to speak more clearly.

Along with working to get my voice back, I was also doing exercises to help with walking, balance and range of motion of my right arm. I was in the rehabilitation hospital as an inpatient and outpatient for about five months (June thru October 2002) relearning all of these things at the same time.

Now, in 2013, my recovery is extremely good. I can get around without a wheelchair, walker or cane. And, I don't drag my right foot any more. I remember they wrapped the toe of my right shoe with tape to keep it from sticking on the floor, so I could slide it while practicing walking, because I couldn't lift my foot when walking in the beginning. I can't run or play tennis or golf anymore as my right side is still weak and the muscles have not totally rejuvenated. I have found that I can swim a little and tread water, if I ever need it, so at least I might not drown!

I reluctantly started to play pool six months after the stroke and have managed have to become somewhat of a skilled player. Playing pool has proved to be good ongoing therapy, mentally as well as physically. And it has provided me a way of monitoring my recovery by my game improvement. Teammates have watched my progress and helped me through many stages, of not having the strength break the rack of balls, to learning new strategies of the game and, in one session winning MVP–– Most Valuable Player!

Having the MVP award doesn't make my pool skills any better. I still can't break the balls as well as I used to prior to the stroke. As I started relearning to play in the winter of 2002, I had to learn new ways of playing the game. Because I lacked control or finesse, due to spasticity of my right hand and arm, instead of a smooth follow-through I would jerk like a rubber band. I was dealing with the loss of strength and control of my right hand and arm, and the mental toughness that it would take to play with more skilled players. Pool has been a good measure of my progress and I have improved. It has been my new sport of choice, which has helped get me through the past 11 years of my recovery.

To elaborate on the past 11 years, I would say that I haven't been able to live my life quite the same as in the past, because there are more things affected and inhibited by the stroke than what I've told you. If I were to give a more honest assessment, some other things would be: being more careful walking on slick surfaces in rain, snow, ice, etc.; not being able to hear with my right ear as well; dealing with balance issues where, at any given time, I may stumble or wobble as if I was drunk *(embarrassing!)*; not being able to ride my trail bike without fear of falling; participating in sports that I was used to play that involve any running– like tennis *(that I played for 35 years!)*, golf– because of the spasticity in my right side which inhibits my swing; and anything that takes more strength than I have due to the weakness of my right side overall.

And then there is my memory, which has been frustrating at times.

Another interesting part of my journey was when I saw Dr. Jack Ryalls from University of Florida on TV being interviewed with another woman with FAS (Foreign Accent Syndrome). I was totally surprised to hear someone with an accent from a stroke like mine. I then emailed the television show "Good Morning America" to find out how I could get in touch with these people. Long story short, I ended up being flown to New York City to be interviewed by Diane Sawyer on *Good Morning America* in January of 2003. I was excited with the anticipation of speaking to someone that was affected by the same thing as me and the possibly of talking with Dr. Ryalls. Beforehand, I had gotten nowhere in my research on the Internet and found nothing more than Dr. Jennifer Gurd's University of Oxford documentation on the subject of FAS.

I made contact with Dr. Ryalls and during one of our conversations we began to discuss the possibility of doing a documentary about FAS. I had been working on projects in video production in my business at the time and was in that mindset. We talked about various ways of getting all the people affected by FAS together in one location to more economically record each person and document their stories. A couple of concepts were roughed out, but to date we have not gotten much farther than that. With all of the new people that have come forward, it seems like more of an appropriate time to move ahead with it now.

Through Jack Ryalls I also got to speak with another person with FAS, from North Carolina, USA. He had been working with Jack on his quest to find answers to why or how FAS happens. He had a French sounding accent similar to mine.

Since then a few stories have been written about me and my accent or FAS. Steve Paul, a writer with the Kansas City Star, had written an article that was published in 2005. After that, a few people from Kansas City responded to Steve wanting to talk to me. This one lady whom I spoke with was from the Northeast area of Kansas City, Missouri and she had more of an Asian or Polynesian accent and was from the United States.

My accent seems to come and go nowadays. But I am still amazed that people hear an accent in my voice and still want to know where I'm from! And then they want to know the details of how my FAS came about. But every so often, after I give them a summarization, they still ask, "But originally where are you from?" Crazy!

Over the course of approximately six to eight years I would talk to stroke groups at the rehab hospital and various other places to tell my story of what I have experienced and how that I never gave up. Even as I was going through all of the different aspects of my recovery process ... such as barely standing, walking by myself, relearning to use my right arm and hand, getting my voice back, struggling to write and type, and using the computer mouse ... I never gave up hope that at some point in time I would get back to normalcy. By the way, I never got the use of my right hand back well enough to maneuver the mouse, so now I'm a lefty ... with a mouse.

It's kind of funny when thinking back to the beginning at the rehab hospital. I thought that I would get better and be home working within a couple of weeks. Boy, how wrong I was!

I didn't really understand that recovering from a stroke or brain injury would take so much time, with a tremendous amount of strength, strong will and hard work along the way to make it back to whom I was before, or close to it. In my recovery, learning ways of coping and managing daily struggles has been occasionally difficult in a world that knows little about what goes on in the mind and life of a stroke survivor. I feel that as a brain injury survivor dealing with the physical and mental challenges, the best thing that could come out of telling my story and publicizing Foreign Accent Syndrome would be the awareness and understanding that is still needed.

What does it mean to be a stroke survivor? Good question.

Judging from my own experience working with stroke groups and hearing other accounts of survivors, there is not always a simple explanation. We're all affected by our injuries in some way. Whether the cause was from a stroke, accident, surgery, anesthesia, whatever may be the case. Some of us come out of it with a so-called "complete recovery." Others are not so lucky.

I am grateful to have my life as it is, making an extraordinary recovery and now appreciating how far I've come. I am alive because of my truly wonderful family, my therapists and good friends who have supported me throughout my recovery.

Overcoming my stroke has taken perseverance, hope, inner drive, strength and confidence to challenge myself to make it to that next level, and the will to never give up as I strive to be the best that I can be. And I am grateful for Beau, for being there to take me to the hospital in the first place and giving me the chance to live . . . with this crazy accent!

Cindylou Vedin Romberg reminds us grippingly of the fragility of human existence, and how tenuous is the thread of our mortal coil. Readers come to understand the overwhelming power of medical authorities and the suffering they can exacerbate through misunderstanding. One again we are reminded of the Hippocratic Oath, and hopefully some medical personnel will re-examine this vow in light of CindyLou's story.

Kindred spirits

CINDYLOU VEDIN ROMBERG
Port Angeles, Washington

Summer of 1981

Went dancing with a friend, and having a great time. Time went by and the evening grew to a close. The moon was shining bright as we got into the car, leaving the parking lot, I had forgotten to buckle my seatbelt, and as we took a 75 degree corner at about 20 miles an hour, my door went open, and out I went! My boot had gotten stuck in the door jamb of the car, so I was dragged about 100 feet. The nightmare began shortly thereafter. I must say if it was not for my Faith in God, this whole story would have a very different outlook. I stood firmly with my feet planted on the word of God, saying 'I will never give you more than you can handle'.

As the story has been told back to me! I lay on the pavement face down, blood coming from my ears, I was unconscious. I only am able to bring into my memory only shadows and fragments of that night. I recall a tall shadow holding my hand, telling me to squeeze as hard as I needed. I remember an extremely loud noise, and my feet being cold. I remember going down a hallway as fast as possible, but everything else is a blur until I woke up in Harborview Medical Center 2 hours away from my home.

I woke up with a headache the size of Texas, thinking 'WOW whatever I did, I must have done it really bad!' I looked around and immediately knew I was not in our local hospital, yeah and I had to pee. Being hooked to monitors I thought 'well to the bathroom, I go, 'and right to the floor I went! My legs did not work in any fashion. Now I am thinking 'Holy Crap, what did I do?' Sitting on the floor, a nurse comes running in. I had obviously set off alarms and she is talking 90 miles a minute and I can't hear any volume from her lips. Meltdown and fear began at that moment. The beginning of many new chapters to come! I am saying 'OK Lord this seems pretty huge to me. I am relying on you to give me strength as we go along.' I don't know what the future holds but I know Lord you will never leave me or forsake me.

The next year was challenging, to say the least. I spent that time in a wheel chair, slowly going from my chair, to 2 crutches, to a cane and then using my legs again. My speech at this time didn't change at all, with the exception of instances of stuttering. I was recovering in some ways and not in others. The Headaches were incredulous! It felt like a vice grip screwing through my ear drum to my brain, there was no relief from that pain! I had no balance, could not take a shower alone. I would fall over, could not look up at air plane, the sky, clouds, nothing or over I would go. Getting out of bed at night was also not an option without a night light; this went on for 26 years.

2007 – August

A friend had been having many of the issues I was having; she suggested I go see a special Doctor who specializes in Atlas Orthogonal. At first, I was very leery of going, I had lived with this for this long, and who could change anything at this point. Well I was so wrong! After just I visit to The Rody Clinic in Puyallup Washington, I was amazed. I had no pain, no headaches, and no balance issues. 'Praise God, this is only through his planning.' I threw away my cane and the medicine I took for balance. For the first time in 26 years, I could look up and see the airplanes without falling over. I could shower alone, if I so chose. I could close my eyes without falling over. I felt like I had a new lease on life! After the Atlas had been adjusted with an air wave, my life was pain-free and I felt awesome! *'MY Faith held me together all this time, and now the blessing is so wonderful. Thank you Jesus!'*

Fast Forward to 2008

This was the year my life took another turn. I had been working in my garden for several days and my back had a dull ache to it. I decided to see my local Chiropractor; I had seen this wonderful doctor multiple times, and I trust him completely– then and now. I had an adjustment both in my back and in my neck. This was a Wednesday afternoon. Thursday evening my neck swelled up a bit, but nothing really notable as far as I was concerned, I had done nothing that I do not usually do. Friday evening February 16, 2008 at 9:00 p.m.; I was in my office up stairs and I look at the clock thinking I need to say goodnight to my daughter Sadrianna. I finished what I was working on, and headed down the stairs. I got to the third step down and say "I love you Pebbles", but my words didn't come out at all! It was all gibberish. So I try again, and still no intelligible English came out of my mouth. Pebbles said to me "Mum, are you alright?" I just looked at her and shook my head yes. Pebbles said to me "I think you should sit down and rest for a bit," thinking maybe this would help. One hour went by and still I could not speak a lick of English.

We waited two more hours and decided to head to the E.R. Pebbles had phoned my brother & wife, Tom & Carol Simons, to meet us there. So when we pulled in, they were waiting for us. The staff got us right into a room and tried to make us comfortable. The doctor's nurse asked "What seems to be the problem tonight?" My daughter said to her, "my mum can't talk. Well she can talk but it isn't English." I could write everything on a pad of paper, I just could not speak. It affected no other part of my body at all. Hours went by at the Hospital, my brother Tom holding my hand telling me everything is going to be fine, not to worry a bit. With his beautiful smile, trying to reassure me that although something was wrong, it was going to be right. He is there with me.

The doctor concluded that I have a migraine (remember there is almost no pain, the only pain was a small tiny throb at the right base of my skull), and that I need to go home and rest. If this still persists tomorrow, I can come back to E.R. Home I go. It is now around 3:30 a.m. Saturday February 17, 2008. 'Lord?' I asked, 'I know you are in control here, please give me strength to walk this walk successfully.'

Morning comes after a few hours, and I awake to find no change at all, no English is available for my speech. We head back to ER around 2:00 pm, and share with the Dr. the facts that have transpired up until now. He checks my vitals, my vision, my heart rate, and so on, nothing new, and concludes that I have had a stroke. No MRI, No CT Scan! I knew in my soul that this was not true, and I was sure I did not have a stroke. But he sent me home!

Monday February, 19, 2008, I go and see my doctor, Dan Addison. Dr. Addison checks me over, and at this time I have very broken English, with extreme accents from Russia, Germany, and Sweden. They would change from sentence to sentence. Dr. Addison sent me directly to Seattle's Virginia Mason Hospital, his words were, "don't go home, don't pass go, just go directly to Seattle!" This is a two hour drive away from the hospital, and now I am worried. Now I am scared that something is really wrong with me! We make a few phone calls to let the children know we will not be coming home, but instead we were going to Seattle.

Upon arrival at Virginia Mason Hospital, they were waiting for us. We were taken right in immediately, and put in a room. The questions began to flow from the Medical Staff, 'Where are you from?' 'No, where are you from?' 'No what country are you from?' Over and over and over again I would tell them I live in Port Angeles, Washington. That I was born in Crescent City, California, I have never been abroad, and "no, I didn't take foreign language in High School!" Then they asked, "Well, why are you here?" REEEEEEEEALLY, I am here because this accent is brand new. I never had it until 4 day ago. I had 13 doctors come into my room and have me touch my finger to their finger to my nose over and over and over again 18 times in all, (in fact we were charged $213 for each of those Doctors), asking me where I am from over and over and over and over again. The doctors ask me "have you ever traveled out of the United States?" I reply "NO!" Then they ask, "Have you attended college abroad" again "NO!" "Do you have family from other countries who have been staying with you?" again "NO!" The decision is made that I need an MRI and an MRA. The tests are done and they inform me that I have a "*collapsed blood vessel going to my brain,*" and I need a surgical procedure. Now I am afraid, they want to operate near my brain. They settle me into a room for the night; it is now around 11:00 pm. 'Heavenly Father I am so afraid right now, scared that there is something wrong inside my head that needs an operation and that terrifies me. Give me strength and wisdom for the future.'

Tuesday February 20, 2008

Today in the late afternoon the doctors want to do a procedure through the groin, they sedate you a bit so that you are sure to be very still; they also restrain me, head, arms, legs, and torso. I am a bit afraid of what they will find and what happens next. A small camera is inserted into the groin and it goes all the way up through to the brain, seems like forever I am laying there, but we get through it OK. When the procedure is completed, I am taken back to my room where now I have to lay still for 6 hour. I lay flat in my bed for about an hour, when a Doctor come and share with me what their findings were. Their statement to me was "*well we didn't find what we were looking for, there is no collapsed blood vessel at all, it must have been a faulty film and now you need to rest for the night*". 'Hallulejah Jesus, what a relief, thank you Lord!'

I sent my husband home since I know now that I have to just rest for the night. We have been up for over 2 day now and he needs a shower a change of clothes and a good night sleep. He gives me a kiss and leaves for the 2 21/2 hour ride home it is about 7:00pm in the evening. At 11:00 pm that evening a doctor come to tell me that I must leave the hospital the test show there is nothing wrong with me. *Yep, I said that right!*, they were kicking me out of the hospital in a strange city, no ID, no money, not to mention that I could barely speak any English in a clear notion. I was shocked, appalled, and horrified! Here I had just sent my husband Glenn home 2 -2 1/2 hours away, and I have no idea what to do! I had never been so disrespected in my whole life! I had great insurance, I knew the room was already paid for through to the next day, and yet I was kicked out, literally!

I phoned my mum to see if she could find Glenn yeah and tell him to come and pick me up. Nobody had answered at the home when I called. When mum reached Glenn he turned around and came right back to Seattle's Virginia Mason Hospital and found me sitting beside the elevator in a chair! What a nightmare this is! I can't quite believe the last week, trying to wrap my head around all of this is mind boggling!

For the next few weeks, my accent was wild, yeah changing from French, to Russian, to Swedish in the blink of an eye. I had no control over anything that came out of my mouth, yeah how frustrating it was. Many times during the day, my language would just turn to gibberish and I would have no English. At this time, Dr. Addison suggested I go to the Stroke Clinic. This was the one appointment I was not nervous about at all. The Stroke Clinic is also in Seattle, so another 2 1/2 hour drive. The doctor was amazing, and wonderful. He did a full neurological work up, and I was smashingly marvelous impressed on all counts. I passed his tests with flying colors, but I knew I didn't have a stroke. He said to me "Cindylou, you don't have to worry about a stroke, you didn't have one. 'Yeah, thank you Jesus,' but inside my heart I already knew this, but these words were still magic to my mind. I was so happy to see this doctor and when the exam was coming to an end, we sat down to chat about what was wrong. The doctor asked me if I had ever heard of *Foreign Accent Syndrome?* I had about 3 months back saw a gal on the Discovery Channel that after some kind of trauma came out with a British accent. I shared with him the knowledge I had, which was not much at the time. He said "Well my dear, this is what I believe you have." Glenn looked at me, and I at him, and then at the doctor, and I say "Thank you." Not because I have *Foreign Accent Syndrome,* but because he was so reassuring that there was, in fact, no stroke. He smiled at me and said "you know that there are only about 62 of you in the world, so this is rare."

I sat for a moment, taking this in and thought to myself this is not as rare as you think I am sure, but I kept it to myself. He shared that he could not really give me any statistics due to the fact there was not a large amount of research done on this particular topic. However *Professor Jack Ryalls* out of Florida has done some research on it. So many doctors around the world have never heard of this, he shared, and finished with "You are free to go." Wow, this is an eye opener, our local doctors didn't have a clue what was wrong with me, and they gave a diagnosis without knowing truly what was in fact wrong. I am so sure that this is a very common event in the lives of Foreign Accent Syndrome friends, around the world.

When we leave his office I feel so reassured within myself. We had made a decision early on, that as long as this was not cancer or a tumor we would deal with it fine. So onto the next chapter of my life *with Foreign Accent Syndrome.*

The reaction to Foreign Accent Syndrome is the kicker here. Remember you have grown up with the people in your community, your family, and your friends. But when all of a sudden you have a French or European accent, nobody wants to believe that it is real. You go to the grocery store and run into a girlfriend and she wants to know if I am studying for a play. You cannot go down to the Wal-Mart aisle without someone asking you where you are from. "My you have a lovely accent, where is it that you are from?," is such a common phrase. Whenever you are out in public be prepared for the questions, they will, and do come. It got to the point that we could not go out in public anywhere, without constant questions about my accent. We don't mind sharing, but sometimes it got to the point of not wanting to have to explain it over and over and over again, many times a day.

My ancestry is from Wales, so I chose on days when I just didn't feel like answering questions I would just say 'I'm from Wales.' When I was with my best friend Nancy, I would never have to explain she would know by the look on my face, and she would just take over, I loved that so much. People are not meaning to be unkind ever, they are just curious. Many have never ever heard of *Foreign Accent Syndrome.* As time went on, I became very comfortable explaining it over and over again to the hundreds and hundreds of people that happened to cross our paths, whether in our community or those we meet on a day trip, or vacation.

Friends whom you have known for many years, which you do not have contact with on a daily basis, or monthly basis, many hang up on you, or think they have the wrong number, or a new woman is answering the phone. My great niece Kayla phoned as she usually does, and I picked up the phone, saying 'Hello,' and the phone was silent, I again say 'Hello,' and she asks if Cindylou is there? I reply this is her, and complete silence on the other end of the phone. Then she says "well um, OK. Is Uncle Glenn there?" I say "yep, he is here" and she asks to speak with him. This was a very common occurrence happening in our home.

We race Harley-Davidsons so there is a group of friends that we only see during race season, so these friends are stunned that I have this new voice. The new voice really freaked people out. Talking on the phone seems to be more difficult for others to understand me. I had one guy phone and ask for me, and I reply "This is me." So he says "the Cindylou I know, sleeps with a guy named Glenn" and I say "Yep I do," and like the norm now, he asks to speak with Glenn.

Our Grandson Hayden Woods, always has his standard answer when I lose my English and says "Nana we don't speak that language." To this day, it is still his answer when I lose my English and revert to gibberish. I have no idea how long this will continue, but I am so fortunate I do not have many of the problematic behaviors that many of my *Foreign Accent Syndrome friends* have. Many suffer with constant migraines, lack of use of limbs, balance issues, severe memory loss, and terrible pain throughout their bodies. My heart breaks for them!

Late fall, of 2008 I was at work one day when a co-worker and I were talking about me FAS and she say would you mind if I share this with a friend of mine. I said "No, not at all. It is not a secret." Well her friend was a writer for the Seattle Times newspaper, and he came to see me and we chatted for quite a long while. He asked if he could write an article on *Foreign Accent Syndrome* and me, and I said sure. Little did I know it would hit the headlines of the Seattle Times on Monday morning. Little did I know that the media would grasp this in such a HUGE way? The very first phone call was from Good Morning America, I was **stunned**, to say the least. They wanted to come and do a live interview with me and my close friends, my ex-husband, and his wife Herb & Nancy Woods, who just happens to be my prayer partner and best friend.

Gosh the next year was crazy. 'Inside Edition' wanted to do an interview; multiple radio programs phoned and asked me to do live shows with them. I did, and it was so much fun. I did an episode of Mystery ER and it told my story, which was once again fabulous to get the word out there that *Foreign Accent Syndrome* is real! When this show aired, after consulting with multiple neurologists, their belief was that the cerebellum was weakened somehow and then with the chiropractor adjustment things within the brain changed enough to allow the accent. This was not the fault of the chiropractor, it could have happened if I had fallen and hit my head, due to the cerebellum being weakened.

Then one day the phone rang our daughter Sadrianna, (whom we call Pebbles) answered the phone, and say "MUM" it's for you. I asked her to take a message, and she replied "I think you better take this, it is Paramount calling." Wow, two days later my best friend Nancy and I were in a limo headed to SeaTac airport, heading to Los Angeles to do an interview on Oprah's new show "The Doctors". We were spoiled and pampered, having a day fit for a Queen. This was one more avenue to advertise that *"Foreign Accent Syndrome"* is really REAL!

After the interview with Good Morning America, I received a phone call from a girl in New Zealand, she was crying on the phone. I didn't get her name I wished I had, she told me that she had hit her head, I believe in a car wreck, and lost her New Zealand accent totally, and her doctors told her they thought it was a mental condition. She shared with me that she had seen an interview I had done and realized that she too had *Foreign Accent Syndrome*. She was so relieved she thought she was losing her mind and having a breakdown. Never realizing all the interviews I had done, would truly ever reach out and help someone, I was rather shocked. Being able to support another person was such a wonderful feeling.

Then I had the privilege of meeting "Nancy Haller" who also suffers for *FAS*. I invited my sister Signe Beadle to come to Silverdale Washington to meet my new friend Nancy Haller for lunch. It was amazing being with someone who not only talked like I do, but she understood so much and shared so much information with me. My first person to person contact with an FAS person was great. Nancy was extremely supportive, and helping me to understand many specifics of *Foreign Accent Syndrome*.

Our Waitress came over to take our order and say" you look familiar, have we met before" and I say no I don't think we have. With Nancy and I both speaking with severe accents, she asked the obvious question," where are you ladies from, I love your accents", before I could even speak, Nancy blurts out, "We have brain damage" the waitress looked at us, then Nancy say "We both have Foreign Accent Syndrome", the waitress looked at me and say "that is how I know you, I saw you on TV!" Nancy was so integral in my understanding what it meant to have Foreign Accent Syndrome, and how she has worked through many of her own issues, she has more strength over this thing which some might call a disability than one could ever imagine. Her struggles give me strength and hope for the future. Nancy has overcome so much. I find her strength endearing.

I feel like that has been a traveling chapter with experiences that continue to inform other people that Foreign Accent Syndrome is real. Glenn and I were on a charity motorcycle ride down the coastline with about 20 others, and we all stopped for the night to rest and have dinner. We all get seated and I picked up the menu and start to read it, when there is no English at all. Only 2 of these 20 knew about my *FAS,* and all of a sudden everybody knew. Everyone looked at me so strange and say "Where is she from?", Nancy took over for me, and explained to all there what was happening.

The odd thing was, I was speaking in Swedish. I know this only due to the fact that there was a gentleman there from his homeland Sweden, and he could understand me completely. I knew what I was saying, he knew what I was saying, but I could not understand him back. I always know what I am saying when the gibberish hits, but most others do not have a clue. I will say I have 2 friends Nancy Woods, and B White who do understand me quite a bit, and we can work through what I am trying to say, that always brings a smile to my face.

Over time, my accent continues to have a life of its own, still now in 2013, I continue to lose my English and speak in gibberish. Family and friends are now used to this strange voice that came out of nowhere some 5 years ago. There are times that I am still frustrated as there is not a time frame for how long that gibberish lasts. It has ranged from 5 minutes to two days. I could be in the middle of dinner with guests, giving a speech, at a charity fund raiser, and the gibberish has a mind of its own. Just this last year I have noticed a new awareness of the gibberish! Now before I begin to speak I am aware that the English is not going to come out correctly, I stop and try to restart, hoping it will correct itself, however that just isn't the case.

Peninsula Daily News is our local Newspaper and its Publisher John Brewer has taken a great interest in my story. John has been instrumental in covering my story from day one. About every year there is an article published along the way of my journey, which really did a HUGE difference in our community. Folks seemed more curious, yet John asked the questions that gave answers to many questions that the community would have. With Foreign Accent Syndrome awareness articles like the ones that John has published here in Port Angeles, Washington, it gives so much more understanding to FAS, and allows them grace that this truly is real, it is not a Mental Disorder, it is a real diagnosis that is out there around the world, just like diabetes, thyroid disease, Crohn's Disease etc. Foreign Accent Syndrome has its own set of issues that we all deal with. Personally I believe I am one of the fortunate ones that was spared many of the horrific issues that can and do come along with *Foreign Accent Syndrome.*

National Geographic contacted me about my *FAS* and what they believe could be at the root of an accent change. My understanding from them is every person if you go back generations; to see where your "POD" began is the core. Say your great, great, great, great grandparents were born in Wales, and through time the families break apart and move to different parts of the world, and raise their families in that language, that cultural it then gives you a place to go back to. As for me, the belief is that since my biological family originates from Wales, when the head injury happened something was changed within the brain, when the accent came, it is of assumption that it would be a rather European accent due to my family genetics.

My life still remains as normal as it can be. I have not allowed this to slow me down, instead it gives me more incentive to live each day to the fullest, and enjoy this beautiful life God gave me. I became a Pastor, and built a small chapel, and share my faith with those who are put in my path. My thanks to all of you on the website for being so supportive through the year we have been together. Thank you to Dr. Jack Ryalls and Dr. Nick Miller for wanting to share with the world, our stories of how we continue to live with Foreign Accent Syndrome.

Rose Shuff offers us a succinct story firmly set in the regional flavour of a unique area of the United States. It serves to emphasise that no story or human drama is without its particular stage. All of human experience comes with its history and culture, which are so important to understanding the broader story of FAS.

Foreign accent syndrome

ROSE SHUFF
Lafayette, Louisiana

My stroke was October 13, 1996 and I was living in New Iberia, Louisiana at the time. Once I was able to talk, I went through several foreign accents. First, I had Japanese, then Spanish, then a British accent. Visitors were always coming by to see what accent I had taken up next. When I started speech therapy again, my therapist asked me if I was from Louisiana because she thought I had a German accent. She had never heard of Foreign Language syndrome.

My speech pathologist at the Lafayette hospital, researched my condition once she heard me speak a couple times. She said approximately 1 out of every 2,000 people that have aphasia have "Foreign Language Syndrome."

It is possible that my life experiences before my stroke influenced the way Foreign Accent Syndrome affected my speech. I was raised on a small farm in northeast Louisiana. When I was little, we took trips every summer to Cajun country & I was fascinated by the Gulf, the marsh, the culture, and French language. I graduated with a B.S. in Agribusiness from the University of Louisiana at Monroe & flew south to Acadiana, which is where my dad grew up. I worked for the United States Department of Agriculture: Natural Resources Conservation Service, where I served land owners, farmers, and ranchers as their district conservationist.

My heritage is mainly French and German descent. My grandfather spoke German and married a French woman. My dad spoke nothing but French until he was 18. All throughout my life, I was exposed to a variety of other foreign languages including Japanese, British, and Spanish.

My other passion, besides conservation, is karate. In my freshman year, I joined the University of Louisiana Monroe Karate Club, spent 3 and half years earning my black belt, and began teaching there. When I moved to God's Cajun country, I was the assistant instructor in New Iberia & the Lafayette Karate Club until October of 1996.

Before my stroke, I had a drawl, a southern red-neck accent, and people thought I was from deep in the heart of Mississippi or Arkansas. After my stroke, my first words were in a Japanese accent. I think I had the Japanese accent first because of the karate commands and words we speak in traditional karate.

My British accent came second. My cousin, from Washington, and I would speak with a British accent from the second we saw each other in the airport. Then, we would talk British all the time we were together. My Uncle took consulting trips to Finland and he started my cousin and I with the accent.

When I was working in St. Mary's parish, the Louisiana State University Fisheries agent on my office floor greeted me in Spanish all the time. I was interested in learning Spanish because I was planning on going to El Salvador within a two year period. I was a member of a nonprofit organization called "Partners" through which Louisiana is partners with El Salvador. I was planning on going on to teaching different agronomic techniques and agricultural problem-solving. My mother also knew a few phrases too. She had Spanish class in elementary school and she was glad I was interested. I would sometimes quiz her about what I had learned.

I don't remember how long each accent lasted. If I had to guess, I had each accent for about 2 weeks. The German accent lasted the longest. When I began speech therapy again in another city, my therapist thought I was from Germany. She had never heard of the Foreign Accent Syndrome before then.

People's reactions to my accents were different. My family and friends thought it was so unusual, but they liked it. In the hospital, visitors were always coming by to see what accent I had taken up next. One of my sisters said, "Your accent sounds exotic." I was embarrassed when talking to strangers without my family or friends present. I depended on them to interpret for me. When I was alone, often times I was embarrassed due to my speech. People would not be patient enough when I was talking, so I would just give up.

I liked each one of my accents because of its uniqueness. There is no treatment that I know of for the syndrome. I would not have wanted the treatment anyway because the accents are what made my stroke recovery unique. The foreign accent syndrome in my situation lasted around a year and a half to two years. Every patient who has the foreign accent syndrome is different, just as every stroke is different. I requested a Cajun accent from my first speech therapist since my father's family was from South Louisiana. She said, "I can't promise that!" In my own opinion, I have no accent now, but people tell me that I do. They can't figure it out though. I have decided I have a half redneck, half Cajun accent– me.

Ellen Spencer relays a story with humour and joie de vivre, full of hope for overcoming the worst of human conditions. She gives us insight into the existential experience of FAS, what it feels like to be on the subjective side of the medical stethoscope. The patient has the high expectation to be 'cured', only to encounter the limitation of the mere mortality of the physician. Although she experiences severe disappointment, she has managed to turn herself into somewhat of a local radio celebrity.

This is not me!! (10 days)

ELLEN SPENCER

My regular voice is gone! Instead I have to hear these weird accents coming out of my mouth. STILL, I am extremely thankful to have any voice at all. Can you imagine? I have had friends call me on the phone, and then just about hang up as they say "I'm sorry, I have gotten the wrong number." I go into a quick "wait a minute! It is me, Ellen, don't hang up!" Then I must give them details that a stranger wouldn't know, to convince them it is ME!! It IS me!!

It has now been a week and a half since the first numbness showed up, and almost as long that I have been speaking with a foreign accent. I sometimes get a bit down about the situation. No doctor has an answer about what is going on – we just don't see any obvious signs of stroke or any tumor or anything on CT or MRI.

The speech therapist I saw on Wednesday was thinking maybe Bell's palsy, but some of the symptoms do not jive. I have just started finding something called "Foreign Accent Syndrome" mentioned on the web. So I will continue to research as I await my neurologist appointment on the 29th.

I praise God that He never gives us more than we can handle. I am being forced to (1) speak funny OR (2) shut-up. Those of you who know my passion for communication (talking with people and about the Gospel) know which option of those two that I am taking.

Here are some things running through my head a lot lately: "Be still – and KNOW – that I AM GOD!" –We are fearfully and wonderfully made; though' this is scary it IS fascinating! I must laugh because, if I take it too seriously, I will cry. How much faith do I really have? I choose to believe that God IS in control of even this.

What do you think about this? I REALLY want to know. I am seeking any advice, ideas or answers anyone might have.

I have been acquaintances with a couple of personalities from the big Indianapolis Radio station WIBC for a number of years. When my voice changed so suddenly, I thought of calling my girlfriend Terri. She thought it was so fascinating that she asked if I would mind doing an on radio interview with her and 'Big Joe' during the morning show. The next thing you know, they are asking me to return every Tuesday morning for a regular spot. This went on for several weeks until Michael Jackson's sudden death bumped me from the lineup.

The funny thing is, people from all over town were asking me when "Eastside Ellen" was going to be back on again. LOL.

Hello it's me (3 weeks after onset of FAS)

Tuesday was another interview time with WIBC 93.1 FM radio friends Terri Stacey and Big Joe Stayzniak. I'm in a regular spot on Tuesdays at 7:45 a.m. for now. Here is a brief outline.

In the previous weeks' time I saw a brand new doctor/neurologist who said "why are you here?" and who had never heard of Foreign Accent Syndrome before. Having never heard my unaccented voice, he didn't notice the significance of such a drastic voice change. I have been scheduled for an EEG test for the 12th.

We talked in the interview about how very many people hear me and ask "Where are you from?" and my standard answer is "Where do you THINK? We are taking a poll. I'd really like to know what you think." Most people guessed that I am Swedish, French, German, Dutch, Irish, from England or Australia, and even South Africa. I am particularly interested in obtaining guesses from world travelers or actors that work with different languages.

Then I gave Terri and Joe the real wonderful news: my singing voice IS my voice. In other words, after having talked for a while in my accent voice I am getting a bit depressed about this not being MY voice. However, God has given me a gift; He has left me a bit of comfort. When I cannot stand it anymore all I need to do is SING. I then gave a sample of my singing "You are my Sunshine" .... Terri noticed it right away. "Wait a minute Ellen!! That is YOUR singing voice!!" I replied "Yes, that IS my voice ... my real voice". So God has given me the ability to sing in my REAL voice. :)

The interviewers made some kind comments about my singing voice. "Maybe God wants you to sing more." They also commented on my positive attitude and said we'd talk again next week at the same time if it's okay. My answer? "Yah Shuuuure"

Let's Get Serious (4 weeks after onset of FAS)

We are fast approaching a month since I first had this strange accented voice coming out of me during normal speaking times. And yet, there has been very little "medical diagnostic" progress. Since being discharged from the hospital I have been to one appointment with a speech therapist, and another appointment with a new neurologist. Both of these professionals had never even heard of Foreign Accent Syndrome before. Likewise, both of these occasions had people believing that I was simply a foreigner speaking English with a foreign accent. "Where are you from?"

But it was when the new neurologist asked me, "so why are you here?" that I became the most frustrated. These new doctors, who had not known me before the affliction, do not truly grasp the severity of my problem. At least the new neurologist entertained my theory on the matter and took the material I had printed off about F.A.S. He almost seemed to dismiss it though in statements that were similar to "but you did not suffer severe head trauma," as a precursor to the malady. I pointed out that there was one case in particular where a woman had IDENTICAL symptoms in regard to right facial numbness and even down her right arm and hand prior to her diagnosis with F.A.S.

Upon leaving the neurologists office, he had provided me with some links to such organizations as N.I.H. (National Institute of Health) and also set me up for an E.E.G. to be conducted on Friday June 12th. Otherwise, I'm not coming back to see him until 4 to 6 more weeks.

In the meantime, I try to remain upbeat and humorous. However, it IS difficult as I struggle to say some words that don't go along with this heavy accent. Also I notice that the speech pattern and order (way in which words are put together: nouns, verbs, adverbs etc.) and unexpected inflections and stresses are placed in the words or sentences as I speak. If I think about catching all the "errors" I get a headache!! So, a lot of times I just allow myself to "sound funny".

I'm getting the feeling that many doctors are not getting seriously proactive about getting to the bottom of what is going on because they don't appreciate the profound difference it has made in my life. Many of the newer doctors and nurses were basically strangers to me before now and so do not know the "real me".

So, I made an appointment with our family doctor Dr. Patterson. The medical office manager noticed my accent right away. Nicole was also the first person I called when I first woke up with the numbness spreading down my right arm almost a month ago. She is the one who talked to Dr. Patterson and then told me that he wouldn't be able to see me in the office that day and would not be able to diagnose me over the phone so to "go to the Emergency room if you want to." It's a good thing I did. Although, that CT scan did not show a stroke, the ER dept.

did note some of the early symptoms and timeline right as it was happening to me. That was the Methodist Hospital ER on Tuesday, May 12th.

It was the delay of not going to be able to see anyone before Friday along with my new speech difficulties that prompted my Chronic Pain Group friends to assist me in getting to the Clarion West Hospital ER on Wednesday and then I was admitted for two days–final diagnosis after a second CT and an MRI, "slurred speech of unknown origin". I was dismissed with instructions to follow up with a new neurologist and outpatient speech therapist.

Back to the more recent past: last Friday Dr. Patterson talked with me and was shaking his head in disbelief as well as all of my friends. It is profound! This strong accent just isn't 'me'. Yet everyone says, "at least you have a charming accent. I rather like it. I wish I had such a lovely accent." I know they mean well, and it is something that I am grateful for, however, I want to know 'why' and for 'how long' and these kind of things.

In the meantime, I am scouring the internet and growing my research file of articles and names. I was looking for the names of fellow sufferers and the details of their stories, names of doctors, neurologists, and speech pathologists, specialists of all kinds and areas of expertise. Above all, I am looking for contact information. I very much believe that what is going on within my brain is a benefit for research into brain function, or malfunction as it may be.

I am fighting to endure the voice that isn't really me. To make it pronounce the words more correctly, or leave out all the 'ah's" that sneak in between words of a sentence. To shorten those incredibly strong and long "U"s that make so much of the sentence sound Swedish. This week I have managed to finally be able to say "yesterday" without flat out stopping between each and every syllable. I simply have to swallow back the "er" sound that wants to be so pronounced with stress. For you it may sound like "yes-sird-aey". You would not believe the effort it took me, a week to get this down, and I still sometimes get hung on it a bit. At this point I am not scheduled for any other speech therapy. I am making these corrections with the help of my very patient 19 year-old daughter and saintly husband.

So far my trying to contact others via email or linking to this website in an attempt to aggregate the information into one place, have failed to produce a connection to constructive help in regard to medical treatment. However, I have gotten more friendships and definitely been productive in increasing awareness of F.A.S. through interviews and articles that have resulted from my web presence. I do see that the once a week segment that I've been doing with WIBC 93.1 FM on Tuesday mornings at 7:45 a.m. ET have been impacting others.

Because of the radio program I met another case. Then because of my internet searching I made a few friends from across the ocean. It is in these connections and friendships with others who have Foreign Accent Syndrome that I get the most hope. I am not alone in this suffering. I have the gift of understanding and we all have the joy of friendships form all over the world. Even if doctors haven't got a reason or solutions for us, we have the very special friendship of sharing. It is like having a family that really does understand, love and support each other . . . no matter what. That is an answer to prayer! –if I must go through this. AND I ,nor any of my doctors, know "why" . . . then at least, I can marvel at the peculiarity of the situation . . . and laugh at the funny accent that is not my own . . . right along with them I will laugh and marvel. Our laughter together helps bridge the gaps of misunderstanding. There is fellowship in suffering, in facing the unknown with the faith and hope that comes from knowing that God is and always has been in control.

I believe that none of this time is wasted. However, I do want to get moving' here. It's time! Let's get serious about gleaning what information we can medically obtain from this event. Can there be some therapy to help ease the strain of trying to correct the speech so much of the time? Would we learn some valuable information from a functional MRI and PET scan? I am certain that there is something profound happening within my brain in different places, because my singing voice is MY voice, not the accented speaking one.

In any case . . . finally, this week . . . I am seeing a glimmer of hope that at least one, maybe two doctors are taking my problem seriously and are actually going to help "light a fire" of some kind of action to help me do something productive in regard to this thing.

Making Waves with an EEG (5weeks)

I recently underwent another medical test known as an electroencephalogram (EEG) which is a noninvasive test used to evaluate brain function or disorders. Electrodes were attached to my scalp with a special gel or paste. This made for a VERY BAD HAIR DAY! It took forever to get that goop out of my hair. These electrodes recorded my brain's electrical activity and transmitted impulses to an electro-encephalograph, which magnified them and recorded them as brain waves on moving strips of paper. I was asked to close my eyes and be still for most of the test, so it was a semi-rest period for me. However, it was hard to keep my eyes closed when I wanted to open them up to see what was going on. A strobe light was used for a portion of the test, and it created interesting colors or spinning patterns while my eyes were closed. Although most of the test was routine, something of great note to me happened.

The young lady who was administering my EEG interviewed me about what kind of problems I have been having. When she asked me the inevitable "Where are you from" question, I let her try to guess and then asked her if she'd heard of Foreign Accent Syndrome. No, she had not heard of it. I further confounded her when I showed her that I could sing with my "real" voice.

When the test was almost done, this young lady who had so painstakingly wired me up to all these electrodes all over my scalp did something unique. She asked me to go ahead and sing a verse of "You Are My Sunshine" (the song I had sung to her before the test began) AND THEN to just speak the same words to that verse. As I heard myself singing and then saying the words my emotions got the better of me. Just as I said "please don't take my sunshine away," I began to bawl like a baby!

I think part of the reason I was so emotional is that I really heard how drastic a difference there is between my real voice singing, and then the foreign accented saying of the exact same words. However, I believe the biggest reason I cried was because I realized something. This technician had really "heard" me. She noticed how much I believed that something could record the difference between the two modes and that I believed concretely that the singing and the speech are coming from two different places in my brain! I believe this may be the first time such a thing is recorded scientifically, in black and white, ink and paper, proven. Maybe history is being made.

This technician not only listened to what I had to say, but DID something about it. She recorded with the EEG the exact thing I had been talking about. When I asked the lady if this was a normal part of the test she answered, "No, I just decided to do that because of what you had told and shown me." History — history was made. Not only have I demonstrated via audio, or video, NOW they have EEG waves recorded of this interesting phenomenon.

I could hardly wait to see my neurologist on July 1st to get the results. There is surely something recorded on that tape of brain waves to help us understand exactly what is going on in the brain. Now, we are getting somewhere, "making waves," and it feels good!

Disappointment

I was very excited about the EEG test that I had a couple of weeks ago. The technician had wired me up to the machine to record brainwaves as I performed the requested tasks. However, the lady surprised me by having me sing "You are my Sunshine" followed immediately by speaking the words. I was excited to learn that she did this because of my demonstration before the testing began.

It was with great anticipation that I went to see Dr. J Scott, my neurologist for my follow up appointment on Wednesday. I could hardly wait to hear what the EEG scribbling would show. I bet that there would be irrefutable evidence that my speech area was located in a different part of the brain than that which I used to sing. And since I can sing in my "regular" voice, I thought that meant that I would be able to fully recover my normal, unaccented voice.

However, my excitement turned to disappointment when I didn't get such a report. "Your EEG is normal," came the report. Although that is good news in regard to connectivity of brainwaves and such, it didn't help shed light on what is actually going on with me.

When I put the doctor on the spot with, "Well, if I just came to you with these symptoms and I had never even mentioned Foreign Accent Syndrome, what would you do with me?"

Dr. Scott told me that there simply isn't an easy way to figure out what is going on with me. He said that in this local hospital network there simply aren't specialists who deal with speech and how one might suddenly be stricken with a foreign accent. The closest related doctors that he could think of deal more with dementia than speech. There are also doctors who handle speech problems as it relates to psychologically-based maladies, but I don't really fit into that category either.

The bottom line of our follow up appointment is that Dr. Scott was entertaining the idea that it might be Foreign Accent Syndrome, but we are unsure of where to go from here. What testing or studies should be done? Dr. J. Ryalls, of the University of Central Florida is an expert on Foreign Accent Syndrome. My neurologist asked me to have Dr. Ryalls email him with suggestions for tests and then he will consider those recommendations and schedule them accordingly if possible. For example a functional MRI has been known to show which areas of the brain are affected, but there may not be the proper imaging tools located around here.

It is looking more and more like I am going to be dependent on some sort of a School of Medicine to launch an investigation, or include me in a study of some kind, because there doesn't appear to be anyone around here like me. Truly, I am feeling very foreign now, not just in accent, but in the idea that people just don't know what to do with me or this problem.

There are very many people who say that I have a beautiful sounding accent. They all are intrigued by the very idea that I have this affliction. It truly is bizarre, however what to do about it? That is the question. All in all, I didn't get the report that I was hoping for.

That is why I continue to scour the internet for more information on what may explain this. I am amassing quite a lot of documentation, but not getting to the answers yet. There is so little known about such a rarity. Still, I press on . . . there are others who are looking for the same answers out there. Still there are others who don't know who to turn to for help. I at least know of some doctors who are investigating F.A.S. in the world. Although they have not personally seen me, I can continue to hope that their research will help us all understand what is happening and why as well as hopefully give us some kind of way to prevent it from happening in the future or at least making it more accurately medically identified and treated. In the meantime, I am happy to have a voice . . . . no matter what accent . . . . that I can use to help comfort those in distress, speak up for those who are mistreated and misunderstood, speak out against the cruel statements made by the ignorant, inform those who are willing to learn and always inquire, there is so much more to learn.

Bernadette West manages to bring us along on her incredible journey full of wrong turns and misdiagnosis. We feel that we always have the road in mind on the map, but never quite get there. Important in her story is the exacerbating factor of medications prescribed in an effort to ameliorate which only obscure and even exacerbate her condition. How deeply we are reminded that each of us is an individual and that our own individual chemistry reacts very differently to each and every medication. Unfortunately, as Bernadette so poignantly portrays, we end up involuntarily being the 'lab rats' and 'test tubes' of procedures that we thought were well past in medical trials. But West offers us useful signposts, with humour and resolve along her journey.

Living out dreams

MS. BERNADETTE WEST
Tucson, AZ

March 15, 2004. I will never forget that day. I woke up able to walk and talk, by noon, I needed help with balance, and my speech was difficult to get out. The short version is that I was experiencing my body in a state of Toxicity due to medications. What followed was an enfoldment that one could only think they would view in a Lifetime Movie! If movies were taken from real life, this would be a great one. The failure to launch was a fact-finding mission and report to headquarters (aka the doctors), resulted in my continued deterioration and lack of care for the under-lying conditions. Houston, we definitely have a problem here, a very complex problem. Missed diagnosis and mis-diagnosed!

I developed the following symptoms:

Pain from my neck to shoulder, right side
Loss of reflexes, right side
Insomnia
Serotonin syndrome
Possible Tardive Dyskinesia
Possible Neuroleptic Malignant Syndrome
Serve vomiting
Pressure and Pain in my head
Intermittent mute (referred to as a 'difficult patient', non-cooperative!)
Facial drooping and episodes of distortion
Involuntary movement of my arms
Sensation of a tight cap around my head
Audio and visual hallucinations (one of each) yep, look Ma, no drugs needed!
    Au natural! This is common with poisoning.
The ability to use my arms above my waist, walk and stand, hold objects, again,
    these were intermittent
Frequent falls

Tremors
Emotional sensitivity
Difficulty understanding concepts
Memory and Cognitive Issues
Visual signs misread

My speech changed, not just the sound, but as well the sentence structure. I was speaking perfect "pigeon English," along with what sounded like an accent. This perplexed the medical community. They thought this was a good act, a psychological / psychiatric manifestation. The second round of poisoning happens 5 to 6 weeks later, this time was near fatal. The next day, I find I have a "swing" to my right leg when I walked. Physical Therapy is called in to teach me how to climb steps using "my good leg" and "my weak leg." An exam before release showed no reflexes on my right side. (Elbow, knee) I am told that nothing happened to me, go home, and rest.

If this were an act, I would be on the Red Carpet thanking my fans for the many rewards, correction, awards, see what I mean! After many trips back to the ER with an attempt to get some relief, I was given to option of either a voluntary or a committed stay to a psychiatric hospital. I chose to go. What else was there to do? At one point, my family is told that I have multiple personalities that go with my accents! I knew that there was something wrong physically with me, however, doctors held the power. I was saying things like" My brain hurts" and "It hurts to think." It was a living nightmare for my family and me.

It did not help matters that the Toxicity was not put into my medical records. The redeeming feature is that my Medical Power of Attorney (who just so happened to be a doctor) and my daughter were told of the poisoning and the near fatal status. I was not conscious and therefore unable to sign for care, so my daughter signed the consent forms. The hospital claims to have no record of this consent. Were they trying to make me crazy, I wonder? The code of White, like the code of Blue, some do not tell the truth in matters where one may responsible for a patients condition. Testing done a few years later (Brain Map) confirms a pattern rarely seen outside the presence of a stroke, neurotoxicity, neoro-encephalitis, neurological function disconnect in the brain, an acquired brain injury.

After a year and a half, my voice and speech return to "The sound of Bernadette." During that time, it was gradual, slow, and unsteady return to my own voice. There would be days where I had FAS for the most part, days where part of the day I could hear my own voice. At one point, most of the day I had my own voice, rather, what I knew I sounded like, to me. The Social Security representative asked me how long I have been in the country. You should have seen the look on her face when I said I was born here, priceless!

Moving forward to 2006, two years later, after six months of feeling better, I get to have this wonderful experience again. I forgot that I had taken a fall and did not put it together with the change of my speech. A few days later, while in a cab, my speech returns again to the sound of a mystery woman. I do not know this sound as my own voice. Here we go, round two. Many of the previous symptoms return. I am acutely aware that my brain is not working correctly. I knew this the first time around, but to no avail. This time, I push for answers.

Symptoms and side attractions :(Yes, I do mean to say it that way!)

Vision changes
Speech changes
Balance
Dizziness
Memory issues
Visual Stimulation Overload
Depth perception

I lose the use of my left side this time. I am hospitalized for a few days. Once again, the accent throws the doctors, I am considered as a physiological case. The doctors keep volleying back to medication being an issue; I know this is not the case. I finally get a doctor who gets it: This is Neurological, all of it. A Brain Map is done, (2007) confirming what actually did happen in 2004. There is more going on at this time however. The question of having TIAs comes into play.

Since no brain lesions are found at this time, I am given the diagnosis of Pseudo Foreign Accent Syndrome and it is suggested that I focus on the mental health. Mean while, back at the ranch, another doctor adds Conversion Disorder, even after finding Executive function impairment in brain function.

What???? Yes, that must be it; I am seeking comfort in another identity with a different cultural leaning and way of speech. In to 2009, after continuing to have neurological episodes and repeated reactions to many medications, I press on for an answer regarding the issue of TIAs. A MRI with contrast reveals a Vertebral Basilliar Insufficiency. I have insomnia, weakness, extreme fatigue. I can hardly walk up a flight of steps. Before the testing, I am offered Ambian to take care of the insomnia. Hello? Can we say, "Look at my medical history please?" After the results are in from the test, I see a vascular surgeon in two days, scheduled for surgery in three more days.

When the surgery is underway, a blood clot is discovered in the artery, at the base on my neck, going up to my brain. It is safely removed. The MRI with contrast did not indicate its presence. The tear in the artery is repaired with a stent, the clot removed. Surely now it has to be over, but hold your hats, round three is still to come. It takes another year and a half to recover from the 2006 chapter. My own voice returns, welcome back Sweetheart!

Round three, now I get to win the lottery. The chances of that happening are higher than another round of FAS! It is July 2011; I am riding on a bus, speaking with a woman from Sweden. She still has her accent after many years in the states. My ancestors, on one side of the family, come from that part of the country as well. I turned my neck to the left side to have eye contact with her. I felt a pain in my neck, going down my mid-back, followed by pressure behind my eyes.

Interesting to note, I was once again near toxic levels one month before this and was reducing the dosage of a medication to control Migraines. How does one experience this condition after being on the same medication for almost 7 years? The first indicator of a migraine for me is pressure behind my eyes.

I experience the following symptoms:

Floaters in my eyes
Return of FAS
Balance Issues

I begin Speech Therapy at an Outpatient Rehab. Two approaches to help the speech are non-successful, oh; I am so surprised, since this has happened before! The person I was working with never heard of this FAS or Pseudo Foreign Accent Syndrome, so she looked it up on line. The fact that I did indeed have a lesion changed the status (in their opinion based on info from 2007) that this was FAS, not a conversion disorder. You can predict the outcome of this one as well.

I knew that speech therapy has not proven helpful to me in the past and it was not helping now. I chose not to continue, especially after being told that perhaps they could refer me to maybe better able to help me. In a five months time, my speech returned to my norm. There have been no answers this time. My own thoughts, a TIA? A mild seizure? Something happened for sure and it triggered my speech area into an old pattern. This is my story and I'm sticking to it.

Here we go again . . . .February, 2012, I awake to the return of Foreign Accent Syndrome, along with a migraine and my left pupil is dilated. I am seen by the neurology department, and ophthalmologist, results . . . . .this is neurological . . . my eye has no tears in the retina; I am referred to the Mayo Clinic. No need for an appointment, they don't take my insurance. This episode lasts about a month. My speech returns to my normal . . . so happy to hear my own voice!

We are not quite done yet, another visit from the land of Foreign Accent Syndrome takes place in August 2012. This time, the left pupil is dilated again, balance issues return, I am alert and aware, cognition is spot on, migraines off and on for 3 weeks. I have a new physician; she has never seen this before. She asks my friend if he has noticed on any personality changes in me, he shakes his head "no!"

Based on old records, I am given the diagnosis, not from her, but due to historical records (misdiagnosed, no less) of 'Intermittent Altered Mental Status, Speech Disorder' . . . I explained what this is; she helpfully added it to the record. I am referred again to the ophthalmologist. He says to me, Bernadette, you are not crazy, you are keenly aware of your body, this is neurological, they need to get to the bottom of this. He sends his findings to the primary; the neurologist isn't very interested in seeing me anytime soon.

In 3–4 weeks, slowly, at interim, my speech returns to once again, to the sound of my own voice. I feel at home! Hello my sweet self, hello! Migraines become less frequent, then cease.

This experience with a rare disorder and loss of my own speech, left me feeling very much like and outsider, add to it, the comments and reactions from uneducated doctors who did more harm than good to my well-being. I found it easier not to speak most of the time, I felt myself pulling inward, like a turtle tucks her head inside her body.

As of this writing, I have no Foreign Accent syndrome. I do have on-going neurological issues, had a lack of blood flow to the brain in November 2012. More rehab for balance, now onto the spine clinic to address issues with my back and neck.

It is my highest hope that my story will help others, those who face the many facets of dealing with FAS and the doctors who treat them, for better or for worse, we all get to learn together about this rare and complicate disorder. To all the doctors who keep an open mind, thank you. To my fellow friends with FAS, we are strong, intelligent people who have been given a very special mission, to be a teacher. There are no degrees given for our experience, however, we are experts in what we know to be true for our own bodies.

Paula Westberry really allows the reader to step into her shoes, which sometimes seem to change dramatically before the ball is over. Remarkable is the insight she manages to convey of how FAS is much deeper than a change of accent but has consequences for personality as well. She tells us how she gave different names to her changes. But do not be deceived: this is the story of a remarkably intelligent woman who makes the near-superhuman effort to help us understand her condition. Her husband **Chuck** gives us a no-nonsense account of a loving husband's attempt to understand the profound upheaval FAS has dealt his wife.

FAS – my experience

PAULA WESTBERRY

2007

The last six months of my life have become more and more a blur. Demanding bosses wanting projects done in deadlines even the Gods on Mt. Olympus could not accomplish. Doctors looking at me at each appointment with a stare – you know the one that says you are crazy but no one wants to say it out loud. Blood tests, yes the simplest way to appease a patient, "we will run some more tests and see what they show and then we might have some answers". "Let's have you come back in two weeks". "That will be $50.00 please."

I had no energy; all I wanted to do was sleep, combing my hair hurt! Now the migraines were coming back almost daily but at least they were something the doctors recognized as an illness. My body grew no hair and hadn't for almost a year but every hormone test done on me had been "normal".

I pushed myself to work eight to ten hours a day. The mental exhaustion of organizing all the paperwork of a successful company, taking them to the next level; the exactness of the work, the attention to detail required a commitment to excellence very few can do. Normally the process takes four to six months; I was given one; all this while being in charge of a fully functioning company. I was determined to complete the task to "show them all" The migraines worsened.

I did it! I completed the task and was commended by the accreditation company for the thoroughness of my work. I was very proud. The headache was out of control that day; the vision in my left eye gone. As people in the company praised the work, I was huddled in my dark office trying not to come out into the light.

Everything inside my head worked just fine, what came out of my mouth however, was a completely different story! For the past month or so, I was having a problem with words beginning with "c" or "p". As an educator for my company I was responsible for the training of any new program Medicare chose to send down to the masses.

One of its latest trail balloons was a program called "Pay for Performance". This program was going to be tried in certain states and if successful, could dictate how home health agencies would be paid with an extra bump going to the top twenty percent of the agencies based on performance criteria. It was my job to introduce the concept of the payment structures and the criteria that would be used to judge the top 20% of the agencies. Unfortunately when I got to the "p" words instead of my usual smooth flowing voice – a stammer was developing. Bea, a very close friend and colleague, had noticed this and had come to learn my training routine and would pick up the sentence for me as if we had planned to present the class that way. I was becoming more and more frightened as to what was going on within my head.

Monday morning October 8, 2007, Bea came to my office as she usually did, just to check in on me. She regularly had taken me to the doctors and knew my condition well. She looked at my face and with that I was off to the hospital. My left eyelid was closed and the left side of my face was drooping like a bad Dali painting. I could not speak. When I tried garbled grunts came out. I was terrified. A nurse of thirty-nine years I knew what was happening to me! There was no time to call my husband of only two years to let him know how much he meant to me, I was just swooped up and placed in the car and off we went.

So much of that day is still a blur to me. Tests, IV insertions, people asking questions but what I remember the most is the headache! The jackhammers on the left side of my head drowning out the sounds of everyone who was talking to me; the vision in my left eye that is normal just white light is now black. If I want to see anything or anyone to the left I have to turn my head.

The nurse came in to ask the "admission questions" I thought I had this under control as I have all my medications memorized. I opened my mouth to speak but what came out, well let me just say was not a human sound and certainly not my sound. The nurse asked the question again as if I were deaf and I tried to answer again and that same terrible noise came out of my mouth again. The nurse in her frustration slammed the pad of paper on the bedside table and threw the pen across the room. As she left I heard her say"why do they always give these problems to me". I looked at the people surrounding my bed and I started to cry.

The parade of doctors in and out of my room over the next few says did not help my pain or disposition in any way. The Jackhammers in my head continued round the clock without any relief despite the different chemical trials the doctors assured me "this one will definitely stop the pain my dear." The vision to my left eye was slowly changing from black back to white but I was still very leery to drive. The big problem was my speech. I stammered and babbled like a baby. I could write just fine but not one intelligible word came out of my mouth.

The Neurologist arrived daily. Today he said "I don't think you had a stroke" "I think you just have a severe migraine headache" I wrote to him "why can't I speak then" His next words began the biggest battle I have fought in my life! "I believe you are recovering from some childhood trauma and are hiding behind it in your voice." While there is a great deal of truth behind some of what he said – I did have a great deal of trauma in my childhood! I spent hours of therapy to get to a wonderful place in my life so that I can counsel others about it. If this person, who knew nothing about me, thought he could just waltz into my hospital room and just drop a diagnosis of conversion disorder (medical code for crazy) on the floor and leave, well he was not going to get away with it with me. There had to be another explanation; the real explanation.

Over the next few weeks my language improved to the point that I spoke without verbs. My husband said I sounded like "Chief Sitting Bull". I could feel the frustration building within me as I could see the object I wanted to say in my mind but the word would not come out of my mouth. The condition is called expressive aphasia. Prior to my "condition" my husband and I could read each other's minds and finish each other's sentences now he is doing the best he can to figure out the babble coming out of my mouth. He is so patient and gentle; I never thought I would find someone as precious as him.

The next trip to the doctor was for neuropsychiatry testing. I was very angry at this visit. I was tired of everyone trying to prove that I was "crazy" when I knew that I was not. Something was wrong inside my head and nobody was looking. It is very easy to just write someone off but to go looking for something that is a little difficult to find now that requires work and dedication! Half way through this silly appointment of building blocks and trains going and coming from Chicago and New York I walked out! I was not crazy, I just could not talk correctly, no amount of having me play with blocks was going to bring it back! Frustrating me with Johnny and Billy selling apples and having me figure out what amount was left in their checking account was the last straw!

The blocks were the worst – there never were enough to make the picture he wanted me to make. After going round and round – I finally gave him all the blocks and told him to show me!

Shortly before my first incident I had been working on my second PhD and one of my colleagues was working on Dysphagia in Parkinson's disease. When she heard me speak, she told me I have that disease "Foreign Accent Syndrome" (FAS). She said it is very rare but she is sure I have it. After doing my own research I discovered that Dr Jack Ryalls was located not to far from my home. My husband made the call to him and they spoke for some time.

All morning as we drove to Orlando I was excited and nervous. 'What if he said I was crazy too?" By the time I met Dr Ryalls, "Natasha" was in her full glory, she sounded just like she got off the boat from mother Russia. I found it easier to give the accent a name for the country of the accent and so that I could keep other remembering it was not Paula. I was put through all the standard testing for FAS – the Grandfather paragraph and all and I left with a diagnosis of FAS from a stroke that hit my Broca's area on October 8, 2007. It is a very rare condition, but there none the less. This was confirmed by my PCP who had also worked in neurology. He took the time to pull my MRI films and looked at the area and saw the damage, small as it was in the area pointed out to him by Dr. Ryalls. Officially I was not crazy! Little did I know my life was about to embark on quite a different journey, one determined to enlighten the world on the little known but life altering illness.

As the holidays started to approach, my husband decided it was finally time to take our honeymoon. He booked us on a Royal Caribbean cruise. He booked a suite with concierge class service; everything a princess could dream of, after all this was my very first cruise. Natasha was in her glory! Little did we know what we were in for on this one week tour. Paula was a very quiet, reserved stick to her husband's side kind of woman. On the first night out, Natasha got on the elevator with Chuck on the way to the Concierge lounge before dinner. She immediately took over the elevator buttons and started engaging all the passengers. "Where might you be going? Off for a little drink before dinner are you now? Have you made your shore excursion plans? Can't leave you here on the ship you know! Why not join us in the lounge it going to be a great evening!" When we got to our floor and got off the elevator, Chuck looked at me and asked, "What was that and are you going to do that again?" I just replied in horror,"I don't know". The remainder of the cruise, Natasha was the life of the party and she collected business cards from everyone! All wanted to sail with her again, they just thought she was just lovely. My husband was just in awe that his meek little wife had turned into the life of the party! I was in shock wondering who had I become.

Everyday was an adventure for "Natasha", so outgoing, full of life, so different from Paula as I had been told. I just wanted to"go home" be myself again". I asked everyone "what was Paula like?" People were so vague in their answers, almost like Paula had slipped away from their memory. As more time went by, the more urgent it was for me to know what the real me was like, I did not want to lose her!

I had all the diplomas and awards from all the education Paula had achieved. But I wanted to know more than that; I wanted to know what made her tick! I just could not remember that! I saw the Certificate for the Daughters of the American Revolution on the wall and I knew that Paula was very proud of that, the family came over on the Mayflower! There are books in the family library on Paula's family tracing her routes to founding towns throughout New England. Family members told me how proud Paula was the day she was accepted into the DAR. Now I am Russian! My mind can not comprehend that!

People responded to me in one of two ways, both completely fascinated with my condition and they wanted me to "perform my accents and the personality quirks that come with it" or they thought I was crazy and wanted to be as far away from me as they could and convince as many other people as they could that I was crazy too.

2012

Now it is July 2012, and it is nearly five years since my first attack and experience with FAS. Natasha (my Russian persona) has never returned as of yet. But I can tell you that my Left Hemi Migraine (yes I received that diagnosis in 2010) has been with me from the beginning, without as much as a minute of rest since that August day in 2007.

May 6, 2010 – I started to cry at work, my body started to shake and I ran out of the office and how I drove home was a blur. Later that night I had the worst seizure I had had to date. I was brought to the hospital and there I remained for the next week.

After many tests and lord knows what, the conclusion was you can not mix Topamax and tegretol together – at least at the dosages I was taking. And oh yes BTW – we believe all your problems are that you have Hemiplegic Migraines. When I asked what I should do about that – the response was "keep doing what your doing!"

The stress and the seizures continued for the next two months, I was terminated from my job. Then I learned from the Short Term Disability CO. that part of their recovery effort of the disability policy is that you can earn 80% of your former salary and still be allowed to collect your claim. 2010 the year I wish to forget!

I have struggled to continue on but when you are now an independent contractor with no guarantees of hours, benefits or medical coverage, the added stress makes the FAS kick into high gear. For me that meant that everyone who met me got to meet a whole host of characters. Let me introduce them to you.

My main and most accent – Elizabeth (very proper British woman, dress is very conservative and polished. Shoes and bag matches, Dresses for work, dress pants for casual, DOES NOT OWN a pair of JEAN, jewelry is classic and real).

Liza – (a cockney British accent, dress is very casual, jeans, tie die, scarf in hair, anything artsy, sneakers, boat shoes, or sandals, sometimes a bag or not, Jewelry big plastic bead necklaces, long bead earring the artier the better)

FiFi – (Feisty, fun loving French Parisian, short skirts, low blouses, Couture always!, Lots of Bling and it is all real!, Loves the Champagne. If FiFi thinks there is some injustice being done she will be right in the middle of it fighting for the underdog. Otherwise she will be in the middle of the best party table)

Scarlett – (Straight from Gone with the Wind, all the Southern charm you could possibly want! knows just how to faint on queue! Every woman in the room immediately wants to be her and every Man wants to go home with her – but she is forever loyal to her man – but in the meantime – she is such a flirt!!)

These are the main four characters I change between everyday. It is not just an accent it is a personality change, a vocabulary attainment, a way of dressing and a state of mind. Who ever is in my head when I dress in the morning is who I will be reflecting in dress for the entire day but they definitely will not be staying with me the entire day.

I have observed over the years that as my stress level elevates, my accent will change, If I am in a frighten state – I can count on FiFi being the one to show up – she seems to be my defender.

Now before you start thinking multiple personality disorder, I am aware they are all me and I am always aware of all of them. The thing that is happening is with my speech, not a complete change of who I am, just a change in how I talk and the words I say and how I use them. I am still me

So Where am I now?

So now that you have a bit of a peek into the pieces of my life what am I doing now? I am still fighting the Migraine every day without any relief. My next appointment I am going to be tested for the possibility of being fitted with a internal Morphine pump. I must tell you that it does scare me a lot. While the pain is so debilitating –the pain that I do not leave my home unless I am going to the doctors or my husband has begged so much I feel like I don't dare say no one more time. The minute I am out of the house I am so anxious I just want to get home – the pain is that bad. I used to love going out! What I miss the most is going to church service so I know HE will find a way for me. I will get the pump – but I don't want to be a walking zombie. We Will See God Willing!

I am now 13 months into the wait for my hearing for Social Security Disability – they have until January 2013 to grant me a hearing for Disability.

I have had 4 strokes, have no Short Term Memory no math ability any longer imaging I have 2 PhD's and can no longer add 6 + 8 or 9 * 5. 7 College degrees all with 4.0 GPA and I have no idea what day of the week it is and even if you tell me – in five minutes I will ask you again. Most of the time my mind is like the movie 50 first dates – can enjoy a wonderful day but when I get up the next day – have no memory of what happened the day before. Note taking does very little to help jog my memory. But the Government has their plans for people like me I guess????

I still have a very positive outlook for Foreign Accent Syndrome – I have a great deal of faith that with research they will find a way to help people like me. You see I am not going to go home with intervention by researchers. Don't get me wrong I like the accents if that was the only thing that changed with this Syndrome but this has also robbed me of my core Identity. While those of you who can read this can look back fondly at your high school or wedding pictures and sit and reminisce. Those of us with FAS no longer can do that. I can look at the picture and see a familiar reflection but then it stops. Who is that woman? What did she dream about? What was important to her? What was she like? What did she hope to achieve? All of that within me is gone and the more time that it has been since my event – the less the people around me remember the "old Me" So perhaps the research can find away to get it back for us.

I am willing to tell you my story so that you understand this thing called Foreign Accent Syndrome so that if you meet someone with it – you are not afraid. Or if God Forbid it happens to you or someone in your family you will have a place to go for support and help. I help found a support page of Facebook – it is a closed group only for people affected by FAS and their families. When the group started we did a fundraiser and raised $500.00 to give to the University of Central Florida Communication Department. This is where Dr. Jack Ryalls and his students are working on FAS and we hoped this would help bring more awareness.

My future will continue to be spent looking for more answer for FAS and continue the outreach through the Facebook support group. I offer my information for anyone who needs to talk 1 on 1

Paula I Westberry, PhD, RN
Sebring, FL

FAS: a husband's perspective

CHUCK WESTBERRY

I cannot begin to tell you how frustrating it is to live with someone who has a different accent from one day to the next. If my wife could stick with just one accent for a little while, I might have a chance to understand what she is trying to say. But when she starts changing accents according to how tired she gets, then it becomes difficult to learn the different inflections. I spent 10 years in St Thomas of the US Virgin Islands. The first two years I did not understand that they were actually speaking English, with the stress points of the word in all the wrong places conflicting with what you are customarily used to. It was like around the relation to hear my own native language spoken in such a way that I could not even recognize it anymore! Now imagine what it's like to hear that same language in five different forms depending on if you're listening to a French, British, Russian, Norwegian or Southern Belle accent. I did okay with the British and Southern Belle but I still haven't developed an ear for the other ones. Yes it does take time and quite a bit of effort to 'develop' an ear to distinguish the different sounds and variables of a spoken accent.

And that brings me to the continuous flow of 'What?' and 'Huhs?' from my responses to what she just said. This only adds to both her and my levels of frustration. So now I have a habit of repeating what I thought I heard if it doesn't many any sense to me, so she can clarify. It's a good thing she is patient and understanding with me. Depending on what I repeat back to her it can get quite hilariously different from what she actually said to me. And it doesn't help that I also suffer a measurable hearing loss from years of loud band music and concerts. Combined with my tinnitus (constant ringing in the ears), hearing loss and lack of understanding her accent; I'm surprised we can communicate at all. Thinking back to when we first met, we used to be able to complete each other's sentences. That was how well we knew how each of us thought. But after the first stroke, we have never had that comfort of communication since.

Right after her first stroke, she suffered a total loss of speech – aphasia. She could visualize what she needed to say but could only write on a page of paper to get her thoughts across. I told her, 'Don't worry about anything right now, just rest a while and come back to me.' She now tells me that was when I pinned an angel pendant onto her gown, and that's why she cherishes that pendant so much today.

While in that hospital the first time, the doctors assigned to her case could not identify exactly where in the brain the stroke had occurred, so they simply dismissed it and discharged her without really treating her for anything, even though she still had the classic signs of a stroke. We live in a small town in central Florida, and even though we rank the second highest geriatric population of the country percentage-wise, the doctors were still befuddled by my wife's case. Their only course of treatment was to have her make an appointment with a psychologist of all things! She wasn't crazy, she only had weeks before she could start to make utterances of only one- and two-word phrases and I would have to play a word game with her until she approvingly nodded her head.

Those first words were hard to make out because she would never say a verb with any of it. Her speech was akin to the Hollywood version of 'Chief Sitting Bull'. She was raised in Boston from childhood and always had a prominent New England accent, so when her speech improved little by little I was surprised that her short sentences were sounding like a Russian instead of her usual voice. And along with this new accent came a change in my wife's attitude as well. The strain on her efforts to communicate presented itself in the form of anger and frustration so much that we named this Russian-sounding person 'Natasha'. She had a 'spunkiness' to her demeanor that had never come out in her personality before. This was the first time I thought of her as a totally different person than who I married only a couple years earlier.

I need to tell you here that I still love my wife and I made a heartfelt commitment to her when I voiced my wedding vows. She has done nothing wrong so why should my feelings for her change? In fact they have grown stronger due to this condition that we are both going through. She is still the same intelligent lady with two Ph.D.s who I can talk to as my best friend. I try to keep my affections 'securely guarded' so I don't get hurt as badly as I have in the past. But when I thought of 'losing' my wife to a stroke or worse, she finally saw me break down by her hospital bed and she has seen for herself just how deeply I feel for her. I believe that by letting her see just how truly in love with her I am, it has helped to strengthen our affection for each other and has helped us adapt to the changing situations and conditions as this progresses.

As my wife's condition continued to improve, her speech became even more pronounced in 'Russian' inflection and accent. At this point, it became confusing to both me and to her as to why she was sounding this way. I was thinking to myself that I should at least be grateful that she is speaking and communicating again. So I now have a wife who gives me a change so I can have variety in my life! How little did I know then just how much variety was about to happen.

VENEZUELA

Finally, **Olga Boscán** rounds out our global perspective of FAS, with her deeply personal account. Her story is one of overcoming great odds, with faith and perseverance. One feels how many medical conditions she has suffered but come through as an essential and uncompromising individual. She has travelled in quest of answers as far as has her accent. She does not find satisfactory answers but has discovered her FAS family around the world in her quest. While her story perhaps leaves us with more questions than it provides answers, it leaves us with the hope that through sharing her story with unswerving honesty we may help find the answers that will one day diminish the suffering of her future FAS family.

My history of foreign accent syndrome

OLGA BOSCÁN
Translated by Caroline Krohne, M.A.
Edited by Astrid Soriano, B.S.

Background

My name is Olga Boscán, born in Venezuela, South America, in 1957. I had a normal childhood, loved by my parents and my three older sisters. Although my father was not a believer, seeking the best education for his four daughters, we studied at the Salesian Catholic College 'María Auxiliadora'.

At 11 years old, I felt a sharp pain that turned out to be a twisted ovary and right fallopian tube, which required emergency surgery. My case was taken to a medical conference since there was no record of a similar case in a child.

At 17 years, I had the first of three spinal operations and immediately was diagnosed with systemic lupus erythematosus, which kept me on bed rest for a year and a half. I underwent an experimental treatment, which gave results and my antinuclear antibodies and LE cells have been negative since many years ago.

As my life continued between my studies in Human Resources and my work in this field, I went through the operating room 12 times, that is, I had 16 operations between the ages of 11 and 52 years. Later, I had two more operations related to Foreign Accent Syndrome.

Related to all these operations, I have several chronic diseases: open-angle glaucoma, hypothyroidism, hyper-insulinism, supraventricular arrhythmia, osteoporosis, dolichocolon and migraines.

The beauty of my life is that none of these circumstances stopped me from living fully, I've always had a positive attitude to adversity, and I have sought to not complain but enjoy the wonderful moments that life has given me. I've never stopped working, except when required by medical orders, I have traveled to many places, lived a life full of God's love, feeling his presence each of my days. There is nothing more wonderful to wake up and realize that I'm still here, experiencing the joy of living.

The start of my experience with the Foreign Accent Syndrome

On March 28, 2009, I suffered a fall and fractured my radius and ulna in my left arm. I had an emergency surgery because I had maimed my hand. Weeks passed and the pain was becoming more acute, intense, continuous and agonizing. The orthopedic surgeon referred me to an anesthesiologist, a pain management specialist who diagnosed 'Complex Regional Pain Syndrome Type I', also known as 'Reflex Sympathetic Dystrophy Syndrome', so he decided perform a ganglion blocks with ultrasound guidance and definitive neurolytic blockade of the stellate ganglion guided by ultrasound and fluoroscopy.

On April 28, 2009, they performed the first stellate ganglion block and that same day, my tongue started to feel very heavy and I could not articulate the words, then I presented with something very strange, I could not speak normally, every time I tried to speak I did so with many accents. My physician attributed it to the pain medication.

Living this experience which I did not understand was a very difficult moment for me. Thank God I never lost my sanity. I considered that this strange event in my life had to have a real clinical reason, and everyone around me started to think it was an emotional or mental problem. Six months later, I decided to be evaluated by a neurologist, who recommended having a Electroencephalogram Digital Map and Cerebral MRI with gadolinium. I was diagnosed with a 'severe cerebral irritability in the central left region'. He recommended valproic acid to prevent seizures. I asked the neurologist why I spoke with several foreign accents and got no response. I spoke of the 'Foreign Accent Syndrome' that I had been researching on the Internet and he told me that it did not exist. I took valproic acid for a month. I lived sleeping all the time and when I spoke it was with multiple accents.

I kept looking for answers and I went to a neurosurgeon, who told me that my brain was perfect and there was no evidence of any injury on the MRI. When I asked him why I spoke with multiple accents he told me that he had no idea and that I should go to a neurologist.

But I would not give up that easily; I continued with my quest to find answers to my condition or at least find a doctor that would listen so I went to see a very prestigious neurologist in the city where I live. I brought my cell phone which I had used to record all the accents that I had spoken (when these accents changed I recorded them as evidence, under the illusion that they would believe me). He explained that I had no damage at the cerebral level, that this 'Foreign Accent Syndrome' that I spoke of did not exist, and that it was all in my mind. He prescribed an antidepressant and a benzodiazepine, which is used to treat schizophrenia and acute mania bipolar disorder (I decided not to take these drugs). He referred me to a psychiatrist. He told me that a person with a life with so much suffering could not be well, that I for sure had open processes that had not healed and my way of gaining attention was by inventing these accents.

Since starting this disorder, in the morning I had trouble initiating talking, that is, I spoke with difficulty, until I began to speak with one of the accents that my brain randomly decided: American, French, Portuguese, Italian and a regional dialect of Madrid, Spain. Sometimes I spoke so badly that I seemed to have small strokes. I had trouble getting the words in my mind to express myself.

It had been 12 months since I started talking with multiple accents. I remember one day I got home and I immersed myself in a deep prayer. I asked the Holy Spirit for light (I am of the Catholic faith) and suddenly remembered having seen the YouTube video of Dr. Jack Ryalls. I opened a Facebook account (I did not like this social network at all) and I wrote to Dr. Ryalls on March 9, 2010; the following day he replied. For the first time someone understood me, listened to me, and supported me. Thanks to Dr. Ryalls, I understood that I had neurological damage. I hypothesized that I spoke with accents that my brain had heard before (I have traveled several times to the USA, France, Italy, Brazil and Spain). As complex as the Foreign Accent Syndrome was, it all somehow made sense to me.

During these three and half years, I have small lapses of a few days in that I've spoken almost normally and then I return again to feel the same sensation, heavy tongue, difficulty articulating words and multiple accents. I do not remember as it was my voice; everyone tells me it was very smooth.

Sometimes I speak with difficulty, other times I do not talk because I get very tired or it is difficult to articulate the words and find them in my mind. Sometimes I speak with a very beautiful sophisticated French accent, other times I speak with a Spanish accent from Madrid (it's so strange because I traveled to Spain in 1996 and went to seven cities, but in my brain, the Madrid accent was the only one that stuck). I also speak with a Brazilian Portuguese accent (for work, I frequently traveled to Brazil); at other times I speak with an American accent (this is the accent that appears most often) and the other is an Italian accent. I think that in my brain there are little boxes that contain files where I have stored information about the languages I have encountered and that my altered brain randomly chooses how I speak. I can speak up to five accents in a day or stay several days with one, as well as alternate between them. When I read aloud the accents are less marked. I have problems correctly speaking Spanish as I had spoken before I had Foreign Accent Syndrome. In the grammatical construction of sentences, the order of the article, verb, and adjective is inverted. That is, I use the article at the end of the sentence and not at the beginning. The adjective that goes to the end of the sentence, I often say before the verb. This affects me because I love my language – it is very beautiful – and now I speak it poorly.

My family has supported me a lot with their unconditional love. My mother and my sisters have been understanding and supporting. They always thought that what happened to me was emotional. Now they understand that it is neurological. I am glad my father, who died 12 years ago, did not know of my condition.

In my work things are more complicated. After working in HR for 25 years in a multinational company, I changed my business and I now work as a property advisor. This is really hard for me since I have to tell all the customers I serve what happened to me because they always ask me where I am from, and if we talk on the phone several times I usually do not speak with the same accent, which in a way reduces my professionalism: they think I'm a stranger; besides, if I am presenting with an Italian accent and I assist an Italian client, he will speak to me in Italian. It also happens with other customers who speak a language I do not speak but because of the accent, they think that I do speak it.

Although I was sure that I had the Foreign Accent Syndrome, thanks to Dr. Jack Ryalls I decided to make one last attempt in my country and in June 2012, I went to Caracas, the capital of Venezuela, for the consultation with a neurologist-neurosurgeon, who is about 75 years old and still operates on brain tumors. It was a beautiful experience; we talked for an hour, I told him about my life, and he only heard me talking in my American accent. At the end he said, 'Thanks to you, today I learned that there really is a Foreign Accent Syndrome; tonight I have decided to research it on the Internet.' He said he had never had a patient who, having suffered so much, had a heart full of such joy, and my treatment was to continue having that positive attitude and faith in God that allowed me to overcome all obstacles. For the first time in my country, a doctor did not consider me to be mentally ill and had the humility to accept that he knew, even with all his experience, that there was a Foreign Accent Syndrome. He made it one of the most beautiful days of my life.

Sometimes I feel like I want to speak normally, and I wish that my tongue did not weigh so much that it causes me to not get the words in my mind out; that every day people wouldn't ask me where I am from, but I'm actually very happy and grateful because I can communicate even though I speak strangely, and this is wonderful. I always try to see the glass half full, never half empty.

I am convinced that what has helped me accept myself as I am today is the attitude I've always had in difficult physical or spiritual situations; it is what has allowed me to continue my life with joy. I thank God for His presence in my life that I loved with my lights and my shadows, which has always been by my side; I have heard Him; He has made me feel centered; He has given me the strength to choose to be good.

My eternal gratitude goes out to Dr. Jack Ryalls, who has generously supported me since March 10, 2010. Without his help I would never have come to understand what was happening in my brain. May God reward all the good he is doing and may the Holy Spirit fill him with the wisdom and intelligence to continue researching and contributing to the good of humanity.

Olga Boscán
Valencia, Venezuela, July 17, 2012

Part III

Additional resources

The psychosocial impact of FAS questionnaire – prototype

Jill Taylor, Chloe Howe and Nick Miller

This questionnaire is a prototype developed by Nick Miller, Chloe Howe and Jill Taylor based on conversations with people with FAS and with speech-language clinicians, both who had and who had not met anyone with FAS. Its purpose is to support case history taking and help gain some insights into the origins, status and beliefs around FAS for a given individual. It aims to stimulate exploration of ways in which FAS might have affected the individual and facilitate recognition of areas of support they may need. The present version could be given to the person with the accent change to fill in themselves, but probably is better used as a guide to questioning.

General background

1. How long have you been speaking with a different accent?

    _____

2. What seems to have caused your different accent?

    Stroke ☐　　Head trauma ☐　　Other ☐　　Unknown ☐

    If other please state

    _____

3. Did your accent change straight away with the stroke/head trauma/other?

    _____

4. If not right away, how long after you were diagnosed with your condition did it change?

    _____

5. How would you describe your accent before it changed?

    _____

6. How would you describe your accent now (what does it sound like to you)?

    _____

7. How do other people describe your accent now?

    _____

8. How aware are you of the accent?

    Not aware　　　　　　☐
    Slightly aware　　　　☐
    Moderately aware　　☐
    Very aware　　　　　☐
    Extremely aware　　☐

9. Has your awareness of the accent changed since you first acquired it?

    Much more aware   ☐
    More aware   ☐
    No change   ☐
    Less aware   ☐
    Much less aware   ☐

10. What do you feel is different about your speech now? (Tick all that apply)

    Faster   ☐
    Slower   ☐
    Softer   ☐
    Louder   ☐
    Slurred   ☐
    Requires more effort   ☐
    Difficulty with certain sounds   ☐

    Which ones do you think? _____

    Difficulty with certain words   ☐

    Which ones do you think? _____

    Difficulty giving the right tone of voice   ☐

    In what way? _____

    Difficulty stressing the words I want to   ☐

    Other (please state) _____

    _____

    _____

    _____

    _____

11. Do you feel your accent changes from day to day?

    No ☐   A little ☐   Moderately ☐   A lot ☐

12. Do other people feel your accent changes from day to day?

    No ☐   A little ☐   Moderately ☐   A lot ☐

13. Have you received any help/therapy for your new accent?

    Yes ☐   No ☐

These questions are about any other changes you have noticed apart from the accent

1. Have you noticed anything else that has changed **apart from your speech?** Tick all that apply and rate the extent to which you feel they have changed.

    1 = No, 2 = A little, 3 = Moderately, 4 = A lot, 5 = Severely

☐ Mobility, walking	1	2	3	4	5
☐ Vision	1	2	3	4	5
☐ Hearing	1	2	3	4	5
☐ Memory	1	2	3	4	5
☐ Language (finding words; grammar)	1	2	3	4	5
☐ Co-ordination	1	2	3	4	5
☐ Fatigue/tiredness	1	2	3	4	5

    Other: If there are other aspects not mentioned here, please add them and rate 1 to 5 as above:

_____	1	2	3	4	5
_____	1	2	3	4	5
_____	1	2	3	4	5

2. Have the changes **apart from your speech** affected any of the following areas of your life and to what extent?

    Employment
    Not at all ☐   Somewhat ☐   Moderately ☐   Very ☐   Extremely ☐

    Day to day life
    Not at all ☐   Somewhat ☐   Moderately ☐   Very ☐   Extremely ☐

    Interests/hobbies
    Not at all ☐   Somewhat ☐   Moderately ☐   Very ☐   Extremely ☐

    Socially
    Not at all ☐   Somewhat ☐   Moderately ☐   Very ☐   Extremely ☐

    Other
    Not at all ☐   Somewhat ☐   Moderately ☐   Very ☐   Extremely ☐

If other please state and rate them too:

_____

_____

_____

3. How much do you agree with this statement about changes **apart from speech**:

    'I have coped well with the changes.'

    Strongly agree ☐   Agree ☐   Disagree ☐   Strongly disagree ☐

These questions ask about the effects of <u>the speech changes</u>

1. How much do you feel the change in accent has impacted on you?

    Not at all ☐   Somewhat ☐   Moderately ☐   Very ☐   Extremely ☐

2. How do you rate the changed accent in relation to other changes because of your condition? Tick which single one applies

    It is my number one concern   ☐

    It is my second most important concern   ☐

    It is my third most important concern   ☐

    It concerns me but is not a major factor   ☐

    It doesn't concern me   ☐

3. On a scale of 1 to 5, how much have <u>**the speech changes**</u> affected your life?

Not at all		Somewhat affected		Greatly affected
1	2	3	4	5

4. If relevant: How did you feel about receiving a diagnosis of FAS?

Relieved		Indifferent		Devastated
1	2	3	4	5

5. Which areas of your life have <u>**the speech changes**</u> had an impact on and to what extent?

    Employment

    Not at all ☐   Somewhat ☐   Moderately ☐   Very ☐   Extremely ☐

    Day to day life

    Not at all ☐   Somewhat ☐   Moderately ☐   Very ☐   Extremely ☐

Interests/hobbies

Not at all ☐   Somewhat ☐   Moderately ☐   Very ☐   Extremely ☐

Socially

Not at all ☐   Somewhat ☐   Moderately ☐   Very ☐   Extremely ☐

Other

Not at all ☐   Somewhat ☐   Moderately ☐   Very ☐   Extremely ☐

If other please state and rate them too:

_____

_____

_____

6. Has talking with your family changed because of **the speech changes**?

	No change		Some change		A lot of change
	1	2	3	4	5

7. Has talking with your friends/colleagues changed because of **the speech changes**?

	No change		Some change		A lot of change
	1	2	3	4	5

8. Has talking with strangers changed because of **the speech changes**?

	No change		Some change		A lot of change
	1	2	3	4	5

9. How do you feel your interaction with others in general has changed due to **the speech changes** (tick all that apply)?

No longer speak on phone   ☐
Conversations focus on my speech disability   ☐
Everything is much slower   ☐
Everything takes more effort   ☐
People ignore me much more   ☐
Other, please state:

_____

_____

_____

10. Have **the speech changes** affected how you feel you get on with family members?

Not at all ☐   Somewhat ☐   Moderately ☐   Very ☐   Extremely ☐

11. Have **the speech changes** affected how you feel you get on with friends/colleagues?

Not at all ☐   Somewhat ☐   Moderately ☐   Very ☐   Extremely ☐

12. Have **the speech changes** affected how you feel you get on with strangers?

Not at all ☐   Somewhat ☐   Moderately ☐   Very ☐   Extremely ☐

13. How much have **the speech changes** affected you emotionally?

Not at all ☐   Somewhat ☐   Moderately ☐   Very ☐   Extremely ☐

14. If you think they have affected you, can you say in what ways?
(Tick all that apply and add more if you feel there are more.)

Poor motivation   ☐
Lonely   ☐
Frustration   ☐
Anger   ☐
Depression   ☐
Easily upset   ☐
Loss of confidence   ☐
Other, please state:

_____

_____

_____

15. How well do you feel you have coped with the changes **to your speech** since it all started?

Very well ☐   Well ☐   Somewhat ☐   Badly ☐   Very badly ☐

16. Which of the following emotions have an effect on how your accent sounds and to what extent?

     1 = Not at all, 2 = A little, 3 = Moderately, 4 = A lot, 5 = Severely

     ☐ Stress   1 2 3 4 5

     ☐ Upset   1 2 3 4 5

     ☐ Tiredness   1 2 3 4 5

     ☐ Arguing   1 2 3 4 5

     ☐ Excitement   1 2 3 4 5

     ☐ Other: If other, please state

     _____   1 2 3 4 5

     _____   1 2 3 4 5

     _____   1 2 3 4 5

17. Which of the following contexts affect how your accent sounds and to what extent?

     1 = Not at all, 2 = A little, 3 = Moderately, 4 = A lot, 5 = Severely

     ☐ Time of day   1 2 3 4 5

     ☐ Reading something aloud   1 2 3 4 5

     ☐ Length of conversation   1 2 3 4 5

     ☐ Singing   1 2 3 4 5

     ☐ Amount of concentration   1 2 3 4 5

     Other: If other, please state

     _____   1 2 3 4 5

     _____   1 2 3 4 5

     _____   1 2 3 4 5

18. How far do you agree with the statement: 'FAS has stopped me from doing certain things in my life'?

     Strongly agree ☐   Agree ☐   Disagree ☐   Strongly disagree ☐

19. How do you feel about the changes the accent has caused to your life? (Tick which one is most like you)

     I have accepted the changes and learnt to adapt my life   ☐

     I still find it difficult to accept but am learning to adapt   ☐

     I cannot accept the changes   ☐

Other, please state:

_____

_____

_____

20. How has the accent change made you feel? Please rate on a scale of I to 5.

I = Strongly agree, 2 = Agree, 3 = Neither agree nor disagree,
4 = Disagree, 5 = Strongly disagree

☐ Self-conscious	I	2	3	4	5
☐ Embarrassed	I	2	3	4	5
☐ Frustrated	I	2	3	4	5
☐ Angry	I	2	3	4	5
☐ Depressed	I	2	3	4	5
☐ Demotivated	I	2	3	4	5
☐ Lonely/isolated	I	2	3	4	5
☐ Worried	I	2	3	4	5
☐ Lacking feeling in control	I	2	3	4	5
☐ Lacking confidence	I	2	3	4	5
☐ More interesting	I	2	3	4	5
☐ Centre of attention	I	2	3	4	5
☐ More expressive	I	2	3	4	5
☐ Unique/an individual	I	2	3	4	5

Other, please state

_____   I   2   3   4   5

_____   I   2   3   4   5

_____   I   2   3   4   5

21. How do you feel about your new accent (please tick all those that apply)?

Dislike it	☐
Hard work	☐
An inconvenience	☐
Grateful	☐
Protective of the accent (as it is now part of your identity)	☐
Makes life easier	☐
Amused	☐

Doesn't bother me ☐

Other, please state:

_____

_____

_____

How far do you agree with the following statements:

22. 'If I had a stronger accent it would be more of a problem for me.'

| Strongly agree | Agree | Neither agree nor disagree | Disagree | Strongly disagree |

23. 'My attitude towards the accent has changed over time.'

| Strongly agree | Agree | Neither agree nor disagree | Disagree | Strongly disagree |

If it has changed: is that for the better or for the worse?

Better   Worse

24. 'The accent has changed the kind of person I am.'

| Strongly agree | Agree | Neither agree nor disagree | Disagree | Strongly disagree |

25. 'People's awareness of FAS needs to be raised.'

| Strongly agree | Agree | Neither agree nor disagree | Disagree | Strongly disagree |

What do you think could be done to help you?

_____

_____

_____

_____

_____

These questions are about others' reactions to your accent

1. Do you feel that you stand out as being 'foreign' in the area you live in?

Strongly agree	Agree	Neither agree nor disagree	Disagree	Strongly disagree

2. Do you feel the new accent has stopped you from talking to people as willingly as you would have before the accent change?

Strongly agree	Agree	Neither agree nor disagree	Disagree	Strongly disagree

3. How often do you feel you avoid conversation/interaction with others because of what they may say/think/do because of your accent?

    Frequently ☐   Often ☐   Sometimes ☐   Seldom ☐   Never ☐

4. What types of reactions have you had from the general public? Please rate below how frequently:

    1 = Frequently, 2 = Quite often, 3 = Sometimes, 4 = Seldom, 5 = Never

		1	2	3	4	5
☐	Negative/bad reaction	1	2	3	4	5
☐	Positive reaction	1	2	3	4	5

5. Please indicate if you have encountered any of the following types of reactions. Please rate how often:

    1 = Frequently, 2 = Quite often, 3 = Sometimes, 4 = Seldom, 5 = Never

		1	2	3	4	5
☐	Racism	1	2	3	4	5
☐	Interest	1	2	3	4	5
☐	Reaction linked to poor knowledge about FAS	1	2	3	4	5
☐	Encouraging/supportive reaction	1	2	3	4	5
☐	Disbelief	1	2	3	4	5
☐	Humour (positive)	1	2	3	4	5
☐	Humour (negative – e.g. making fun of you)	1	2	3	4	5
☐	Rude/inconsiderate	1	2	3	4	5

    Other, please state

	1	2	3	4	5
_____	1	2	3	4	5
_____	1	2	3	4	5
_____	1	2	3	4	5

6. To what extent has **the accent** affected relationships with your family?

Not at all ☐　Somewhat ☐　Moderately ☐
Greatly ☐　Extremely ☐

7. To what extent has **the accent** affected relationships with your friends?

Not at all ☐　Somewhat ☐　Moderately ☐
Greatly ☐　Extremely ☐

8. To what extent do your family now view you as 'different' due to **the accent**?

Frequently ☐　Often ☐　Sometimes ☐　Seldom ☐　Never ☐

9. How far do you agree with the following statements:

'My family have shown concern and support following my accent change.'

Strongly agree	Agree	Neither agree nor disagree	Disagree	Strongly disagree

'My family make jokes about the accent and it doesn't bother me.'

Strongly agree	Agree	Neither agree nor disagree	Disagree	Strongly disagree

'To begin with my family and friends thought I was putting the accent on.'

Strongly agree	Agree	Neither agree nor disagree	Disagree	Strongly disagree

'My family are not bothered about the accent, they are just happy I am okay.'

Strongly agree	Agree	Neither agree nor disagree	Disagree	Strongly disagree

Are there any other observations you would like to make?

_____

_____

_____

_____

_____

Index

Note: Page numbers in *italics* are for tables.

accent accommodation 24, 50
aetiology *see* causes of FAS
Alzheimer, Alois 16
anarthria 21, 22
aphasia 5, 6, 15, 21, 37, 47, 55;
    conduction 18, 61
apraxia: ideational 16; of speech 18, 37,
    47, 60, 61, 62
Aronson, A. 37
articulators/articulation 28, 36, 60,
    64
Ås, Arvid 21, 39, 40
assessment 47, 58–65; of articulation 60;
    case history 59; delayed auditory
    feedback 63; diadochokinetic speech
    tasks 60; neurological 59;
    neurophysiological 59; phonetic
    analysis 60, 61; of propositionality 60,
    63; of prosody 60; radiological 59; of
    speech sounds 60; of tongue
    movements 6; of voice production 60;
    white noise masking 63; *see also*
    differential diagnosis
attitudes of others 54–5; *see also* listener
    perceptions

Bastian, Henry 20–1, 38
bite block 63
brain damage/injury 21, 24–5, 27, 36–7,
    41, 52; expected symptoms 60;
    movement changes after 33; recovery
    after 67

breathing 35, 44
Broadbent, Sir William 38–9

causes of FAS 24–52; brain areas and
    conditions associated with 36, 37;
    descriptive accounts 25–7; explanatory
    accounts 25–7; neurogenic 3–4, 5, 6,
    24–5, 27, 28, 34, 35–40, 47, 52, 59,
    61, 62, 63, 64–5; psychogenic 5,
    19–20, 24, 27, 40, 41–9, 61, 62, 63;
    re-emergence of a former accent
    38–40; sociolinguistic 24, 49–51;
    structural-mechanical 5, 24, 27, 41–2
Charcot, Jean-Martin 20
clinical presentation 9–10; duration of
    condition 14; grammar, use of 13;
    lips/lip movement 12, 26, 28, 29, 35,
    36, 37, 41, 60, 61; manual gestures,
    alterations in 31, 33, 34; nasality 22,
    30, 35, 63, 64; persistence of FAS
    47–8; pronunciation, shifts in 12;
    rhythm of speech 12; soft palate 28,
    36; speech rate 12; tongue movement
    6, 25, 26, 28, 37, 41, 60; vocal cords
    26, 41
conditions associated with FAS: aphasia
    6, 37; autism 51; bipolar disorder 42;
    brain atrophy 37; brain damage/injury
    36–7, 41, 52; cerebral vasculitis 27,
    37; childhood speech disorders 27;
degenerative neurological conditions 11,
    14, 37, 47, 52; dystonia 4, 27, 37;

electrocution 27, 37; fronto-temporal dementia 37; migraine 4, 27; multiple sclerosis 27, 37; Parkinson's disease 27, 37; progressive aphasia 37; psychogenic fugue or conversion disorder 42; schizophrenia 16, 42; shared symptoms or beliefs 48; stroke 24, 25, 26, 37, 38, 47, 52
conduction aphasia 18, 61
coping with FAS 52–8
Critchley, Macdonald 19, 21, 22, 39

demotic speech 21
differential diagnosis 58–65; delayed auditory feedback (DAF) 63, 64; frequency-shifted auditory feedback (FAF) 64; general guidelines 61, 62; listener perceptions of foreignness 64; propositionality 60, 63; situational variability 63; white noise masking 63
dysarthria 37
dysprosody 3, 22, 28, 37, 47, 60; see also intonation

ear of the listener effect see listener perceptions
emotions/emotional states 40, 43, 57, 63; see also coping with FAS
eye of the listener effect 33

Fischer, Otto 17
folie à deux (à trois or à plusieurs) 48
foreignness: listener perceptions of 14, 28–32
(and differential diagnosis 64)
Fromm, Erika 21, 39–40
functional disorders see psychogenic FAS

gender differences 6, 15–16
Goldstein, Kurt 5
group identification/membership 48–9

historical perspective 16–24

incidence 6, 13–14, 15
infantilism 20, 22
interventions 44, 49, 52, 64–5; behaviour modification approaches

65; pharmacological 65; speech therapy 7, 18; talking therapies 65
intonation 12, 13, 19, 21, 22, 23, 29, 34, 35, 36, 37, 54, see also dysprosody; prosody
irritable larynx syndrome 44

Kussmaul, Adolph 20

Lichtheim, Ludwig 20, 21
listener perceptions, role in diagnosis of FAS 14, 18, 23, 28–32, 34, 49–50, 54
loss, sense of 55, 57; see also coping with FAS

McKeown, M. 23, 29
Marie, Pierre 3, 17, 21
media portrayals 9, 11, 14, 56
Monrad-Krohn, Georg 3, 21–2

neurogenic FAS 3–4, 5, 6, 24–5, 27, 28, 34, 35–40, 47, 52, 59; conditions associated with see conditions associated with FAS; distinguished from psychogenic FAS 61, 62; interventions 64–5;
situational variations in 63
Nielsen, J.M. 23, 29

Osborne, Jonathan 12, 17–18, 23

palilalia 61
Pick, Arnold 16–17, 20, 22
prevalence/incidence 6, 13–14, 15
prosody 19, 21, 22, 60; rhythm of speech 12, 13, 22, 37, 61; stress 12, 19, 21, 22, 23, 29, 34–5, 37, 54; tone of voice 35, 36, 55, 56; see also dysprosody; intonation
pseudoaccent 22, 31
psychogenic FAS 5, 19–20, 24, 27, 40, 41–9, 58, 63; distinguished from neurogenic FAS 61, 62; feigning 43, 44, 63; identity issues 46, 51; malingering 43
psychogenic fugue disorder 42
psychosocial consequences of FAS 52–8; alienation 49, 57, 58; attitudes of

others 54–5; media reactions 56; personality change 19, 53; sense of loss 55, 57
psychotic episodes 42

reactions of others 54–5; *see also* listener perceptions
regional accents 18–19, 21
rehabilitation *see* interventions

shared symptoms/beliefs 48
social accents 18–19, 21, 46–7
social distancing 24, 46, 51
sociolinguistic aspects of FAS 24, 49–51
spasmodic dysphonia 61
speech differential diagnosis 59–65
speech rate 12, 34, 36, 54, 63; *see also* prosody

structural-mechanical causes of FAS 5, 24, 27, 41–2
stuttering 15, 37, 38, 46; acquired psychogenic 44–5

therapy *see* interventions

unlearned foreign accent 22

van Thal, Joan 19
ventriloquism and auditory illusion 31, 41
voice disorders 15, 35, 44, 45, 46

Wernicke, Carl 20, 21
Westberry, Paula 4
Whitaker, Henry 3–4, 5, 22
Whitty, C.W.M. 33